Fluent C
Principles, Practices, and Patterns

Christopher Preschern

Beijing · Boston · Farnham · Sebastopol · Tokyo

Fluent C

by Christopher Preschern

Copyright © 2023 Christopher Preschern. All rights reserved.

Published by O'Reilly Media, Inc., 1005 Gravenstein Highway North, Sebastopol, CA 95472.

O'Reilly books may be purchased for educational, business, or sales promotional use. Online editions are also available for most titles (*https://oreilly.com*). For more information, contact our corporate/institutional sales department: 800-998-9938 or *corporate@oreilly.com*.

Acquisitions Editor: Brian Guerin
Development Editor: Corbin Collins
Production Editor: Jonathon Owen
Copyeditor: Piper Editorial Consulting, LLC
Proofreader: Justin Billing

Indexer: Judith McConville
Interior Designer: David Futato
Cover Designer: Karen Montgomery
Illustrator: Kate Dullea

October 2022:   First Edition

Revision History for the First Edition
2022-10-14:   First Release

See *https://oreilly.com/catalog/errata.csp?isbn=9781492097334* for release details.

978-1-492-09733-4

[LSI]

Table of Contents

Preface

You picked up this book to move your programming skills one step forward. That is good, because you'll definitely benefit from the hands-on knowledge provided in this book. If you have a lot of experience programming in C, you'll learn the details of good design decisions and about their benefits and drawbacks. If you are fairly new to C programming, you'll find guidance about design decisions, and you'll see how these decisions are applied bit by bit to running code examples for building larger scale programs.

The book answers questions such as how to structure a C program, how to cope with error handling, or how to design flexible interfaces. As you learn more about C programming, questions often pop up, such as the following:

- Should I return any error information I have?

- Should I use the global variable `errno` to do that?

- Should I have few functions with many parameters or the other way around?

- How do I build a flexible interface?

- How can I build basic things like an iterator?

For object-oriented languages, most of these questions are answered to a great extent by the Gang of Four book *Design Patterns: Elements of Reusable Object-Oriented Software* by Erich Gamma, Richard Helm, Ralph Johnson, and John Vlissides (Prentice Hall, 1997). Design patterns provide a programmer with best practices on how objects should interact and which object owns which other kinds of objects. Also, design patterns show how such objects can be grouped together.

However, for procedural programming languages like C, most of these design patterns cannot be implemented in the way described by the Gang of Four. There are no native object-oriented mechanisms in C. It is possible to emulate inheritance or polymorphism in the C programming language, but that might not be the first choice, because such emulation makes things unfamiliar for programmers who are used to programming C and are not used to programming with object-oriented languages like C++ and using concepts like inheritance and polymorphism. Such programmers may want to stick to their native C programming style that they are used to. However, with the native C programming style, not all object-oriented design patterns guidance is usable, or at least the specific implementation of the idea presented in a design pattern is not provided for non-object-oriented programming languages.

And that is where we stand: we want to program in C, but we cannot directly use most of the knowledge documented in design patterns. This book shows how to bridge this gap and implement hands-on design knowledge for the C programming language.

Why I Wrote This Book

Let me tell you why the knowledge gathered in this book turned out to be very important for me and why such knowledge is hard to find.

In school I learned C programming as my first programming language. Just like every new C programmer, I wondered why arrays start with index 0, and I first rather randomly tried out how to place the operators * and & in order to finally get the C pointer magic working.

At university I learned how C syntax actually works and how it translates to bits and bytes on the hardware. With that knowledge I was able to write small programs that worked very well. However, I still had trouble understanding why longer code looked the way it did, and I certainly wouldn't have come up with solutions like the following:

```
typedef struct INTERNAL_DRIVER_STRUCT* DRIVER_HANDLE;
typedef void (*DriverSend_FP)(char byte);
typedef char (*DriverReceive_FP)();
typedef void (*DriverIOCTL_FP)(int ioctl, void* context);

struct DriverFunctions
{
  DriverSend_FP fpSend;
  DriverReceive_FP fpReceive;
  DriverIOCTL_FP fpIOCTL;
};

DRIVER_HANDLE driverCreate(void* initArg, struct DriverFunctions f);
void driverDestroy(DRIVER_HANDLE h);
void sendByte(DRIVER_HANDLE h, char byte);
char receiveByte(DRIVER_HANDLE h);
void driverIOCTL(DRIVER_HANDLE h, int ioctl, void* context);
```

Looking at code like that prompted many questions:

- Why have function pointers in the `struct`?
- Why do the functions need that `DRIVER_HANDLE`?
- What is an IOCTL, and why would I not have separate functions instead?
- Why have explicit create and destroy functions?

These questions came up as I began writing industrial applications. I regularly came across situations where I realized I did not have the C programming knowledge, for example, to decide how to implement an iterator or to decide how to cope with error handling in my functions. I realized that although I knew C syntax, I had no clue how to apply it. I tried to achieve something but just managed to do it in a clumsy way or not at all. What I needed were best practices on how to achieve specific tasks with the C programming language. For example, I needed to know things like the following:

- How can I acquire and release resources in an easy way?
- Is it a good idea to use `goto` for error handling?
- Should I design my interface to be flexible, or should I simply change it when the need arises?
- Should I use an `assert` statement, or should I return an error code?
- How is an iterator implemented in C?

It was very interesting for me to realize that while my experienced work colleagues had many different answers for these questions, nobody could point me to anything that documented these design decisions and their benefits and drawbacks.

So next I turned to the internet, and yet again I was surprised: it was very hard to find sound answers to these questions even though the C programming language has been around for decades. I found out that while there is much literature on the C programming language basics and its syntax, there's not much on advanced C programming topics or how to write beautiful C code that holds up to industrial applications.

And that is exactly where this book comes in. This book teaches you how to advance your programming skills from writing basic C programs to writing larger-scale C programs that consider error handling and that are flexible regarding certain future changes in requirements and design. This book uses the concept of design patterns to provide you bit by bit with design decisions and their benefits and drawbacks. These design patterns are applied to running code examples that teach you how code like the earlier example evolves and why it ends up looking the way it does.

The presented patterns can be applied to any C programming domains. As I come from the domain of embedded programming in a multithreaded real-time environment, some of the patterns are biased towards that domain. Anyways, you'll see that the general idea of the patterns can be applied to other C programming domains and even beyond the scope of C programming.

Patterns Basics

The design guidance in this book is provided in the form of patterns. The idea of presenting knowledge and best practices in the form of patterns comes from the architect Christopher Alexander in *The Timeless Way of Building* (Oxford University Press, 1979). He uses small pieces of well-proven solutions to tackle a huge problem in his domain: how to design and construct cities. The approach of applying patterns was adopted by the software development domain, where pattern conferences like the conference on Pattern Languages of Programs (PLoP) are held to extend the body of knowledge of patterns. In particular, the book *Design Patterns: Elements of Reusable Object-Oriented Software* by the Gang of Four (Prentice Hall, 1997) had a significant impact and made the concept of design patterns well known to software developers.

But what exactly is a pattern? There are many definitions out there, and if you are deeply interested in the topic, then the book *Pattern-Oriented Software Architecture: On Patterns and Pattern Languages* by Frank Buschmann et al. (Wiley, 2007) can provide you with accurate descriptions and details. For the purposes of this book, a pattern provides a well-proven solution to a real-life problem. The patterns presented in this book have the structure shown in Table P-1.

Table P-1. How patterns are broken down in this book

Pattern section	Description
Name	This is the name of the pattern, which should be easy to remember. The aim is that this name will be used by programmers in their everyday language (as is the case with the Gang of Four patterns, where you hear programmers say, "And the Abstract Factory creates the object"). Pattern names are capitalized in this book.
Context	The context section sets the scene for the pattern. It tells you under which circumstances this pattern can be applied.
Problem	The problem section gives you information about the issue you want to tackle. It starts with the major problem statement written in bold font type and then adds details on why the problem is hard to solve. (In other pattern formats, these details go into a separate section called "forces.")
Solution	This section provides guidance on how to tackle the problem. It starts with stating the main idea of the solution written in bold font type and continues with details about the solution. It also provides a code example in order to give very concrete guidance.
Consequences	This section lists the benefits and drawbacks of applying the described solution. When applying a pattern, you should always confirm that the consequences that arise are OK with you.
Known uses	The known uses give you evidence that the proposed solution is good and actually works in real-life applications. They also show you concrete examples to help you understand how to apply the pattern.

A major benefit of presenting design guidance in the form of patterns is that these patterns can be applied one after another. If you have a huge design problem, it's hard to find the one guidance document and the one solution that addresses exactly that problem. Instead, you can think of your huge and very specific problem as a sum of many smaller and more generic problems, and you can tackle these problems bit by bit by applying one pattern after the other. You simply check the problem descriptions of the patterns and apply the one that fits your problem and that has consequences you can live with. These consequences might lead to another problem that you can then address by applying another pattern. That way you incrementally design your code instead of trying to come up with a complete up-front design before even writing the first line of code.

How to Read This Book

You should already know C programming basics. You should know the C syntax and how it works—for example, this book won't teach you what a pointer is or how to use it. This book delivers hints and guidance on advanced topics.

The chapters in this book are self-standing. You can read them in an arbitrary order, and you can simply pick out the topics you are interested in. You'll find an overview of all patterns in the next section, and from there you can jump to the patterns you are interested in. So if you know exactly what you are looking for, you can start right there.

If you are not looking for one particular pattern, but instead want to get an overview of possible C design options, read through Part I of the book. Each chapter there focuses on a particular topic, starting with basic topics like error handling and memory managment, and then moving to more advanced and specific topics like interface design or platform-independent code. The chapters each present patterns related to that topic and a running code example that shows bit by bit how the patterns can be applied.

Part II of this book shows two larger running examples that apply many of the patterns from Part I. Here you can learn how to build up some larger piece of software bit by bit through the application of patterns.

Overview of the Patterns

You'll find an overview of all patterns presented in this book in Tables P-2 through P-10. The tables show a short form of the patterns that only contains a brief description of the core problem, followed by the keyword "Therefore," followed by the core solution.

Table P-2. Patterns for error handling

Pattern name	Summary
"Function Split" on page 6	The function has several responsibilities, which makes the function hard to read and maintain. Therefore, split it up. Take a part of a function that seems useful on its own, create a new function with that, and call that function.
"Guard Clause" on page 9	The function is hard to read and maintain because it mixes pre-condition checks with the main program logic of the function. Therefore, check if you have mandatory pre-conditions, and immediately return from the function if these pre-conditions are not met.
"Samurai Principle" on page 12	When returning error information, you assume that the caller checks for this information. However, the caller can simply omit this check and the error might go unnoticed. Therefore, return from a function victorious or not at all. If there is a situation for which you know that an error cannot be handled, then abort the program.
"Goto Error Handling" on page 16	Code gets difficult to read and maintain if it acquires and cleans up multiple resources at different places within a function. Therefore, have all resource cleanup and error handling at the end of the function. If a resource cannot be acquired, use the `goto` statement to jump to the resource cleanup code.
"Cleanup Record" on page 19	It is difficult to make a piece of code easy to read and maintain if this code acquires and cleans up multiple resources, particularly if those resources depend on one another. Therefore, call resource acquisition functions as long as they succeed, and store which functions require cleanup. Call the cleanup functions depending on these stored values.
"Object-Based Error Handling" on page 22	Having multiple responsibilities in one function, such as resource acquisition, resource cleanup, and usage of that resource, makes that code difficult to implement, read, maintain, and test. Therefore, put initialization and cleanup into separate functions, similar to the concept of constructors and destructors in object-oriented programming.

Table P-3. Patterns for returning error information

Pattern name	Summary
"Return Status Codes" on page 32	You want to have a mechanism to return status information to the caller, so that the caller can react to it. You want the mechanism to be simple to use, and the caller should be able to clearly distinguish between different error situations that could occur. Therefore, use the Return Value of a function to return status information. Return a value that represents a specific status. Both of you as the callee and the caller must have a mutual understanding of what the value means.
"Return Relevant Errors" on page 39	On the one hand, the caller should be able to react to errors; on the other hand, the more error information you return, the more your code and the code of your caller have to deal with error handling, which makes the code longer. Longer code is harder to read and maintain and brings in the risk of additional bugs. Therefore, only return error information to the caller if that information is relevant to the caller. Error information is only relevant to the caller if the caller can react to that information.
"Special Return Values" on page 45	You want to return error information, but it's not an option to explicitly Return Status Codes because that implies that you cannot use the Return Value of the function to return other data. You'd have to return that data via Out-Parameters, which would make calling your function more difficult. Therefore, use the Return Value of your function to return the data computed by the function. Reserve one or more special values to be returned if an error occurs.
"Log Errors" on page 48	You want to make sure that in case of an error you can easily find out its cause. However, you don't want your error-handling code to become complicated because of this. Therefore, use different channels to provide error information that is relevant for the calling code and error information that is relevant for the developer. For example, write debug error information into a log file and don't return the detailed debug error information to the caller.

Table P-4. Patterns for memory management

Pattern name	Summary
"Stack First" on page 62	Deciding the storage class and memory section (stack, heap, …) for variables is a decision every programmer has to make often. It gets exhausting if for each and every variable, the pros and cons of all possible alternatives have to be considered in detail. Therefore, simply put your variables on the stack by default to profit from automatic cleanup of stack variables.
"Eternal Memory" on page 65	Holding large amounts of data and transporting it between function calls is difficult because you have to make sure that the memory for the data is large enough and that the lifetime extends across your function calls. Therefore, put your data into memory that is available throughout the whole lifetime of your program.
"Lazy Cleanup" on page 69	Having dynamic memory is required if you need large amounts of memory and memory where you don't know the required size beforehand. However, handling cleanup of dynamic memory is a hassle and is the source of many programming errors. Therefore, allocate dynamic memory and let the operating system cope with deallocation by the end of your program.
"Dedicated Ownership" on page 72	The great power of using dynamic memory comes with the great responsibility of having to properly clean that memory up. In larger programs, it becomes difficult to make sure that all dynamic memory is cleaned up properly. Therefore, right at the time when you implement memory allocation, clearly define and document where it's going to be cleaned up and who is going to do that.
"Allocation Wrapper" on page 76	Each allocation of dynamic memory might fail, so you should check allocations in your code to react accordingly. This is cumbersome because you have many places for such checks in your code. Therefore, wrap the allocation and deallocation calls, and implement error handling or additional memory management organization in these wrapper functions.
"Pointer Check" on page 81	Programming errors that lead to accessing an invalid pointer cause uncontrolled program behavior, and such errors are difficult to debug. However, because your code works with pointers frequently, there is a good chance that you have introduced such programming errors. Therefore, explicitly invalidate uninitialized or freed pointers and always check pointers for validity before accessing them.
"Memory Pool" on page 84	Frequently allocating and deallocating objects from the heap leads to memory fragmentation. Therefore, hold a large piece of memory throughout the whole lifetime of your program. At runtime, retrieve fixed-size chunks of that memory pool instead of directly allocating new memory from the heap.

Table P-5. Patterns for returning data from C functions

Pattern name	Summary
"Return Value" on page 95	The function parts you want to split are not independent from one another. As usual in procedural programming, some part delivers a result that is then needed by some other part. The function parts that you want to split need to share some data. Therefore, simply use the one C mechanism intended to retrieve information about the result of a function call: the Return Value. The mechanism to return data in C copies the function result and provides the caller access to this copy.
"Out-Parameters" on page 99	C only supports returning a single type from a function call, and that makes it complicated to return multiple pieces of information. Therefore, return all the data with a single function call by emulating by-reference arguments with pointers.
"Aggregate Instance" on page 103	C only supports returning a single type from a function call, and that makes it complicated to return multiple pieces of information. Therefore, put all data that is related into a newly defined type. Define this Aggregate Instance to contain all the related data that you want to share. Define it in the interface of your component to let the caller directly access all the data stored in the instance.

Pattern name	Summary
"Immutable Instance" on page 108	You want to provide information held in large pieces of immutable data from your component to a caller. Therefore, have an instance (for example, a `struct`) containing the data to share in static memory. Provide this data to users who want to access it and make sure that they cannot modify it.
"Caller-Owned Buffer" on page 111	You want to provide complex or large data of known size to the caller, and that data is not immutable (it changes at runtime). Therefore, require the caller to provide a buffer and its size to the function that returns the large, complex data. In the function implementation, copy the required data into the buffer if the buffer size is large enough.
"Callee Allocates" on page 116	You want to provide complex or large data of unknown size to the caller, and that data is not immutable (it changes at runtime). Therefore, allocate a buffer with the required size inside the function that provides the large, complex data. Copy the required data into the buffer and return a pointer to that buffer.

Table P-6. Patterns for data lifetime and ownership

Pattern name	Summary
"Stateless Software-Module" on page 123	You want to provide logically related functionality to your caller and make that functionality as easy as possible for the caller to use. Therefore, keep your functions simple and don't build up state information in your implementation. Put all related functions into one header file and provide the caller this interface to your software-module.
"Software-Module with Global State" on page 127	You want to structure your logically related code that requires common state information and make that functionality as easy as possible for the caller to use. Therefore, have one global instance to let your related functions share common resources. Put all functions that operate on this instance into one header file, and provide the caller this interface to your software-module.
"Caller-Owned Instance" on page 132	You want to provide multiple callers or threads access to functionality with functions that depend on one another, and the interaction of the caller with your functions builds up state information. Therefore, require the caller to pass an instance, which is used to store resource and state information, along to your functions. Provide explicit functions to create and destroy these instances, so that the caller can determine their lifetime.
"Shared Instance" on page 138	You want to provide multiple callers or threads access to functionality with functions that depend on one another, and the interaction of the caller with your functions builds up state information, which your callers want to share. Therefore, require the caller to pass an instance, which is used to store resource and state information, along to your functions. Use the same instance for multiple callers and keep the ownership of that instance in your software-module.

Table P-7. Patterns for flexible APIs

Pattern name	Summary
"Header Files" on page 149	You want functionality that you implement to be accessible to code from other implementation files, but you want to hide your implementation details from the caller. Therefore, provide function declarations in your API for any functionality you want to provide to your user. Hide any internal functions, internal data, and your function definitions (the implementations) in your implementation file and don't provide this implementation file to the user.
"Handle" on page 152	You have to share state information or operate on shared resources in your function implementations, but you don't want your caller to see or even access all that state information and shared resources. Therefore, have a function to create the context on which the caller operates and return an abstract pointer to internal data for that context. Require the caller to pass that pointer to all your functions, which can then use the internal data to store state information and resources.

Pattern name	Summary
"Dynamic Interface" on page 156	It should be possible to call implementations with slightly deviating behaviors, but it should not be necessary to duplicate any code, not even the control logic implementation and interface declaration. Therefore, define a common interface for the deviating functionalities in your API and require the caller to provide a callback function for that functionality, which you then call in your function implementation.
"Function Control" on page 159	You want to call implementations with slightly deviating behaviors, but you don't want to duplicate any code, not even the control logic implementation or the interface declaration. Therefore, add a parameter to your function that passes meta-information about the function call and that specifies the actual functionality to be performed.

Table P-8. Patterns for flexible iterator interfaces

Pattern name	Summary
"Index Access" on page 168	You want to make it possible for the user to iterate elements in your data structure in a convenient way, and it should be possible to change internals of the data structure without resulting in changes to the user's code. Therefore, provide a function that takes an index to address the element in your underlying data structure and return the content of this element. The user calls this function in a loop to iterate over all elements.
"Cursor Iterator" on page 172	You want to provide an iteration interface to your user which is robust in case the elements change during the iteration and which enables you to change the underlying data structure at a later point without requiring any changes to the user's code. Therefore, create an iterator instance that points to an element in the underlying data structure. An iteration function takes this iterator instance as argument, retrieves the element the iterator currently points to, and modifies the iteration instance to point to the next element. The user then iteratively calls this function to retrieve one element at a time.
"Callback Iterator" on page 177	You want to provide a robust iteration interface which does not require the user to implement a loop in the code for iterating over all elements and which enables you to change the underlying data structure at a later point without requiring any changes to the user's code. Therefore, use your existing data structure—specific operations to iterate over all your elements within your implementation, and call some provided user-function on each element during this iteration. This user-function gets the element content as a parameter and can then perform its operations on this element. The user calls just one function to trigger the iteration, and the whole iteration takes place inside your implementation.

Table P-9. Patterns for organizing files in modular programs

Pattern name	Summary
"Include Guard" on page 189	It's easy to include a header file multiple times, but including the same header file leads to compile errors if types or certain macros are part of it, because during compilation they get redefined. Therefore, protect the content of your header files against multiple inclusion so that the developer using the header files does not have to care whether it is included multiple times. Use an interlocked #ifdef statement or a #pragma once statement to achieve this.
"Software-Module Directories" on page 192	Splitting code into different files increases the number of files in your codebase. Having all files in one directory makes it difficult to keep an overview of all the files, particularly for large codebases. Therefore, put header files and implementation files that belong to a tightly coupled functionality into one directory. Name that directory after the functionality that is provided via the header files.
"Global Include Directory" on page 197	To include files from other software-modules, you have to use relative paths like ../othersoftwaremodule/file.h. You have to know the exact location of the other header file. Therefore, have one global directory in your codebase that contains all software-module APIs. Add this directory to the global include paths in your toolchain.

Pattern name	Summary
"Self-Contained Component" on page 201	From the directory structure it is not possible to see the dependencies in the code. Any software-module can simply include the header files from any other software-module, so it's impossible to check dependencies in the code via the compiler. Therefore, identify software-modules that contain similar functionality and that should be deployed together. Put these software-modules into a common directory and have a designated subdirectory for their header files that are relevant for the caller.
"API Copy" on page 207	You want to develop, version, and deploy the parts of your codebase independently from one another. However, to do that, you need clearly defined interfaces between the code parts and the ability to separate that code into different repositories. Therefore, to use the functionality of another component, copy its API. Build that other component separately and copy the build artifacts and its public header files. Put these files into a directory inside your component and configure that directory as a global include path.

Table P-10. Patterns for escaping #ifdef hell

Pattern name	Summary
"Avoid Variants" on page 220	Using different functions for each platform makes the code harder to read and write. The programmer is required to initially understand, correctly use, and test these multiple functions in order to achieve a single functionality across multiple platforms. Therefore, use standardized functions that are available on all platforms. If there are no standardized functions, consider not implementing the functionality.
"Isolated Primitives" on page 224	Having code variants organized with #ifdef statements makes the code unreadable. It is very difficult to follow the program flow, because it is implemented multiple times for multiple platforms. Therefore, isolate your code variants. In your implementation file, put the code handling the variants into separate functions and call these functions from your main program logic, which then contains only platform-independent code.
"Atomic Primitives" on page 227	The function that contains the variants and is called by the main program is still hard to comprehend because all the complex #ifdef code was only put into this function in order to get rid of it in the main program. Therefore, make your primitives atomic. Only handle exactly one kind of variant per function. If you handle multiple kinds of variants, for example, operating system variants and hardware variants, then have separate functions for that.
"Abstraction Layer" on page 231	You want to use the functionality which handles platform variants at several places in your codebase, but you do not want to duplicate the code of that functionality. Therefore, provide an API for each functionality that requires platform-specific code. Define only platform-independent functions in the header file and put all platform-specific #ifdef code into the implementation file. The caller of your functions includes only your header file and does not have to include any platform-specific files.
"Split Variant Implementations" on page 236	The platform-specific implementations still contain #ifdef statements to distinguish between code variants. That makes it difficult to see and select which part of the code should be built for which platform. Therefore, put each variant implementation into a separate implementation file and select per file what you want to compile for which platform.

Conventions Used in This Book

The following typographical conventions are used in this book:

Italic
> Indicates new terms, URLs, email addresses, filenames, and file extensions.

Bold
> Used to highlight the problem and solution for each pattern.

`Constant width`
> Used for program listings, as well as within paragraphs to refer to program elements such as variable or function names, databases, data types, environment variables, statements, and keywords.

 This element signifies a general note.

 This element indicates a warning or caution.

Using Code Examples

The code examples in this book show short code snippets which focus on the core idea to showcase the patterns and their application. The code snippets by themselves won't compile, because to keep it simple several things are omitted (for example, include files). If you are interested in getting the full code which does compile, you can download it from GitHub at *https://github.com/christopher-preschern/fluent-c*.

If you have a technical question or a problem using the code examples, please send email to *bookquestions@oreilly.com*.

This book is here to help you get your job done. In general, if example code is offered with this book, you may use it in your programs and documentation. You do not need to contact us for permission unless you're reproducing a significant portion of the code. For example, writing a program that uses several chunks of code from this book does not require permission. Selling or distributing examples from O'Reilly books does require permission. Answering a question by citing this book and quoting example code does not require permission. Incorporating a significant amount of example code from this book into your product's documentation does require permission.

We appreciate, but generally do not require, attribution. An attribution usually includes the title, author, publisher, and ISBN. For example: "*Fluent C* by Christopher Preschern (O'Reilly). Copyright 2023 Christopher Preschern, 978-1-492-09733-4."

If you feel your use of code examples falls outside fair use or the permission given above, feel free to contact us at *permissions@oreilly.com*.

The patterns in this book all present existing code examples which apply these patterns. The following list shows the references to these code examples:

- The game NetHack (*https://oreil.ly/nzO5W*)
- OpenWrt Project (*https://oreil.ly/qeppo*)
- OpenSSL library (*https://oreil.ly/zzsMO*)
- Wireshark network sniffer (*https://oreil.ly/M55B5*)
- Portland Pattern repository (*https://oreil.ly/wkZzb*)
- Git version control system (*https://oreil.ly/7F9Oz*)
- Apache Portable Runtime (*https://oreil.ly/ysaM6*)
- Apache Webserver (*https://oreil.ly/W6SMn*)
- B&R Automation Runtime operating system (proprietary and undisclosed code of the company B&R Industrial Automation GmbH)
- B&R Visual Components automation system visualization editor (proprietary and undisclosed code of the company B&R Industrial Automation GmbH)
- NetDRMS data management system (*https://oreil.ly/eR0EV*)
- MATLAB programming and numeric computing platform (*https://oreil.ly/UpvJK*)
- GLib library (*https://oreil.ly/QoUwT*)
- GoAccess real-time web analyzer (*https://oreil.ly/L1Eij*)
- Cloudy physical calculation software (*https://oreil.ly/phLBb*)
- GNU Compiler Collection (GCC) (*https://oreil.ly/KK4jY*)
- MySQL database system (*https://oreil.ly/YKXxs*)
- Android ION memory manager (*https://oreil.ly/2JV7h*)
- Windows API (*https://oreil.ly/nnzyX*)
- Apple's Cocoa API (*https://oreil.ly/sQuaI*)
- VxWorks real-time operating system (*https://oreil.ly/UMUaj*)

- sam text editor (*https://oreil.ly/k3SQI*)
- C standard library functions: glibc implementation (*https://oreil.ly/9Qr95*)
- Subversion project (*https://oreil.ly/sg9sz*)
- Netdata real-time performance monitoring and visualization system (*https://oreil.ly/1sDZz*)
- Nmap network tool (*https://oreil.ly/8Yz5R*)
- OpenZFS file system (*https://oreil.ly/VWeQL*)
- RIOT operating system (*https://oreil.ly/LhZM4*)
- Radare reverse engineering framework (*https://oreil.ly/TUYfh*)
- Education First digital learning products (*https://www.ef.com*)
- VIM text editor (*https://github.com/vim/vim*)
- GNUplot graphing utility (*https://oreil.ly/PlQPj*)
- SQLite database engine (*https://oreil.ly/5Knfz*)
- gzip data compression program (*https://oreil.ly/it40Z*)
- lighttpd web server (*https://github.com/lighttpd*)
- U-Boot bootloader (*https://oreil.ly/IKVYV*)
- Smpl discrete event simulation system (*https://oreil.ly/NJnCH*)
- Nokia's Maemo platform (*https://oreil.ly/RwDtt*)

O'Reilly Online Learning

 For more than 40 years, *O'Reilly Media* has provided technology and business training, knowledge, and insight to help companies succeed.

Our unique network of experts and innovators share their knowledge and expertise through books, articles, and our online learning platform. O'Reilly's online learning platform gives you on-demand access to live training courses, in-depth learning paths, interactive coding environments, and a vast collection of text and video from O'Reilly and 200+ other publishers. For more information, visit *https://oreilly.com*.

How to Contact Us

Please address comments and questions concerning this book to the publisher:

O'Reilly Media, Inc.
1005 Gravenstein Highway North
Sebastopol, CA 95472
800-998-9938 (in the United States or Canada)
707-829-0515 (international or local)
707-829-0104 (fax)

We have a web page for this book, where we list errata, examples, and any additional information. You can access this page at *https://oreil.ly/fluent-c*.

Email *bookquestions@oreilly.com* to comment or ask technical questions about this book.

For news and information about our books and courses, visit *https://oreilly.com*.

Find us on LinkedIn: *https://linkedin.com/company/oreilly-media*

Follow us on Twitter: *https://twitter.com/oreillymedia*

Watch us on YouTube: *https://www.youtube.com/oreillymedia*

Acknowledgments

I want to thank my wife Silke who by now even knows what patterns are :-) and I want to thank my daughter Ylvi. They both make my life happier, and they both make sure that I don't end up sitting in front of my computer working all the time, but that I instead enjoy life.

This book would not have come to life without the help of many pattern enthusiasts. I want to thank all the participants of Writers' Workshops at the European Conference on Pattern Languages of Programs for providing me with feedback on the patterns. In particular, I want to thank the following people, who provided me with very helpful feedback during the so-called shepherding process of that conference: Jari Rauhamäki, Tobias Rauter, Andrea Höller, James Coplien, Uwe Zdun, Thomas Raser, Eden Burton, Claudius Link, Valentino Vranić, and Sumit Kalra. Special thanks also to my work colleagues, in particular to Thomas Havlovec, who made sure that I got the C programming details in my patterns right. Robert Hanmer, Michael Weiss, David Griffiths, and Thomas Krug spent a lot of time for reviewing this book and provided me with additional ideas how to improve it—thank you very much! Thanks also to the whole team at O'Reilly who helped me a lot in making this book happen. In particular, I want to thank my development editor, Corbin Collins, and my production editor, Jonathon Owen.

The content of this book is based on the following papers that were accepted at the European Conference on Pattern Languages of Programs and published with ACM. These papers can be accessed for free at the website *http://www.preschern.com.*

- "A Pattern Story About C Programming," EuroPLoP '21: 26th European Conference on Pattern Languages of Programs, July 2015, article no. 53, 1–10, *https://dl.acm.org/doi/10.1145/3489449.3489978.*

- "Patterns for Organizing Files in Modular C Programs," EuroPLoP '20: Proceedings of the European Conference on Pattern Languages of Programs, July 2020, article no. 1, 1–15, *https://dl.acm.org/doi/10.1145/3424771.3424772.*

- "Patterns to Escape the #ifdef Hell," EuroPLop '19: Proceedings of the 24th European Conference on Pattern Languages of Programs, July 2019, article no. 2, 1–12, *https://dl.acm.org/doi/10.1145/3361149.3361151.*

- "Patterns for Returning Error Information in C," EuroPLop '19: Proceedings of the 24th European Conference on Pattern Languages of Programs, July 2019, article no. 3, 1–14, *https://dl.acm.org/doi/10.1145/3361149.3361152.*

- "Patterns for Returning Data from C Functions," EuroPLop '19: Proceedings of the 24th European Conference on Pattern Languages of Programs, July 2019, article no. 37, 1–13, *https://dl.acm.org/doi/10.1145/3361149.3361188.*

- "C Patterns on Data Lifetime and Ownership," EuroPLop '19: Proceedings of the 24th European Conference on Pattern Languages of Programs, July 2019, article no. 36, 1–13, *https://dl.acm.org/doi/10.1145/3361149.3361187.*

- "Patterns for C Iterator Interfaces," EuroPLoP '17: Proceedings of the 22nd European Conference on Pattern Languages of Programs, July 2017, article no. 8, 1–14, *https://dl.acm.org/doi/10.1145/3147704.3147714.*

- "API Patterns in C," EuroPlop '16: Proceedings of the 21st European Conference on Pattern Languages of Programs, July 2016, article no. 7, 1–11, *https://dl.acm.org/doi/10.1145/3011784.3011791.*

- "Idioms for Error Handling in C," EuroPLoP '15: Proceedings of the 20th European Conference on Pattern Languages of Programs, July 2015, article no. 53, 1–10, *https://dl.acm.org/doi/10.1145/2855321.2855377.*

PART I

C Patterns

Patterns make your life easier. They take the burden of having to cope with each and every design decision from you. Patterns explain to you well-proven solutions, and in this first part of the book, you'll find such well-proven solutions and the consequences that arise when applying these solutions. Each of the following chapters focuses on a particular topic for C programming, presents patterns on that topic, and shows their application to a running example.

CHAPTER 1

Error Handling

Error handling is a big part of writing software, and when it's done poorly, the software becomes difficult to extend and to maintain. Programming languages like C++ or Java provide "Exceptions" and "Destructors" that make error handling easier. Such mechanisms are not natively available for C, and literature on good error handling in C is widely scattered over the internet.

This chapter provides collected knowledge on good error handling in the form of C error-handling patterns and a running example that applies the patterns. The patterns provide good practice design decisions and elaborate on when to apply them and which consequences they bring. For a programmer, these patterns remove the burden of making many fine-grained decisions. Instead, a programmer can rely on the knowledge presented in these patterns and use them as a starting point to write good code.

Figure 1-1 shows an overview of the patterns covered in this chapter and their relationships, and Table 1-1 provides a summary of the patterns.

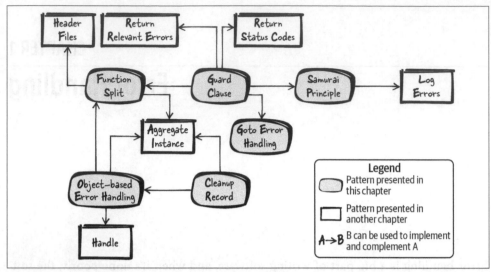

Figure 1-1. Overview of patterns for error handling

Table 1-1. Patterns for error handling

Pattern name	Summary
Function Split	The function has several responsibilities, which makes the function hard to read and maintain. Therefore, split it up. Take a part of a function that seems useful on its own, create a new function with that, and call that function.
Guard Clause	The function is hard to read and maintain because it mixes pre-condition checks with the main program logic of the function. Therefore, check whether you have mandatory pre-conditions and immediately return from the function if these pre-conditions are not met.
Samurai Principle	When returning error information, you assume that the caller checks for this information. However, the caller can simply omit this check and the error might go unnoticed. Therefore, return from a function victorious or not at all. If there is a situation for which you know that an error cannot be handled, then abort the program.
Goto Error Handling	Code gets difficult to read and maintain if it acquires and cleans up multiple resources at different places within a function. Therefore, have all resource cleanup and error handling at the end of the function. If a resource cannot be acquired, use the `goto` statement to jump to the resource cleanup code.
Cleanup Record	It is difficult to make a piece of code easy to read and maintain if this code acquires and cleans up multiple resources, particularly if those resources depend on one another. Therefore, call resource acquisition functions as long as they succeed, and store which functions require cleanup. Call the cleanup functions depending on these stored values.
Object-Based Error Handling	Having multiple responsibilities in one function, such as resource acquisition, resource cleanup, and usage of that resource, makes that code difficult to implement, read, maintain, and test. Therefore, put initialization and cleanup into separate functions, similar to the concept of constructors and destructors in object-oriented programming.

Running Example

You want to implement a function that parses a file for certain keywords and that returns information on which of the keywords was found.

The standard way to indicate an error situation in C is to provide this information via the return value of a function. To provide additional error information, legacy C functions often set the errno variable (see *errno.h*) to a specific error code. The caller can then check errno to get information about the error.

However, in the following code, you simply use return values instead of errno because you don't need very detailed error information. You come up with the following initial piece of code:

```c
int parseFile(char* file_name)
{
  int return_value = ERROR;
  FILE* file_pointer = 0;
  char* buffer = 0;

  if(file_name!=NULL)
  {
    if(file_pointer=fopen(file_name, "r"))
    {
      if(buffer=malloc(BUFFER_SIZE))
      {
        /* parse file content*/
        return_value = NO_KEYWORD_FOUND;
        while(fgets(buffer, BUFFER_SIZE, file_pointer)!=NULL)
        {
          if(strcmp("KEYWORD_ONE\n", buffer)==0)
          {
            return_value = KEYWORD_ONE_FOUND_FIRST;
            break;
          }
          if(strcmp("KEYWORD_TWO\n", buffer)==0)
          {
            return_value = KEYWORD_TWO_FOUND_FIRST;
            break;
          }
        }
        free(buffer);
      }
      fclose(file_pointer);
    }
  }
  return return_value;
}
```

In the code, you have to check the return values of the function calls to know whether an error occurred, so you end up with deeply nested if statements in your code. That presents the following problems:

- The function is long and mixes error-handling, initialization, cleanup, and functional code. This makes it difficult to maintain the code.

- The main code that reads and interprets the file data is deeply nested inside the if clauses, which makes it difficult to follow the program logic.

- The cleanup functions are far separated from their initialization functions, which makes it easy to forget some cleanup. This is particularly true if the function contains multiple return statements.

To make things better, you first perform a Function Split.

Function Split

Context

You have a function that performs multiple actions. For example, it allocates a resource (like dynamic memory or some file handle), uses this resource, and cleans it up.

Problem

The function has several responsibilities, which makes the function hard to read and maintain.

Such a function could be responsible for allocating resources, operating on these resources, and cleaning up these resources. Maybe the cleanup is even scattered over the function and duplicated in some places. In particular, error handling of failed resource allocation makes such a function hard to read, because quite often that ends up in nested if statements.

Coping with allocation, cleanup, and usage of multiple resources in one function makes it easy to forget cleanup of a resource, particularly if the code is changed later on. For example, if a return statement is added in the middle of the code, then it is easy to forget cleaning up the resources that were already allocated at that point in the function.

Solution

Split it up. Take a part of a function that seems useful on its own, create a new function with that, and call that function.

To find out which part of the function to isolate, simply check whether you can give it its own meaningful name and whether the split isolates responsibilities. That could, for example, result in one function containing just functional code and one containing just error-handling code.

A good indicator for a function to be split is if it contains cleanup of the same resource at multiple places in the function. In such a case, it is a lot better to split the code into one function that allocates and cleans up the resources and one function that uses these resources. The called function that uses the resources can then easily have multiple return statements without the need to clean up the resources before each return statement, because that is done in the other function. This is shown in the following code:

```
void someFunction()
{
  char* buffer = malloc(LARGE_SIZE);
  if(buffer)
  {
    mainFunctionality(buffer);
  }
  free(buffer);
}

void mainFunctionality()
{
  // implementation goes here
}
```

Now, you have two functions instead of one. That means, of course, that the calling function is not self-contained anymore and depends on the other function. You have to define where to put that other function. The first step is to put it right in the same file as the calling function, but if the two functions are not closely coupled, you can consider putting the called function into a separate implementation file and including a Header File declaration of that function.

Consequences

You improved the code because two short functions are easier to read and maintain compared to one long function. For example, the code is easier to read because the cleanup functions are closer to the functions that need cleanup and because the resource allocation and cleanup do not mix with the main program logic. That makes the main program logic easier to maintain and to extend its functionality later on.

The called function can now easily contain several return statements because it does not have to care about cleanup of the resources before each return statement. That cleanup is done at a single point by the calling function.

If many resources are used by the called function, all these resources also have to be passed to that function. Having a lot of function parameters makes the code hard to read, and accidentally switching the order of the parameters when calling the function might result in programming errors. To avoid that, you can have an Aggregate Instance in such a case.

Known Uses

The following examples show applications of this pattern:

- Pretty much all C code contains parts that apply this pattern and parts that do not apply this pattern and that are thus difficult to maintain. According to the book *Clean Code: A Handbook of Agile Software Craftsmanship* by Robert C. Martin (Prentice Hall, 2008), each function should have exactly one responsibility (single-responsibility principle), and thus resource handling and other program logic should always be split into different functions.

- This pattern is called Function Wrapper in the Portland Pattern Repository.

- For object-oriented programming, the Template Method pattern also describes a way to structure the code by splitting it up.

- The criteria for when and where to split the function are described in *Refactoring: Improving the Design of Existing Code* by Martin Fowler (Addison-Wesley, 1999) as the Extract Method pattern.

- The game NetHack applies this pattern in its function `read_config_file`, in which resources are handled and in which the function `parse_conf_file` is called, which then works on the resources.

- The OpenWrt code uses this pattern at several places for buffer handling. For example, the code responsible for MD5 calculation allocates a buffer, passes this buffer to another function that works on that buffer, and then cleans that buffer up.

Applied to Running Example

Your code already looks a lot better. Instead of one huge function you now have two large functions with distinct responsibilities. One function is responsible for retrieving and releasing resources, and the other is responsible for searching for the keywords as shown in the following code:

```
int searchFileForKeywords(char* buffer, FILE* file_pointer)
{
  while(fgets(buffer, BUFFER_SIZE, file_pointer)!=NULL)
  {
    if(strcmp("KEYWORD_ONE\n", buffer)==0)
    {
```

```
        return KEYWORD_ONE_FOUND_FIRST;
      }
      if(strcmp("KEYWORD_TWO\n", buffer)==0)
      {
        return KEYWORD_TWO_FOUND_FIRST;
      }
    }
    return NO_KEYWORD_FOUND;
  }

  int parseFile(char* file_name)
  {
    int return_value = ERROR;
    FILE* file_pointer = 0;
    char* buffer = 0;

    if(file_name!=NULL)
    {
      if(file_pointer=fopen(file_name, "r"))
      {
        if(buffer=malloc(BUFFER_SIZE))
        {
          return_value = searchFileForKeywords(buffer, file_pointer);
          free(buffer);
        }
        fclose(file_pointer);
      }
    }
    return return_value;
  }
```

The depth of the `if` cascade decreased, but the function `parseFile` still contains three `if` statements that check for resource allocation errors, which is way too many. You can make that function cleaner by implementing a Guard Clause.

Guard Clause

Context

You have a function that performs a task that can only be successfully completed under certain conditions (like valid input parameters).

Problem

The function is hard to read and maintain because it mixes pre-condition checks with the main program logic of the function.

Allocating resources always requires their cleanup. If you allocate a resource and then later on realize that another pre-condition of the function was not met, then that resource also has to be cleaned up.

It is difficult to follow the program flow if there are several pre-condition checks scattered across the function, particularly if these checks are implemented in nested `if` statements. When there are many such checks, the function becomes very long, which by itself is a code smell.

Code Smell

A code "smells" if it is badly structured or programmed in a way that makes the code hard to maintain. Examples of code smells are very long functions or duplicated code. More code smell examples and countermeasures are covered in the book *Refactoring: Improving the Design of Existing Code* by Martin Fowler (Addison-Wesley, 1999).

Solution

Check if you have mandatory pre-conditions and immediately return from the function if these pre-conditions are not met.

For example, check for the validity of input parameters or check if the program is in a state that allows execution of the rest of the function. Carefully think about which kind of pre-conditions for calling your function you want to set. On the one hand, it makes life easier for you to be very strict on what you allow as function input, but on the other hand, it would make life easier for the caller of your function if you are more liberal regarding possible inputs (as described by Postel's law: "Be conservative in what you do, be liberal in what you accept from others").

If you have many pre-condition checks, you can call a separate function for performing these checks. In any case, perform the checks before any resource allocation has been done because then it is very easy to return from a function as no cleanup of resources has to be done.

Clearly describe the pre-conditions for your function in the function's interface. The best place to document that behavior is in the header file where the function is declared.

If it is important for the caller to know which pre-condition was not met, you can provide the caller with error information. For example, you can Return Status Codes, but make sure to only Return Relevant Errors. The following code shows an example without returning error information:

someFile.h

```
/* This function operates on the 'user_input', which must not be NULL */
void someFunction(char* user_input);
```

someFile.c

```
void someFunction(char* user_input)
{
  if(user_input == NULL)
  {
    return;
  }
  operateOnData(user_input);
}
```

Consequences

Immediately returning when the pre-conditions are not met makes the code easier to read compared to nested `if` constructs. It is made very clear in the code that the function execution is not continued if the pre-conditions are not met. That makes the pre-conditions very well separated from the rest of the code.

However, some coding guidelines forbid returning in the middle of a function. For example, for code that has to be formally proved, return statements are usually only allowed at the very end of the function. In such a case, a Cleanup Record can be kept, which also is a better choice if you want to have a central place for error handling.

Known Uses

The following examples show applications of this pattern:

- The Guard Clause is described in the Portland Pattern Repository.

- The article "Error Detection" by Klaus Renzel (Proceedings of the 2nd EuroPLoP conference, 1997) describes the very similar Error Detection pattern that suggests introducing pre-condition and post-condition checks.

- The NetHack game uses this pattern at several places in its code, for example, in the `placebc` function. That function puts a chain on the NetHack hero that reduces the hero's movement speed as punishment. The function immediately returns if no chain objects are available.

- The OpenSSL code uses this pattern. For example, the `SSL_new` function immediately returns in case of invalid input parameters.

- The Wireshark code `capture_stats`, which is responsible for gathering statistics when sniffing network packets, first checks its input parameters for validity and immediately returns in case of invalid parameters.

Applied to Running Example

The following code shows how the `parseFile` function applies a Guard Clause to check pre-conditions of the function:

```c
int parseFile(char* file_name)
{
  int return_value = ERROR;
  FILE* file_pointer = 0;
  char* buffer = 0;

  if(file_name==NULL) ❶
  {
    return ERROR;
  }
  if(file_pointer=fopen(file_name, "r"))
  {
    if(buffer=malloc(BUFFER_SIZE))
    {
      return_value = searchFileForKeywords(buffer, file_pointer);
      free(buffer);
    }
    fclose(file_pointer);
  }
  return return_value;
}
```

❶ If invalid parameters are provided, we immediately return and no cleanup is required because no resources were acquired yet.

The code Returns Status Codes to implement the Guard Clause. It returns the constant `ERROR` in the specific case of a `NULL` parameter. The caller could now check the Return Value to know whether an invalid `NULL` parameter was provided to the function. But such an invalid parameter usually indicates a programming error, and checking for programming errors and propagating this information within the code is not a good idea. In such a case, it is easier to simply apply the Samurai Principle.

Samurai Principle

Context

You have some code with complicated error handling, and some errors are very severe. Your system does not perform safety-critical actions, and high availability is not very important.

Problem

When returning error information, you assume that the caller checks for this information. However, the caller can simply omit this check and the error might go unnoticed.

In C it is not mandatory to check return values of the called functions, and your caller can simply ignore the return value of a function. If the error that occurs in your function is severe and cannot be gracefully handled by the caller, you don't want your caller to decide whether and how the error should be handled. Instead, you'd want to make sure that an action is definitely taken.

Even if the caller handles an error situation, quite often the program will still crash or some error will still occur. The error might simply show up somewhere else—maybe somewhere in the caller's caller code that might not handle error situations properly. In such a case, handling the error disguises the error, which makes it much harder to debug the error in order to find out the root cause.

Some errors in your code might only occur very rarely. To Return Status Codes for such situations and handle them in the caller's code makes that code less readable, because it distracts from the main program logic and the actual purpose of the caller's code. The caller might have to write many lines of code to handle very rarely occurring situations.

Returning such error information also poses the problem of how to actually return the information. Using the Return Value or Out-Parameters of the function to return error information makes the function's signature more complicated and makes the code more difficult to understand. Because of this, you don't want to have additional parameters for your function that only return error information.

Solution

Return from a function victorious or not at all (samurai principle). If there is a situation for which you know that an error cannot be handled, then abort the program.

Don't use Out-Parameters or the Return Value to return error information. You have all the error information at hand, so handle the error right away. If an error occurs, simply let the program crash. Abort the program in a structured way by using the assert statement. Additionally, you can provide debug information with the assert statement as shown in the following code:

```
void someFunction()
{
  assert(checkPreconditions() && "Preconditions are not met");
  mainFunctionality();
}
```

This piece of code checks for the condition in the assert statement and if it is not true, the assert statement including the string on the right will be printed to stderr and the program will be aborted. It would be OK to abort the program in a less structured way by not checking for NULL pointers and accessing such pointers. Simply make sure that the program crashes at the point where the error occurs.

Quite often, the Guard Clauses are good candidates for aborting the program in case of errors. For example, if you know that a coding error occurred (if the caller provided you a NULL pointer), abort the program and log debug information instead of returning error information to the caller. However, don't abort the program for every kind of error. For example, runtime errors like invalid user input should definitely not lead to a program abort.

The caller has to be well aware of the behavior of your function, so you have to document in the function's API the cases in which the function aborts the program. For example, the function documentation has to state whether the program crashes if the function is provided a NULL pointer as parameter.

Of course, the Samurai Principle is not appropriate for all errors or all application domains. You wouldn't want to let the program crash in case of some unexpected user input. However, in case of a programming error, it can be appropriate to fail fast and let the program crash. That makes it as simple as possible for the programmers to find the error.

Still, such a crash need not necessarily be shown to the user. If your program is just some noncritical part of a larger application, then you might still want your program to crash. But in the context of the overall application, your program might fail silently so as not not disturb the rest of the application or the user.

Asserts in Release Executables

When using assert statements, the discussion comes up of whether to only have them active in debug executables or whether to also have them active in release executables. Assert statements can be deactivated by defining the macro NDEBUG in your code before including *assert.h* or by directly defining the macro in your toolchain. A main argument for deactivating assert statements for release executables is that you already catch your programming errors that use asserts when testing your debug executables, so there is no need to risk aborting programs due to asserts in release executables. A main argument for also having assert statements active in release executables is that you use them anyway for critical errors that cannot be handled gracefully, and such errors should never go unnoticed, not even in release executables used by your customers.

Consequences

The error cannot go unnoticed because it is handled right at the point where it shows up. The caller is not burdened with having to check for this error, so the caller code becomes simpler. However, now the caller cannot choose how to react to the error.

In some cases aborting the application is OK because a fast crash is better than unpredictable behavior later on. Still, you have to consider how such an error should be presented to the user. Maybe the user will see it as an abort statement on the screen. However, for embedded applications that use sensors and actors to interact with the environment, you have to take more care and consider the influence an aborting program has on the environment and whether this is acceptable. In many such cases, the application might have to be more robust and simply aborting the application will not be acceptable.

To abort the program and to Log Errors right at the point where the error shows up makes it easier to find and fix the error because the error is not disguised. Thus, in the long term, by applying this pattern you end up with more robust and bug-free software.

Known Uses

The following examples show applications of this pattern:

- A similar pattern that suggests adding a debug information string to an `assert` statement is called Assertion Context and is described in the book *Patterns in C* by Adam Tornhill (Leanpub, 2014).

- The Wireshark network sniffer applies this pattern all over its code. For example, the function `register_capture_dissector` uses `assert` to check that the registration of a dissector is unique.

- The source code of the Git project uses `assert` statements. For example, the functions for storing SHA1 hash values use `assert` to check whether the path to the file where the hash value should be stored is correct.

- The OpenWrt code responsible for handling large numbers uses `assert` statements to check pre-conditions in its functions.

- A similar pattern with the name Let It Crash is presented by Pekka Alho and Jari Rauhamäki in the article "Patterns for Light-Weight Fault Tolerance and Decoupled Design in Distributed Control Systems" (*https://oreil.ly/x0tQW*). The pattern targets distributed control systems and suggests letting single fail-safe processes crash and then restart quickly.

- The C standard library function `strcpy` does not check for valid user input. If you provide the function with a `NULL` pointer, it crashes.

Applied to Running Example

The `parseFile` function now looks a lot better. Instead of returning an Error Code, you now have a simple `assert` statement. That makes the following code shorter, and the caller of the code does not have the burden of checking against the Return Value:

```c
int parseFile(char* file_name)
{
  int return_value = ERROR;
  FILE* file_pointer = 0;
  char* buffer = 0;

  assert(file_name!=NULL && "Invalid filename");
  if(file_pointer=fopen(file_name, "r"))
  {
    if(buffer=malloc(BUFFER_SIZE))
    {
      return_value = searchFileForKeywords(buffer, file_pointer);
      free(buffer);
    }
    fclose(file_pointer);
  }
  return return_value;
}
```

While the `if` statements that don't require resource cleanup are eliminated, the code still contains nested `if` statements for everything that requires cleanup. Also, you don't yet handle the error situation if the `malloc` call fails. All of this can be improved by using Goto Error Handling.

Goto Error Handling

Context

You have a function that acquires and cleans up multiple resources. Maybe you already tried to reduce the complexity by applying Guard Clause, Function Split, or Samurai Principle, but you still have a deeply nested `if` construct in the code, particularly because of resource acquisition. You might even have duplicated code for resource cleanup.

Problem

Code gets difficult to read and maintain if it acquires and cleans up multiple resources at different places within a function.

Such code becomes difficult because usually each resource acquisition can fail, and each resource cleanup can just be called if the resource was successfully acquired. To implement this, a lot of if statements are required, and when implemented poorly, nested if statements in a single function make the code hard to read and maintain.

Because you have to clean up the resources, returning in the middle of the function when something goes wrong is not a good option. This is because all resources already acquired have to be cleaned up before each return statement. So you end up with multiple points in the code where the same resource is being cleaned up, but you don't want to have duplicated error handling and cleanup code.

Solution

Have all resource cleanup and error handling at the end of the function. If a resource cannot be acquired, use the goto statement to jump to the resource cleanup code.

Acquire the resources in the order you need them, and at the end of your function clean the resources up in the reverse order. For the resource cleanup, have a separate label to which you can jump for each cleanup function. Simply jump to the label if an error occurs or if a resource cannot be acquired, but don't jump multiple times and only jump forward as is done in the following code:

```
void someFunction()
{
  if(!allocateResource1())
  {
    goto cleanup1;
  }
  if(!allocateResource2())
  {
    goto cleanup2;
  }
  mainFunctionality();
cleanup2:
  cleanupResource2();
cleanup1:
  cleanupResource1();
}
```

If your coding standard forbids the usage of goto statements, you can emulate it with a do{ ... }while(0); loop around your code. On error use break to jump to the end of the loop where you put your error handling. However, that workaround is usually a bad idea because if goto is not allowed by your coding standard, then you should also not be emulating it just to continue programming in your own style. You could use a Cleanup Record as an alternative to goto.

In any case, the usage of goto might simply be an indicator that your function is already too complex, and splitting the function, for example with Object-Based Error Handling, might be a better idea.

goto: Good or Evil?

There are many discussions about whether the usage of goto is good or bad. The most famous article against the use of goto is by Edsger W. Dijkstra (*https://oreil.ly/yXkyq*), who argues that it obscures the program flow. That is true if goto is being used to jump back and forth in a program, but goto in C cannot be as badly abused as in the programming languages Dijkstra wrote about. (In C you can only use goto to jump within a function.)

Consequences

The function is a single point of return, and the main program flow is well separated from the error handling and resource cleanup. No nested if statements are required anymore to achieve this, but not everybody is used to and likes reading goto statements.

If you use goto statements, you have to be careful, because it is tempting to use them for things other than error handling and cleanup, and that definitely makes the code unreadable. Also, you have to be extra careful to have the correct cleanup functions at the correct labels. It is a common pitfall to accidentally put cleanup functions at the wrong label.

Known Uses

The following examples show applications of this pattern:

- The Linux kernel code uses mostly goto-based error handling. For example, the book *Linux Device Drivers* (*https://oreil.ly/linux-device-drivers*) by Alessandro Rubini and Jonathan Corbet (O'Reilly, 2001) describes goto-based error handling for programming Linux device drivers.

- *The CERT C Coding Standard* by Robert C. Seacord (Addison-Wesley Professional, 2014) suggests the use of goto for error handling.

- The goto emulation using a do-while loop is described in the Portland Pattern Repository as the Trivial Do-While-Loop pattern.

- The OpenSSL code uses the goto statement. For example, the functions that handle X509 certificates use goto to jump forward to a central error handler.

- The Wireshark code uses goto statements to jump from its main function to a central error handler at the end of that function.

Applied to Running Example

Even though quite a few people highly disapprove of the use of goto statements, the error handling is better compared to the previous code example. In the following code there are no nested if statements, and the cleanup code is well separated from the main program flow:

```
int parseFile(char* file_name)
{
  int return_value = ERROR;
  FILE* file_pointer = 0;
  char* buffer = 0;

  assert(file_name!=NULL && "Invalid filename");
  if(!(file_pointer=fopen(file_name, "r")))
  {
    goto error_fileopen;
  }
  if(!(buffer=malloc(BUFFER_SIZE)))
  {
    goto error_malloc;
  }
  return_value = searchFileForKeywords(buffer, file_pointer);
  free(buffer);
error_malloc:
  fclose(file_pointer);
error_fileopen:
  return return_value;
}
```

Now, let's say you don't like goto statements or your coding guidelines forbid them, but you still have to clean up your resources. There are alternatives. You can, for example, simply have a Cleanup Record instead.

Cleanup Record

Context

You have a function that acquires and cleans up multiple resources. Maybe you already tried to reduce the complexity by applying Guard Clause, Function Split, or Samurai Principle, but you still have a deeply nested if construct in the code, because of resource acquisition. You might even have duplicated code for resource cleanup. Your coding standards don't allow you to implement Goto Error Handling, or you don't want to use goto.

Problem

It is difficult to make a piece of code easy to read and maintain if this code acquires and cleans up multiple resources, particularly if those resources depend on one another.

This is difficult because usually each resource acquisition can fail, and each resource cleanup can just be called if the resource was successfully acquired. To implement this, a lot of `if` statements are required, and when implemented poorly, nested `if` statements in a single function make the code hard to read and maintain.

Because you have to clean up the resources, returning in the middle of the function when something goes wrong is not a good option. This is because all resources already acquired have to be cleaned up before each return statement. So you end up with multiple points in the code where the same resource is being cleaned up, but you don't want to have duplicated error handling and cleanup code.

Solution

Call resource acquisition functions as long as they succeed, and store which functions require cleanup. Call the cleanup functions depending on these stored values.

In C, lazy evaluation of `if` statements can be used to achieve this. Simply call a sequence of functions inside a single `if` statement as long as these functions succeed. For each function call, store the acquired resource in a variable. Have the code operating on the resources in the body of the `if` statement, and have all resource cleanup after the `if` statement only if the resource was successfully acquired. The following code shows an example of this:

```
void someFunction()
{
  if((r1=allocateResource1()) && (r2=allocateResource2()))
  {
    mainFunctionality();
  }
  if(r1) ❶
  {
    cleanupResource1();
  }
  if(r2) ❶
  {
    cleanupResource2();
  }
}
```

❶ To make the code easier to read, you can alternatively put these checks inside the cleanup functions. This is a good approach if you have to provide the resource variable to the cleanup function anyway.

Consequences

You now have no nested if statements anymore, and you still have one central point at the end of the function for resource cleanup. That makes the code a lot easier to read because the main program flow is no longer obscured by error handling.

Also, the function is easy to read because it has a single exit point. However, the fact that you have to have many variables for keeping track of which resources were successfully allocated makes the code more complicated. Maybe an Aggregate Instance can help to structure the resource variables.

If many resources are being acquired, then many functions are being called in the single if statement. That makes the if statement very hard to read and even harder to debug. Therefore, if many resources are being acquired, it is a much better solution to have Object-Based Error Handling.

Another reason for having Object-Based Error Handling instead is that the preceding code is still complicated because it has a single function that contains the main functionality as well as resource allocation and cleanup. So one function has multiple responsibilities.

Known Uses

The following examples show applications of this pattern:

- In the Portland Pattern Repository, a similar solution where each of the called functions registers a cleanup handler to a callback list is presented. For cleanup, all functions from the callback list are called.

- The OpenSSL function dh_key2buf uses lazy evaluation in an if statement to keep track of allocated bytes that are then cleaned up later on.

- The function cap_open_socket of the Wireshark network sniffer uses lazy evaluation of an if statement and stores the resources allocated in this if statement in variables. At cleanup, these variables are then checked, and if the resource allocation was successful, the resource is cleaned up.

- The nvram_commit function of the OpenWrt source code allocates its resources inside an if statement and stores these resources to a variable right inside that if statement.

Applied to Running Example

Now, instead of `goto` statements and nested `if` statements, you have a single `if` statement. The advantage of not using `goto` statements in the following code is that the error handling is well separated from the main program flow:

```
int parseFile(char* file_name)
{
  int return_value = ERROR;
  FILE* file_pointer = 0;
  char* buffer = 0;

  assert(file_name!=NULL && "Invalid filename");
  if((file_pointer=fopen(file_name, "r")) &&
     (buffer=malloc(BUFFER_SIZE)))
  {
    return_value = searchFileForKeywords(buffer, file_pointer);
  }
  if(file_pointer)
  {
    fclose(file_pointer);
  }
  if(buffer)
  {
    free(buffer);
  }
  return return_value;
}
```

Still, the code does not look nice. This one function has a lot of responsibilities: resource allocation, resource deallocation, file handling, and error handling. These responsibilities should be split into different functions with Object-Based Error Handling.

Object-Based Error Handling

Context

You have a function that acquires and cleans up multiple resources. Maybe you already tried to reduce the complexity by applying Guard Clause, Function Split, or Samurai Principle, but you still have a deeply nested `if` construct in the code, because of resource acquisition. You might even have duplicated code for resource cleanup. But maybe you already got rid of nested `if` statements by using Goto Error Handling or a Cleanup Record.

Problem

Having multiple responsibilities in one function, such as resource acquisition, resource cleanup, and usage of that resource, makes that code difficult to implement, read, maintain, and test.

All of that becomes difficult because usually each resource acquisition can fail, and each resource cleanup can just be called if the resource was successfully acquired. To implement this, a lot of if statements are required, and when implemented poorly, nested if statements in a single function make the code hard to read and maintain.

Because you have to clean up the resources, returning in the middle of the function when something goes wrong is not a good option. This is because all resources already acquired have to be cleaned up before each return statement. So you end up with multiple points in the code where the same resource is being cleaned up, but you don't want to have duplicated error handling and cleanup code.

Even if you already have a Cleanup Record or Goto Error Handling, the function is still hard to read because it mixes different responsibilities. The function is responsible for acquisition of multiple resources, error handling, and cleanup of multiple resources. However, a function should only have one responsibility.

Solution

Put initialization and cleanup into separate functions, similar to the concept of constructors and destructors in object-oriented programming.

In your main function, simply call one function that acquires all resources, one function that operates in these resources, and one function that cleans up the resources.

If the acquired resources are not global, then you have to pass the resources along the functions. When you have multiple resources, you can pass an Aggregate Instance containing all resources along the functions. If you want to instead hide the actual resources from the caller, you can use a Handle for passing the resource information between the functions.

If resource allocation fails, store this information in a variable (for example, a NULL pointer if memory allocation fails). When using or cleaning up the resources, first check whether the resource is valid. Perform that check not in your main function, but rather in the called functions, because that makes your main function a lot more readable:

```
void someFunction()
{
  allocateResources();
  mainFunctionality();
  cleanupResources();
}
```

Consequences

The function is now easy to read. While it requires allocation and cleanup of multiple resources, as well as the operations on these resources, these different tasks are still well separated into different functions.

Having object-like instances that you pass along functions is known as an "object-based" programming style. This style makes procedural programming more similar to object-oriented programming, and thus code written in such a style is also more familiar to programmers who are used to object-orientation.

In the main function, there is no reason for having multiple return statements anymore, because there are no more nested if statements for the logic of resource allocation and cleanup. However, you did not eliminate the logic regarding resource allocation and cleanup, of course. All this logic is still present in the separated functions, but it is not mixed with the operation on the resources anymore.

Instead of having a single function, you now have multiple functions. While that could have a negative impact on performance, it usually does not matter a lot. The performance impact is minor, and for most applications it is not relevant.

Known Uses

The following examples show applications of this pattern:

- This form of cleanup is used in object-oriented programming where constructors and destructors are implicitly called.
- The OpenSSL code uses this pattern. For example, the allocation and cleanup of buffers is realized with the functions BUF_MEM_new and BUF_MEM_free that are called across the code to cover buffer handling.
- The show_help function of the OpenWrt source code shows help information in a context menu. The function calls an initialization function to create a struct, then operates on that struct and calls a function to clean up that struct.
- The function cmd__windows_named_pipe of the Git project uses a Handle to create a pipe, then operates on that pipe and calls a separate function to clean up the pipe.

Applied to Running Example

You finally end up with the following code, in which the parseFile function calls other functions to create and clean up a parser instance:

```
typedef struct
{
  FILE* file_pointer;
```

```c
  char* buffer;
}FileParser;

int parseFile(char* file_name)
{
  int return_value;
  FileParser* parser = createParser(file_name);
  return_value = searchFileForKeywords(parser);
  cleanupParser(parser);
  return return_value;
}

int searchFileForKeywords(FileParser* parser)
{
  if(parser == NULL)
  {
    return ERROR;
  }
  while(fgets(parser->buffer, BUFFER_SIZE, parser->file_pointer)!=NULL)
  {
    if(strcmp("KEYWORD_ONE\n", parser->buffer)==0)
    {
      return KEYWORD_ONE_FOUND_FIRST;
    }
    if(strcmp("KEYWORD_TWO\n", parser->buffer)==0)
    {
      return KEYWORD_TWO_FOUND_FIRST;
    }
  }
  return NO_KEYWORD_FOUND;
}

FileParser* createParser(char* file_name)
{
  assert(file_name!=NULL && "Invalid filename");
  FileParser* parser = malloc(sizeof(FileParser));
  if(parser)
  {
    parser->file_pointer=fopen(file_name, "r");
    parser->buffer = malloc(BUFFER_SIZE);
    if(!parser->file_pointer || !parser->buffer)
    {
      cleanupParser(parser);
      return NULL;
    }
  }
  return parser;
}

void cleanupParser(FileParser* parser)
{
  if(parser)
```

```
    {
      if(parser->buffer)
      {
        free(parser->buffer);
      }
      if(parser->file_pointer)
      {
        fclose(parser->file_pointer);
      }
      free(parser);
    }
}
```

In the code, there is no more `if` cascade in the main program flow. This makes the `parseFile` function a lot easier to read, debug, and maintain. The main function does not cope with resource allocation, resource deallocation, or error handling details anymore. Instead, those details are all put into separate functions, so each function has one responsibility.

Have a look at the beauty of this final code example compared to the first code example. The applied patterns helped step-by-step to make the code easier to read and maintain. In each step, the nested `if` cascade was removed and the method of how to handle errors was improved.

Summary

This chapter showed you how to perform error handling in C. Function Split tells you to split your functions into smaller parts to make error handling of these parts easier. A Guard Clause for your functions checks pre-conditions of your function and returns immediately if they are not met. This leaves fewer error-handling obligations for the rest of that function. Instead of returning from the function, you could also abort the program, adhering to the Samurai Principle. When it comes to more complex error handling—particularly in combination with acquiring and releasing resources—you have several options. Goto Error Handling makes it possible to jump forward in your function to an error-handling section. Instead of jumping, Cleanup Record stores the info, which resources require cleanup, and performs it by the end of the function. A method of resource acquisition that is closer to object-oriented programming is Object-Based Error Handling, which uses separate initialization and cleanup functions similar to the concept of constructors and destructors.

With these error-handling patterns in your repertoire, you now have the skill to write small programs that handle error situations in a way that ensures the code stays maintainable.

Further Reading

If you're ready for more, here are some resources that can help you further your knowledge of error handling.

- The Portland Pattern Repository (*https://oreil.ly/qFLdA*) provides many patterns and discussions on error handling as well as other topics. Most of the error-handling patterns target exception handling or how to use assertions, but some C patterns are also presented.

- A comprehensive overview of error handling in general is provided in the master's thesis "Error Handling in Structured and Object-Oriented Programming Languages" by Thomas Aglassinger (University of Oulu, 1999). This thesis describes how different kinds of errors arise; discusses error-handling mechanisms of the programming languages C, Basic, Java, and Eiffel; and provides best practices for error handling in these languages, such as reversing the cleanup order of resources compared to the order of their allocation. The thesis also mentions several third-party solutions in the form of C libraries providing enhanced error handling features for C, like exception handling by using the commands `setjmp` and `longjmp`.

- Fifteen object-oriented patterns on error handling tailored for business information systems are presented in the article "Error Handling for Business Information Systems" (*https://oreil.ly/bQnfx*) by Klaus Renzel, and most of the patterns can be applied for non-object-oriented domains as well. The presented patterns cover error detection, error logging, and error handling.

- Implementations including C code snippets for some Gang of Four design patterns are presented in the book *Patterns in C* by Adam Tornhill (Leanpub, 2014). The book further provides best practices in the form of C patterns, some of them covering error handling.

- A collection of patterns for error logging and error handling is presented in the articles "Patterns for Generation, Handling and Management of Errors" and "More Patterns for the Generation, Handling and Management of Errors" by Andy Longshaw and Eoin Woods (*https://oreil.ly/7Yj8h*). Most of the patterns target exception-based error handling.

Outlook

The next chapter shows you how to handle errors when looking at larger programs that return error information across interfaces to other functions. The patterns tell you which kind of error information to return and how to return it.

CHAPTER 2

Returning Error Information

The previous chapter focused on error handling. This chapter continues this discussion, but focuses on how to inform users of your code about the errors detected.

For every larger program, programmers have to decide how to react to errors arising in their own code, how to react to errors arising in third-party code, how to pass this error information along in the code, and how to present this error information to the user.

Most object-oriented programming languages come with the handy mechanism of exceptions to provide the programmer with an additional channel for returning error information, but C does not natively provide such a mechanism. There are ways to emulate exception handling or even inheritance among exceptions in C, for example as described in the book *Object-Oriented Programming with ANSI-C* (*https://oreil.ly/ YK7x1*) by Axel-Tobias Schreiner (2011). But for C programmers working on legacy C code or for C programmers who want to stick to the native C style they are used to, introducing such exception mechanisms is not the way to go. Instead, such C programmers need guidance on how to use the mechanisms for error handling already natively present in C.

This chapter provides such guidance on how error information can be transported between functions and across interfaces. Figure 2-1 shows an overview of the patterns covered in this chapter and their relationships, and Table 2-1 provides a summary of the patterns.

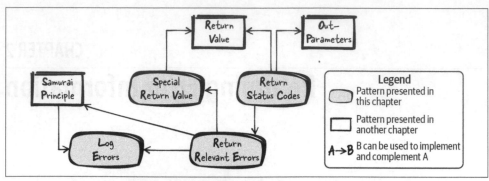

Figure 2-1. Overview of patterns for returning error information

Table 2-1. Patterns for returning error information

Pattern name	Summary
Return Status Codes	You want to have a mechanism to return status information to the caller, so that the caller can react to it. You want the mechanism to be simple to use, and the caller should be able to clearly distinguish between different error situations that could occur. Therefore, use the Return Value of a function to return status information. Return a value that represents a specific status. Both of you as the callee and the caller must have a mutual understanding of what the value means.
Return Relevant Errors	On the one hand, the caller should be able to react to errors; on the other hand, the more error information you return, the more your code and the code of your caller have to deal with error handling, which makes the code longer. Longer code is harder to read and maintain and brings in the risk of additional bugs. Therefore, only return error information to the caller if that information is relevant to the caller. Error information is only relevant to the caller if the caller can react to that information.
Special Return Values	You want to return error information, but don't want to explicitly Return Status Codes, because that makes it difficult for your function to return other data. You could add Out-Parameters to your function, but it would make calling the function more difficult. Therefore, use the Return Value of your function to return the data computed by the function. Reserve one or more special values to be returned if an error occurs.
Log Errors	You want to make sure that in case of an error you can easily find out its cause. However, you don't want your error-handling code to become complicated because of this. Therefore, use different channels to return error information that is relevant for the calling code and error information that is relevant for the developer. For example, write debug error information into a log file and don't return the detailed debug error information to the caller.

Running Example

You want to implement a software-module that provides functionality to store string-values for keys identified via strings. In other words, you want to implement a functionality similar to the Windows registry. To keep things simple, the following code will not contain hierarchical relationships between the keys, and only functions to create registry elements will be discussed:

Registry API

```
/* Handle for registry keys */
typedef struct Key* RegKey;

/* Create a new registry key identified via the provided 'key_name' */
RegKey createKey(char* key_name);

/* Store the provided 'value' to the provided 'key' */
void storeValue(RegKey key, char* value);

/* Make the key available for being read (by other
   functions that are not part of this code example) */
void publishKey(RegKey key);
```

Registry implementation

```
#define STRING_SIZE 100
#define MAX_KEYS 40

struct Key
{
  char key_name[STRING_SIZE];
  char key_value[STRING_SIZE];
};

/* file-global array holding all registry keys */
static struct Key* key_list[MAX_KEYS];

RegKey createKey(char* key_name)
{
  RegKey newKey = calloc(1, sizeof(struct Key));
  strcpy(newKey->key_name, key_name);
  return newKey;
}

void storeValue(RegKey key, char* value)
{
  strcpy(key->key_value, value);
}

void publishKey(RegKey key)
{
  int i;
  for(i=0; i<MAX_KEYS; i++)
  {
    if(key_list[i] == NULL)
    {
      key_list[i] = key;
      return;
    }
  }
}
```

With the preceding code, you are not sure how you should provide your caller with error information in case of internal errors or, for example, in case of invalid function input parameter values. Your caller does not really know whether the calls succeeded or whether something failed and ends up with the following code:

```
RegKey my_key = createKey("myKey");
storeValue(my_key, "A");
publishKey(my_key);
```

The caller's code is very short and easy to read, but the caller does not know whether any error occurred and is not able to react to errors. To give the caller that possibilitym you want to introduce error handling in your code and provide your caller with error information. The first idea that comes to your mind is to let the caller know about any errors showing up in your software-module. To do that, you Return Status Codes.

Return Status Codes

Context

You implement a software-module that performs some error handling, and you want to return error and other status information to your caller.

Problem

You want to have a mechanism to return status information to the caller, so that the caller can react to it. You want the mechanism to be simple to use, and the caller should be able to clearly distinguish between different error situations that could occur.

In the old days of C, error information was transported by an error code with the global errno variable. The global errno variable had to be reset by the caller, then a function had to be called, and the function indicated errors by setting the global errno variable, which the caller had to check after the function call.

However, compared to using errno, you want a way to return status information that makes it easier for the caller to check for errors. The caller should see from the function signature how the status information will be returned and which kind of status information to expect.

Also, the mechanism to return status information should be safe to use in a multi-threaded environment, and only the called function should have the ability to influence the returned status information. In other words, it should be possible to use the mechanism and still have a reentrant function.

Solution

Use the Return Value of a function to return status information. Return a value that represents a specific status. Both of you as the callee and the caller must have a mutual understanding of what the value means.

Usually, the returned value is a numeric identifier. The caller can check the function Return Value against that identifier and react accordingly. If the function has to return other function results, provide them to the caller in the form of Out-Parameters.

Define the numeric status identifiers in your API as an enum or by using #define. If there are many status codes or if your software-module consists of more than one header file, you could have a separate header file that just contains the status codes and is included by your other header files.

Give the status identifiers a meaningful name and document their meaning with comments. Make sure to name your status codes in a consistent way across your APIs.

The following code shows an example of using status codes:

Caller's code using status codes

```
ErrorCode status = func();
if(status == MAJOR_ERROR)
{
  /* abort program */
}
else if(status == MINOR_ERROR)
{
  /* handle error */
}
else if(status == OK)
{
  /* continue normal execution */
}
```

Callee API providing status codes

```
typedef enum
{
  MINOR_ERROR,
  MAJOR_ERROR,
  OK
}ErrorCode;

ErrorCode func();
```

Callee implementation providing status codes

```
ErrorCode func()
{
  if(minorErrorOccurs())
  {
    return MINOR_ERROR;
  }
  else if(majorErrorOccurs())
  {
    return MAJOR_ERROR;
  }
  else
  {
    return OK;
  }
}
```

Consequences

You now have a way to return status information that makes it very easy for the caller to check for occurring errors. Compared to errno, the caller does not have to set and check the error information in steps in addition to the function call. Instead, the caller can check the information directly against the return value of the function call.

Returning status codes can safely be used in multithreaded environments. Callers can be sure that only the called function, and no other side-channels, influences the returned status.

The function signature makes it very clear how the status information is returned. This is made clear for the caller and also clear for the compiler or static code analysis tools, which can check if the caller checked the function return value and against all statuses that could occur.

As the function now provides different results in different error situations, these results have to be tested. Compared to a function without any error handling, more extensive testing has to be done. Also, the caller is burdened with having to check these error situations, which might blow up the size of the caller's code.

Any C function can return only one object of the type specified in the function signature, and the function now returns the status code. Thus, you have to use more complicated techniques for returning other function results. You could do this using Out-Parameters, which have the drawback that an additional parameter is required, or you could return an Aggregate Instance that contains the status information and other function results.

Known Uses

The following examples show applications of this pattern:

- Microsoft uses HRESULT to return status information. An HRESULT is a unique status code. Making the status code unique has the advantage that the status information can be transported across many functions while still making it possible to find out where that status originated. But making the status code unique brings in the additional effort of assigning status numbers and keeping track of who is allowed to use which status numbers. Another specialty of HRESULT is that it encodes specific information, such as the severity of an error, into the status code by using some bits dedicated to returning this information.

- The code of the Apache Portable Runtime defines the type apr_status_t to return error information. Any function that returns error information in this way returns APR_SUCCESS on success or any other value to indicate errors. Other values are uniquely defined error codes specified via #define statements.

- The OpenSSL code defines status codes in several header files (*dsaerr.h*, *kdferr.h*, …). As an example, the status codes KDF_R_MISSING_PARAMETER or KDF_R_MISSING_SALT inform the caller in detail about missing or wrong input parameters. The status codes in each of the files are defined only for a specific set of functions that belong to that file, and the status code values are not unique across the whole OpenSSL code.

- The pattern Error Code is described in the Portland Pattern Repository. It describes the idea of returning error information by explicitly using the function's return value.

Applied to Running Example

Now you provide your caller with information in case of errors in your code. In the following code you check for things that could go wrong and provide that information to the caller:

Registry API

```
/* Error codes returned by this registry */
typedef enum
{
  OK,
  OUT_OF_MEMORY,
  INVALID_KEY,
  INVALID_STRING,
  STRING_TOO_LONG,
  CANNOT_ADD_KEY
}RegError;
```

```
/* Handle for registry keys */
typedef struct Key* RegKey;

/* Create a new registry key identified via the provided 'key_name'.
   Returns OK if no problem occurs, INVALID_KEY if the 'key'
   parameter is NULL, INVALID_STRING if 'key_name' is NULL,
   STRING_TOO_LONG if 'key_name' is too long, or OUT_OF_MEMORY
   if no memory resources are available. */
RegError createKey(char* key_name, RegKey* key);

/* Store the provided 'value' to the provided 'key'.
   Returns OK if no problem occurs, INVALID_KEY if the 'key'
   parameter is NULL, INVALID_STRING if 'value' is NULL, or
   STRING_TOO_LONG if 'value' is too long. */
RegError storeValue(RegKey key, char* value);

/* Make the key available for being read. Returns OK if no
   problem occurs, INVALID_KEY if 'key' is NULL, or CANNOT_ADD_KEY
   if the registry is full and no more keys can be published. */
RegError publishKey(RegKey key);
```

Registry implementation

```
#define STRING_SIZE 100
#define MAX_KEYS 40

struct Key
{
  char key_name[STRING_SIZE];
  char key_value[STRING_SIZE];
};

/* file-global array holding all registry keys */
static struct Key* key_list[MAX_KEYS];

RegError createKey(char* key_name, RegKey* key)
{
  if(key == NULL)
  {
    return INVALID_KEY;
  }

  if(key_name == NULL)
  {
    return INVALID_STRING;
  }

  if(STRING_SIZE <= strlen(key_name))
  {
    return STRING_TOO_LONG;
  }
```

```c
    RegKey newKey = calloc(1, sizeof(struct Key));
    if(newKey == NULL)
    {
      return OUT_OF_MEMORY;
    }

    strcpy(newKey->key_name, key_name);
    *key = newKey;
    return OK;
}

RegError storeValue(RegKey key, char* value)
{
  if(key == NULL)
  {
    return INVALID_KEY;
  }

  if(value == NULL)
  {
    return INVALID_STRING;
  }

  if(STRING_SIZE <= strlen(value))
  {
    return STRING_TOO_LONG;
  }

  strcpy(key->key_value, value);
  return OK;
}

RegError publishKey(RegKey key)
{
  int i;
  if(key == NULL)
  {
    return INVALID_KEY;
  }

  for(i=0; i<MAX_KEYS; i++)
  {
    if(key_list[i] == NULL)
    {
      key_list[i] = key;
      return OK;
    }
  }

  return CANNOT_ADD_KEY;
}
```

Now the caller can react to the provided error information and can, for example, provide the user of the application with detailed information about what went wrong:

Caller's code

```
RegError err;
RegKey my_key;

err = createKey("myKey", &my_key);
if(err == INVALID_KEY || err == INVALID_STRING)
{
  printf("Internal application error\n");
}
if(err == STRING_TOO_LONG)
{
  printf("Provided registry key name too long\n");
}
if(err == OUT_OF_MEMORY)
{
  printf("Insufficient resources to create key\n");
}

err = storeValue(my_key, "A");
if(err == INVALID_KEY || err == INVALID_STRING)
{
  printf("Internal application error\n");
}
if(err == STRING_TOO_LONG)
{
  printf("Provided registry value to long to be stored to this key\n");
}

err = publishKey(my_key);
if(err == INVALID_KEY)
{
  printf("Internal application error\n");
}
if(err == CANNOT_ADD_KEY)
{
  printf("Key cannot be published, because the registry is full\n");
}
```

The caller can now react to errors, but the code for the registry software-module as well as the code for the caller have more than doubled in size. The caller code could be cleaned up a little by having a separate function for mapping the error code to error texts, but the majority of that code would still cope with error handling.

You can see that error handling did not come for free. A lot of effort was put into implementing error handling. This can also be seen in the registry API. The comments for the functions became a lot longer because they have to describe which error situations can occur. The caller also has to put a lot of effort into thinking about what to do if a specific error occurs.

When providing such detailed error information to the caller, you burden the caller with reacting to these errors and thinking about which errors are relevant to handle and which are irrelevant. Thus, special care has to be taken to on the one hand, provide the caller with the necessary error information, but on the other hand, not to flood the caller with unnecessary information.

Next, you want to make these considerations in your code, and you only want to provide error information that is actually useful to the caller. Thus, you only Return Relevant Errors.

Return Relevant Errors

Context

You implement a software-module that performs some error handling, and you want to return error information to your caller.

Problem

On the one hand, the caller should be able to react to errors; on the other hand, the more error information you return, the more your code and the code of your caller have to deal with error handling, which makes the code longer. Longer code is harder to read and maintain and brings in the risk of additional bugs.

In order to return error information to your caller, detecting the error and returning the information are not your only tasks. You also have to document in your API which errors are returned. If you don't do that, then your caller will not know which errors to expect and handle. Documenting error behavior is work that has to be done. The more types of errors there are, the more documentation work has to be done.

Returning very detailed, implementation-specific error information and adding additional error information later on in your code if the implementation changes implies that with such an implementation change, you have to semantically change your interface that documents the returned error information. Such changes might not be desirable for your existing callers because they would have to adapt their code to react to the newly introduced error information.

Providing detailed error information is also not always a good thing for the caller either. Each error information returned to the caller means additional work for the caller. The caller has to decide if the error information is relevant and how to handle it.

Solution

Only return error information to the caller if that information is relevant to the caller. Error information is only relevant to the caller if the caller can react to that information.

If the caller cannot react to the error information, then it would be unnecessary to provide the caller the opportunity (or the burden) to do so.

There are several ways to return only relevant error information. One extreme way is to simply not return any error information at all. For example, when you have a function `cleanupMemory (void* handle)` that cleans up memory, there is no need to return information if the cleanup succeeded because the caller cannot react in the code to such a cleanup error (retrying to call a cleanup function is in most cases not a solution). Thus the function simply does not return any error information. To make sure that errors within the function do not go unnoticed, aborting the program in case of error (Samurai Principle) might even be an option.

Or imagine the only reason why you return the error to the caller is so the caller can then log this error. In that case, do not return the error to the caller, but instead simply Log Errors yourself in order to make life easier for the caller.

If you already Return Status Codes, then only the error information that is relevant to the caller should be returned. Other errors that occur can be summarized as one internal error code. Also, detailed error codes from the functions you call need not necessarily all be returned by your function. They can be summarized as one internal error code as shown in the following code:

Caller's code

```
ErrorCode status = func();
if(status == MAJOR_ERROR || status == UNKNOWN_ERROR)
{
  /* abort program */
}
else if(status == MINOR_ERROR)
{
  /* handle error */
}
else if(status == OK)
{
  /* continue normal execution*/
}
```

API

```
typedef enum
{
  MINOR_ERROR,
```

```
      MAJOR_ERROR,
      UNKNOWN_ERROR,
      OK
   }ErrorCode;

   ErrorCode func();
```

Implementation

```
   ErrorCode func()
   {
     if(minorErrorOccurs())
     {
       return MINOR_ERROR;
     }
     else if(majorErrorOccurs())
     {
       return MAJOR_ERROR;
     }
     else if(internalError1Occurs() || internalError2Occurs())
     {
       return UNKNOWN_ERROR;  ❶
     }
     else
     {
       return OK;
     }
   }
```

❶ You return the same error information if `internalError1Occurs` or `internal Error2Occurs` because it is irrelevant to the caller which of the two implementation-specific errors occurs. The caller would react to both errors in the same way (in the preceding example, the reaction is to abort the program).

If more detailed error information is needed for debugging purposes, you could Log Errors. If you realize that there are not many error situations after returning only relevant errors, then instead of error codes, it might be a better solution to simply have Special Return Values to return the error information.

Consequences

Not returning detailed information about which kind of internal errors occurred is a relief for the caller. The caller is not burdened with thinking about how to handle all possible internal errors that occur, and it is more likely that the caller will react to all the errors that are returned because all of the returned errors are relevant for the caller. Also, testers can be happy, because now that fewer error information is returned by the functions, fewer error situations have to be tested.

If the caller uses very strict compilers or static code analysis tools that verify whether the caller checks for all possible return values, the caller does not have to explicitly handle irrelevant errors (for example, a switch statement with many fallthroughs and one central error-handling code for all internal errors). Instead, the caller only handles one internal error code, or if you abort the program on error, the caller does not have to handle any errors.

Not returning the detailed error information makes it impossible for the caller to show this error information to the user or to save this error information for the developer for debugging purposes. However, for such debugging purposes, it would be better to Log Errors directly in the software-module where they occur and not burden the caller with doing that.

If you don't return all information about errors occurring in your function, but instead you return only information that you think is relevant to the caller, then there is the chance that you get it wrong. You might forget some information that is necessary for the caller, and maybe that leads to a change request for adding this information. But if you Return Status Codes, additional error codes can easily be added without changing the function signature.

Known Uses

The following examples show applications of this pattern:

- For security-relevant code it is very common to return only relevant information in case of errors. For example, if a function to authenticate a user returns detailed information about why authentication is not working because the username or password is invalid, then the caller could use this function to check which usernames are already taken. To avoid opening side-channels with this information, it is common to return only the binary information about whether authentication worked or not. For example, the function rbacAuthenticateUserPassword used to authenticate users in the B&R Automation Runtime operating system has the return type bool and returns true if the authentication worked or false if it did not work. No detailed information about why the authentication did not work is returned.

- The function FlushWinFile of the game NetHack flushes a file to the disk calling the Macintosh function FSWrite, which does return error codes. However, the NetHack wrapper explicitly ignores the error code, and FlushWinFile is of return type void because the code using that function cannot react accordingly if an error occurs. Thus, the error information is not passed along.

- The OpenSSL function EVP_CIPHER_do_all initializes cipher suites with the internal function OPENSSL_init_crypto, which Returns Status Codes. However, this detailed error information is ignored by the EVP_CIPHER_do_all function because it is of return type void. So the strategy of returning detailed error information is changed by the wrapping function to only Return Relevant Errors, which in this case is no error information at all.

Applied to Running Example

When you only Return Relevant Errors, your registry code looks like the following. To keep things simple, only the createKey function is shown here:

Implementation of the function createKey

```
RegError createKey(char* key_name, RegKey* key)
{
  if(key == NULL || key_name == NULL)
  {
    return INVALID_PARAMETER; ❶
  }

  if(STRING_SIZE <= strlen(key_name))
  {
    return STRING_TOO_LONG;
  }

  RegKey newKey = calloc(1, sizeof(struct Key));
  if(newKey == NULL)
  {
    return OUT_OF_MEMORY;
  }

  strcpy(newKey->key_name, key_name);
  *key = newKey;
  return OK;
}
```

❶ Instead of returning INVALID_KEY or INVALID_STRING, you now return INVALID_PARAMETER for all these error cases.

Now the caller cannot handle specific invalid parameters differently, which also means the caller does not have to think about how to handle these error situations differently. The caller code becomes simpler because now there is one less error situation to be handled.

That is good, because what would the caller do if the function returns INVALID_KEY or INVALID_STRING? It wouldn't make any sense for the caller to try calling the function again. In both cases the caller could just accept that calling the function did not work and report that to the user or abort the program. As there would be no reason for the caller to react differently to the two errors, you have relieved the caller of the burden of thinking about two different error situations. Now the caller only has to think about one error situation and then react accordingly.

To make things even easier, you next apply the Samurai Principle. Instead of returning all of these error codes, you handle some of the errors by aborting the program:

Declaration of the function createKey

```
/* Create a new registry key identified via the provided 'key_name'
   (must not be NULL, max. STRING_SIZE characters). Stores a handle
   to the key in the provided 'key' parameter (must not be NULL).
   Returns OK on success, or OUT_OF_MEMORY in case of insufficient memory. */
RegError createKey(char* key_name, RegKey* key);
```

Implementation of the function createKey

```
RegError createKey(char* key_name, RegKey* key)
{
  assert(key != NULL && key_name != NULL); ❶
  assert(STRING_SIZE > strlen(key_name)); ❶

  RegKey newKey = calloc(1, sizeof(struct Key));
  if(newKey == NULL)
  {
    return OUT_OF_MEMORY;
  }

  strcpy(newKey->key_name, key_name);
  *key = newKey;
  return OK;
}
```

❶ Instead of returning an INVALID_PARAMETER or STRING_TOO_LONG, you now abort the program if one of the provided parameters is not what you expect it to be.

Aborting in case of too long strings seems a bit drastic at first. However, similar to NULL pointers, a too long string is invalid input for your function. If your registry does not get its string input from a user via a GUI, but instead gets a fixed input from the caller's code, then for too long strings this code only aborts in case of programming errors, which is perfectly fine behavior.

Next, you realize that the createKey function returns only two different error codes: OUT_OF_MEMORY and OK. Your code can be made much more beautiful by simply providing this kind of error information with Special Return Values.

Special Return Values

Context

You have a function that computes some result, and you want to provide error information to your caller if an error occurs when executing the function. You only want to Return Relevant Errors.

Problem

You want to return error information, but don't want to explicitly Return Status Codes because that makes it difficult for your function to return other data. You could add Out-Parameters to your function, but this would make calling the function more difficult.

Returning no error information at all is also not an option for you. You want to provide your caller with some error information, and you want your caller to be able to react to these errors. There is not a lot of error information that you want to provide to your caller. It might be just the binary information about whether the function call worked or not. To Return Status Codes for such simple information would be overkill.

You cannot apply the Samurai Principle and abort the program because the errors occurring in your function are not severe. Or maybe you want to make it possible for the caller to decide how the errors should be handled because the caller can handle the errors gracefully.

Solution

Use the Return Value of your function to return the data computed by the function. Reserve one or more special values to be returned if an error occurs.

If, for example, your function returns a pointer, then you could use the NULL pointer as a reserved special value to indicate that some error occurred. The NULL pointer is by definition an invalid pointer, so you can be sure that this special value is not confused with a valid pointer calculated by your function as a result. The following code shows how to return error information when using pointers:

Callee implementation

```
void* func()
{
  if(somethingGoesWrong())
  {
    return NULL;
  }
  else
  {
```

```
        return some_pointer;
    }
}
```

Caller's code

```
pointer = func();
if(pointer != NULL)
{
    /* operate on the pointer */
}
else
{
    /* handle error */
}
```

You have to make sure to document in the API which returned special value has which meaning. In some cases, a common convention settles which special values indicate errors. For example, very often negative integer values are used to indicate errors. Still, even in such cases the meaning of the specific return values has to be documented.

You have to make sure that the special value that indicates error information is a value that cannot occur in case of no error. For example, if a function returns a temperature value in degrees Celsius as an integer value, then it would not be a good idea to stay with the UNIX convention where any negative value indicates an error. Instead, it would be better to use, for example, the value –300 to indicate an error, because it is physically impossible that a temperature takes a value below –273 degrees Celsius.

Consequences

The function can now return error information via the Return Value even though the Return Value is used to return the computation result of the function. No additional Out-Parameters have to be used just to provide error information.

Sometimes you don't have many special values to encode error information. For example, for pointers there is only the NULL pointer to indicate error information. That leads to the situation in which it is only possible to indicate to the caller whether everything worked well or whether anything went wrong. This has the drawback that you cannot return detailed error information. However, this also has the benefit that you are not tempted to return unnecessary error information. In many cases, it is sufficient to provide only the information that something went wrong, and the caller cannot react to more detailed information anyway.

If, at a later point in time, you realize that you have to provide more detailed error information, then perhaps that is not possible anymore because you have no more unused special values left. You'd have to change the whole function signature and instead Return Status Codes to provide that additional error information. Changing the function signature might not always be an option because your API might have to stay compatible for existing callers. If you expect such future changes, don't use Special Return Values, but instead Return Status Codes right away.

Sometimes programmers assume that it is clear which returned values indicate errors. For example, to some programmers it might be clear that a NULL pointer indicates an error. For some other programmers it might be clear that −1 indicates an error. This brings in the dangerous situation in which the programmers assume that it is clear to everybody which values indicate errors. However, these are just assumptions. In any case it should be well documented in the API which values indicate errors, but sometimes programmers forget to do that, wrongly assuming that it is absolutely clear.

Known Uses

The following examples show applications of this pattern:

- The getobj function of the game NetHack returns the pointer to some object if no error occurs and returns NULL if an error occurs. To indicate the special case that there is no object to return, the function returns the pointer to a global object called zeroobj that is an object of the return type defined for the function and that is also known to the caller. The caller can then check if the returned pointer is the same as the pointer to the global object and can thus distinguish between a pointer to any valid object and a pointer to the zeroobj that carries some special meaning.

- The C standard library function getchar reads a character from stdin. The function has return type int which allows returning much more information than simple characters. If no more characters are available, the function returns EOF, which is usually defined as −1. As characters cannot take negative integer representations, EOF can clearly be distinguished from regular function results and can thus be used to indicate the special situation in which no more characters are available.

- Most UNIX or POSIX function use negative numbers to indicate error information. For example, the POSIX function write returns the number of written bytes or −1 on error.

Applied to Running Example

With Special Return Values, your code looks like the following. To keep it simple, only the createKey function is shown:

Declaration of the function createKey

```
/* Create a new registry key identified via the provided 'key_name'
   (must not be NULL, max. STRING_SIZE characters).
   Returns a handle to the key or NULL on error. */
RegKey createKey(char* key_name);
```

Implementation of the function createKey

```
RegKey createKey(char* key_name)
{
  assert(key_name != NULL);
  assert(STRING_SIZE > strlen(key_name));

  RegKey newKey = calloc(1, sizeof(struct Key));
  if(newKey == NULL)
  {
    return NULL;
  }

  strcpy(newKey->key_name, key_name);
  return newKey;
}
```

The createKey function is much simpler now. It does not Return Status Codes anymore, but instead it directly returns the handle and no Out-Parameter is needed to return this information. The API documentation for the function also becomes much simpler because there is no need to describe the additional parameter and no need to lengthily describe how the function result will be returned to the caller.

Things also are much simpler for your caller. The caller does not have to provide a handle as an Out-Parameter anymore, but instead the caller directly retrieves this handle via the Return Value, which makes the caller's code a lot more readable and thus easier to maintain.

However, now you have the problem that compared to the detailed error information that you can provide if you Return Status Codes, the only error information that comes out of the function is whether it worked or not. The internal details about the error are thrown away, and if you need these details later on, for example, as debugging information, there is no way to get it. To address that issue, you can Log Errors.

Log Errors

Context

You have a function in which you handle errors. You want to only Return Relevant Errors to your caller for reacting to them in the code, but you want to keep detailed error information for later debugging.

Problem

You want to make sure that in case of an error you can easily find out its cause. However, you don't want your error-handling code to become complicated because of this.

One way to do this would be to return very detailed error information, such as error information indicating programming errors, directly to the caller. To do this you can Return Status Codes to the caller, who then displays the detailed error codes to the user. The user might get back to you (for example, via some service hotline) to ask what the error code means and how to fix the problem. Then you'd have your detailed error information to debug the code, and you could figure out what went wrong.

However, such an approach has the major drawback that the caller, who does not care at all about that error information, has to provide the error information to the user only for the sake of providing this error information to you. The user also does not really care about such detailed error information.

In addition, Return Status Codes has the drawback that you have to use the Return Value of the function to return error information, and you have to use additional Out-Parameters to provide the actual function results. In some cases, instead, you can provide error information via Special Return Values, but this is not always possible. You don't want to have additional parameters for your function only to provide error information because it makes your caller's code more complicated.

Solution

Use different channels to provide error information that is relevant for the calling code and error information that is relevant for the developer. For example, write debug error information into a log file and don't return the detailed debug error information to the caller.

If an error occurs, the user of the program has to provide you with the logged debug information so that you can easily find out the cause of the error. For example, the user has to send you a log file via email.

Alternatively, you could log the error at the interface between you and your caller and also Return Relevant Errors to the caller. For example, the caller could be informed that some internal error occurred, but the caller does not see the details of what kind of error occurred. Thus, the caller could still handle the error in the code without requiring knowledge on how to handle very detailed errors, and you still wouldn't be losing valuable debug information.

To not lose valuable debug information, you should log information about programming errors and unexpected errors. For such errors it is valuable to store information about their severity and where the error occurred—for example, the source code filename and the line number, or the backtrace. The C language comes with special macros to get information about the current line number (__LINE__), the current function (__func__), or the current file (__FILE__). The following code uses the __func__ macro for logging:

```
void someFunction()
{
  if(something_goes_wrong)
  {
    logInFile("something went wrong", ERROR_CODE, __func__);
  }
}
```

To get more detailed logging, you could even trace your function calls and log their return information. That makes it easier to reverse-engineer error situations with these logs, but of course that logging also introduces computational overhead. For tracing return values of your function calls, you can use the following code:

```
#define RETURN(x)          \
do {                       \
  logInFile(__func__, x);  \
  return x;                \
} while (0)

int soneFunction()
{
  RETURN(-1);
}
```

The log information can be stored in files, as indicated in the preceding code. You'll have to take care of special situations like not having enough memory to store the file or a crashing program while writing to the file. Handling such situations is not an easy task, but it is very important to have a robust code for your logging mechanism because later on you'll rely on the log files for debugging purposes. If the data in these files is not correct, then you might be misled when hunting down coding errors.

Multiline Macros

By having a do/while loop around the statements in a macro, you can avoid problems like the one shown in the following code:

```
#define MACRO(x) \
x=1;             \
x=2;             \

if(x==0)
  MACRO(x)
```

The code does not use curly braces around its `if` body, and when reading the code you might think that the thing in the macro is only executed in case `x==0`. But actually when the macro expands, you end up with the following code:

```
if(x==0)
    x=1;
x=2;
```

The last line of the code is not inside the body of the `if` statement, which is not what was intended. To avoid problems like this one, it is a best practice to have a `do/while` loop around the statements in a macro.

Consequences

You can obtain debug information without requiring your caller to handle or transport this information. That makes life for the caller a lot easier, because the caller does not have to handle or transport the detailed error information. Instead, you provide the detailed error information yourself.

In some cases, you might just want to log some error or situation that occurred, but that is completely irrelevant to the caller. Thus, you don't even have to return any error information to the caller. For example, if you abort the program if the error occurs, the caller does not have to react to the error at all, and you can still make sure to not lose valuable debug information if you Log Errors. So there are no additional required parameters to your function in order to return error information, which makes calling your function a lot easier and helps the caller to keep the code clean.

You don't lose this valuable error information and can still use it for debugging purposes to hunt down programming errors. To not lose this debug information, you provide it via a different channel, for example, via log files. However, you have to think about how to get to these log files. You could ask the users to send you the log file via email or, more advanced, you could implement some automatic bug report mechanism. Still, with both of these approaches you cannot be 100% sure that the log information really gets back to you. If the users do not want that, they could prevent it.

Known Uses

The following examples show applications of this pattern:

- The Apache web server code uses the function `ap_log_error` that writes errors related to requests or connections to an error log. Such a log entry contains information about the filename and line of code where the error occurred as well as a custom string provided to the function by the caller. The log information is stored in an `error_log` file on the server.

- The B&R Automation Runtime operating system uses a logging system that allows programmers to provide logging information to the user via calling the function eventLogWrite from anywhere in the code. This makes it possible to provide information to the user without having to return this information across the whole calling stack up to some central logging component.

- The pattern Assertion Context from the book *Patterns in C* by Adam Tornhill (Leanpub, 2014) suggests aborting the program in case of errors and also logging information the about the reason for or the position of the crash by adding a string statement inside the assert call. If the assert fails, then the line of code containing the assert statement will be printed, which includes the added string.

Applied to Running Example

After applying the patterns, you'll get the following final code for your registry software-module. This code provides the caller with relevant error information, but does not require the caller to handle any internal error situations:

Registry API

```
/* max. size of string parameters (including NULL-termination) */
#define STRING_SIZE 100

/* Error codes returned by this registry */
typedef enum
{
  OK,
  CANNOT_ADD_KEY
}RegError;

/* Handle for registry keys */
typedef struct Key* RegKey;

/* Create a new registry key identified via the provided 'key_name'
   (must not be NULL, max. STRING_SIZE characters).  Returns a handle
   to the key or NULL on error. */
RegKey createKey(char* key_name);

/* Store the provided 'value' (must not be NULL, max. STRING_SIZE characters)
   to the 'key' (MUST NOT BE NULL) */
void storeValue(RegKey key, char* value);

/* Make the 'key' (must not be NULL) available for being read.
   Returns OK if no problem occurs or CANNOT_ADD_KEY if the
   registry is full and no more keys can be published. */
RegError publishKey(RegKey key);
```

Registry implementation

```c
#define MAX_KEYS 40

struct Key
{
  char key_name[STRING_SIZE];
  char key_value[STRING_SIZE];
};

/* macro to log debug info and to assert */
#define logAssert(X)                        \
if(!(X))                                     \
{                                           \
  printf("Error at line %i", __LINE__);     \
  assert(false);                            \
}

/* file-global array holding all registry keys */
static struct Key* key_list[MAX_KEYS];

RegKey createKey(char* key_name)
{
  logAssert(key_name != NULL)
  logAssert(STRING_SIZE > strlen(key_name))

  RegKey newKey = calloc(1, sizeof(struct Key));
  if(newKey == NULL)
  {
    return NULL;
  }

  strcpy(newKey->key_name, key_name);
  return newKey;
}

void storeValue(RegKey key, char* value)
{
  logAssert(key != NULL && value != NULL)
  logAssert(STRING_SIZE > strlen(value))

  strcpy(key->key_value, value);
}

RegError publishKey(RegKey key)
{
  logAssert(key != NULL)

  int i;
  for(i=0; i<MAX_KEYS; i++)
  {
    if(key_list[i] == NULL)
    {
```

```
            key_list[i] = key;
            return OK;
        }
    }

    return CANNOT_ADD_KEY;
}
```

This code is shorter compared to the earlier code in the running example for these reasons:

- The code does not check for programming errors but aborts the program in case of programming errors. Invalid parameters like NULL pointers are not gracefully handled in the code; instead, the API documents that the handles must not be NULL.

- The code returns only errors that are relevant for the caller. For example, the createKey function does not Return Status Codes, but instead simply returns a handle and NULL in case of error because the caller does not need more detailed error information.

Although the code is shorter, the API comments grew. The comments now specify more clearly how the functions behave in case of errors. Apart from your code, the caller's code also became simpler because now the caller is not burdened with many decisions on how to react to different kinds of error information:

Caller's code

```
RegKey my_key = createKey("myKey");
if(my_key == NULL)
{
    printf("Cannot create key\n");
}

storeValue(my_key, "A");

RegError err = publishKey(my_key);
if(err == CANNOT_ADD_KEY)
{
    printf("Key cannot be published, because the registry is full\n");
}
```

This is shorter compared to the earlier code in the running example because:

- The return value of functions that abort in case of error does not have to be checked.

- Functions in which no detailed error information is required directly return the requested item. For example, createKey() now returns a handle, and the caller no longer has to provide an Out-Parameter.

- Error codes that indicate a programming error, for example, an invalid provided parameter, are not returned anymore and thus do not have to be checked by the caller.

The final code in the running example showed that it is important to think about which kinds of errors should be handled in the code and how these errors should be handled. Simply returning all kinds of errors and requiring the caller to cope with all of them is not always the best solution. The caller might not be interested in the detailed error information, or maybe the caller does not want to react to the error in the application. Maybe the error is severe enough that at the point where the error occurs it can be decided to abort the program. Such measures make the code simpler and have to be considered when designing the API of a software component.

Summary

This chapter showed you how to handle errors across different functions and different parts of your software. The pattern Return Status Codes provides the caller with numeric codes representing an occurring error. Return Relevant Errors only returns error information to the caller if the caller can react to these errors in the code, and Special Return Value is one way to do that. Log Errors provides an additional channel to provide error information that is not intended for the caller, but for the user or for debugging purposes.

These patterns equip you with more tools for tackling error situations and can guide your first steps when implementing a larger piece of code.

Further Reading

If you're ready for more, here are some resources that can help you further your knowledge of returning error information:

- The master's thesis *Error Handling in Structured and Object-Oriented Programming Languages* by Thomas Aglassinger (University of Oulu, 1999) provides a comprehensive overview of error handling in general and describes error handling best practices, with code examples for several programming languages including C.

- The Portland Pattern Repository (*https://oreil.ly/bs9FX*) provides many patterns and discussions on error-handling as well as other topics. Most of the error handling patterns target exception handling, but some C idioms are also presented.

- The articles "Patterns for the Generation, Handling and Management of Errors" and "More Patterns for the Generation, Handling and Management of Errors" by Andy Longshaw and Eoin Woods (*https://oreil.ly/7Yj8h*) present patterns for error logging and error handling with a focus on exception-based error handling.

Outlook

The next chapter gives guidance on how to cope with dynamic memory. In order to return more complex data between your functions and to organize larger data and its lifetime throughout your application, you'll need to deal with dynamic memory, and you'll need advice on how to do that.

CHAPTER 3

Memory Management

Each program stores some values in memory to use them later on in the program. This functionality is so common for programs that modern programming languages make doing it as easy as possible. The C++ programming language, as well as other object-oriented programming languages, provides constructors and destructors, which make it very easy to have a defined place and time to allocate and clean up memory. The Java programming language even comes with a garbage collector, which makes sure that memory that is not used anymore by the program is made available to others.

Compared to that, programming in C is special in the way that the programmer has to manually manage the memory. The programmer has to decide whether to put variables on the stack, on the heap, or in static memory. Also, the programmer has to make sure that heap variables are manually cleaned up afterwards, and there is no mechanism like a destructor or a native garbage collector, which would make some of these tasks much easier.

Guidance on how to perform such tasks is well scattered over the internet, which makes it quite hard to answer questions like the following: "Should that variable go on the stack or on the heap?" To answer that as well as other questions, this chapter presents patterns on how to handle memory in C programs. The patterns provide guidance on when to use the stack, when to use the heap, and when and how to clean up heap memory. To make the core idea of the patterns easier to grasp, the patterns are applied to a running code example throughout the chapter.

Figure 3-1 shows an overview of the patterns discussed in this chapter and their relationships, and Table 3-1 provides a summary of the patterns.

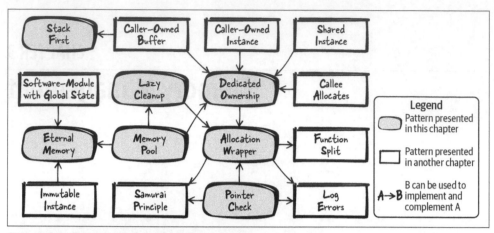

Figure 3-1. Overview of patterns for memory management

Table 3-1. Patterns for memory management

Pattern name	Summary
Stack First	Deciding the storage class and memory section (stack, heap, …) for variables is a decision every programmer has to make often. It gets exhausting if for each and every variable, the pros and cons of all possible alternatives have to be considered in detail. Therefore, simply put your variables on the stack by default to profit from automatic cleanup of stack variables.
Eternal Memory	Holding large amounts of data and transporting it between function calls is difficult because you have to make sure that the memory for the data is large enough and that the lifetime extends across your function calls. Therefore, put your data into memory that is available throughout the whole lifetime of your program.
Lazy Cleanup	Having dynamic memory is required if you need large amounts of memory and memory where you don't know the required size beforehand. However, handling cleanup of dynamic memory is a hassle and is the source of many programming errors. Therefore, allocate dynamic memory and let the operating system cope with deallocation by the end of your program.
Dedicated Ownership	The great power of using dynamic memory comes with the great responsibility of having to properly clean that memory up. In larger programs, it becomes difficult to make sure that all dynamic memory is cleaned up properly. Therefore, right at the time when you implement memory allocation, clearly define and document where it's going to be cleaned up and who is going to do that.
Allocation Wrapper	Each allocation of dynamic memory might fail, so you should check allocations in your code to react accordingly. This is cumbersome because you have many places for such checks in your code. Therefore, wrap the allocation and deallocation calls, and implement error handling or additional memory management organization in these wrapper functions.
Pointer Check	Programming errors that lead to accessing an invalid pointer cause uncontrolled program behavior, and such errors are difficult to debug. However, because your code works with pointers frequently, there is a good chance that you have introduced such programming errors. Therefore, explicitly invalidate uninitialized or freed pointers and always check pointers for validity before accessing them.
Memory Pool	Frequently allocating and deallocating objects from the heap leads to memory fragmentation. Therefore, hold a large piece of memory throughout the whole lifetime of your program. At runtime, retrieve fixed-size chunks of that memory pool instead of directly allocating new memory from the heap.

Data Storage and Problems with Dynamic Memory

In C you have several options for where to put your data:

- You can put the data on the stack. The stack is a fixed-size memory reserved for each thread (allocated when creating the thread). When calling a function in such a thread, a block on the top of the stack is reserved for the function parameters and automatic variables used by that function. After the function call, that memory is automatically cleaned up. To put data on the stack, simply declare variables in the functions where they are used. These variables can be accessed as long as they don't run out of scope (when the function block ends):

```
void main()
{
  int my_data;
}
```

- You can put data into static memory. The static memory is a fixed-size memory in which the allocation logic is fixed at compile time. To use the static memory, simply place the static keyword in front of your variable declaration. Such variables are available throughout the whole lifetime of your program. The same holds true for global variables, even without the static keyword:

```
int my_global_data;
static int my_fileglobal_data;
void main()
{
  static int my_local_data;
}
```

- If your data is of fixed size and immutable, you can simply store it directly in the static memory where the code is stored. Quite often, fixed string values are stored this way. Such data is available throughout the whole lifetime of your program (even though, in the example below, the pointer to that data runs out of scope):

```
void main()
{
  char* my_string = "Hello World";
}
```

- You can allocate dynamic memory on the heap to store the data. The heap is a global memory pool available for all processes on the system, and it is up to the programmer to allocate and deallocate from that pool at any time:

```
void main()
{
  void* my_data = malloc(1000);
  /* work with the allocated 1000 byte memory */
  free(my_data);
}
```

Allocating dynamic memory is the starting point where things can easily go wrong, and tackling the problems that can arise is the focus of this chapter. Using dynamic memory in C programs comes with many problems that have to be solved or at least considered. The following outlines the major problems with dynamic memory:

- Memory that is allocated has to be freed at some point later on. When not doing so for all memory you allocated, you'll consume more memory than you need and have a so-called memory leak. If that happens frequently and your applications runs for a long time, you'll end up having no additional memory.

- Freeing memory more than once is a problem and can lead to undefined program behavior, which is really bad. Worst case, nothing goes wrong in the actual code line where you made the mistake, but at some random point later in time, your program might crash. Such errors are a hassle to debug.

- Trying to access freed memory is a problem as well. It is easy to free some memory and then later on make a mistake and dereference a pointer to that memory (a so-called dangling pointer). Again, this leads to error situations that are a hassle to debug. Best case, the program would simply crash. Worst case, it would not crash and the memory already belongs to somebody else. Errors related to using that memory are a security risk and might show up as some kind of hard-to-understand error later during program execution.

- You have to cope with lifetime and ownership of allocated data. You have to know who cleans up which data when, and that can be particularly tricky in C. In C++ it would be possible to simply allocate data for objects in the constructor and free them in the destructor. In combination with C++ *smart pointers*, you even have the option to automatically clean up an object if it runs out of scope. However, that is not possible in C because we don't have destructors. We are not notified when a pointer runs out of scope and the memory should be cleaned up.

- Working with heap memory takes more time compared to working with memory from the stack or with static memory. The allocation of heap memory has to be protected against race conditions because other processes use the same pool of memory. This makes allocation slower. Accessing the heap memory is also slower because, in comparison, the stack memory is accessed more often and thus more likely already resides in the cache or in CPU registers.

- A huge issue with heap memory is that it becomes fragmented, which is depicted in Figure 3-2. If you allocate memory blocks A, B, and C and later on free memory block B, your overall free heap memory is no longer consecutive. If you want to allocate a large memory block D, you won't get that memory, although there is enough total memory available. However, as that available memory is not consecutive, your malloc call will fail. Fragmentation is a huge issue in memory-constrained systems that run for a long time (like embedded real-time systems).

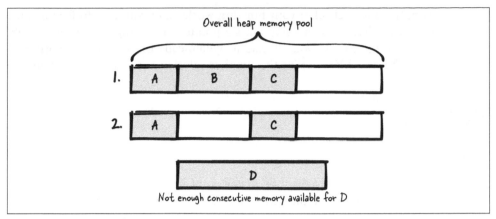

Figure 3-2. Memory fragmentation

Tackling these issues is not easy. The patterns in the following sections describe bit by bit how to either avoid dynamic allocation or live with it in an acceptable way.

Running Example

You want to implement a simple program that encrypts some text with the Caesar cipher. The Caesar cipher replaces each letter with another letter that is some fixed number of positions down the alphabet. For example, if the fixed number of positions is 3, then the letter A would be replaced by letter D. You start to implement a function that performs the Caesar encryption:

```
/* Performs a Caesar encryption with the fixed key 3.
   The parameter 'text' must contain a text with only capital letters.
   The parameter 'length' must contain the length of the text excluding
   NULL termination. */
void caesar(char* text, int length)
{
  for(int i=0; i<length; i++)
  {
    text[i] = text[i]+3; ❶
    if(text[i] > 'Z')
    {
      text[i] = text[i] - 'Z' + 'A' - 1; ❷
    }
  }
}
```

❶ Characters in C are stored as numeric values, and you can shift the character down the alphabet by adding a numeric value to a character.

❷ If we shift beyond the letter Z, we restart at the beginning of the alphabet.

Now you simply want to check if your function works, and you need to feed it some text in order to do that. Your function takes a pointer to a string. But where should you store that string? Should you allocate it dynamically or should you work with memory from the stack? You realize the simplest solution is to use the Stack First to store the string.

Stack First

Context

You want to store data and access it at a later point in your program. You know its maximum size beforehand, and the data is not very large in size (just a few bytes).

Problem

Deciding the storage class and memory section (stack, heap, ...) for variables is a decision every programmer has to make often. It gets exhausting if for each and every variable, the pros and cons of all possible alternatives have to be considered in detail.

For storing data in your C program, you have a myriad of possibilities, of which the most common ones are storage on the stack, in static memory, or in dynamic memory. Each of these possibilities has its own specific benefits and drawbacks, and the decision of where to store the variable is very important. It affects the lifetime of the variable and determines whether the variable is cleaned up automatically or whether you have to manually clean it up.

This decision also affects the required effort and discipline for you as a programmer. You want to make your life as easy as possible, so if you have no special requirements for storing the data, you want to use the kind of memory that requires the least possible effort with allocation, deallocation, and bug fixes due to potential programming errors.

Solution

Simply put your variables on the stack by default to profit from automatic cleanup of stack variables.

All variables declared inside a code block are by default so-called *automatic variables* that are put on the stack and automatically cleaned up once the code block ends (when the variable runs out of scope). It could be made explicit that a variable is declared as an automatic variable by putting the auto storage-class specifier before it, but this is rarely done because it is the default anyway.

You can pass the memory from the stack along to other functions (for example, Caller-Owned Buffer), but make sure not to return the address of such a variable. The variable runs out of scope at the end of the function and is automatically cleaned up. Returning the address of such a variable would lead to a dangling pointer, and accessing it results in undefined program behavior and possibly a crash of the program.

The following code shows a very simple example with variables on the stack:

```
void someCode()
{
  /* This variable is an automatic variable that is put on the stack and
     that will run out of scope at the end of the function */
  int my_variable;

  {
    /* This variable is an automatic variable that is put on the stack and
       that will run out of scope right after this code block, which is
       after the first '}' */
    int my_array[10];
  }
}
```

Variable Length Arrays

The array in the preceding code is of fixed size. It is very common to put only data of fixed size known at compile time on the stack, but it is also possible to decide the size of stack variables during runtime. This is done using functions like alloca() (which is not part of the C standard and which causes stack overflows if you allocate too much) or using variable length arrays (regular arrays whose size is specified by a variable), which are introduced with the C99 standard.

Consequences

Storing the data on the stack makes it easy to access that data. Compared to dynamically allocated memory, there is no need to work with pointers. This makes it possible to eliminate the risk of programming errors related to dangling pointers. Also, there is no heap fragmentation and memory cleanup is easier. The variables are automatic variables, which means they are automatically cleaned up. There is no need to manually free the memory, and that eliminates the risk of memory leaks or accidentally freeing memory multiple times. In general, most of the hard-to-debug errors related to incorrect memory usage can be eliminated by simply putting variables on the stack.

The data on the stack can be allocated and accessed very quickly compared to dynamic memory. For the allocation there is no need to go through complex data structures that manage the available memory. There is also no need to ensure mutual exclusion from other threads because each thread has its own stack. Also, the stack data can usually be accessed quickly because that memory is used often and you usually have it in the cache memory.

However, a drawback of using the stack is that it is limited. Compared to the heap memory, it is very small (depending on your build settings regarding stack size, maybe just a few KB). If you put too much data on the stack, you cause a stack overflow, which usually results in a crashing program. The problem is that you don't know how much stack memory you have left. Depending on how much stack memory is already used by the functions that you called, you might have only a little left. You have to make sure that the data you put on the stack is not too large, and you have to know its size in advance.

Programming errors related to buffers on the stack can be major security issues. If you produce a buffer overflow on the stack, then attackers can easily exploit that to overwrite some other data on the stack. If attackers manage to overwrite the address your code returns to after processing the function, then the attackers can execute any code they want.

Also, having the data on the stack will not suit all your needs. If you have to return large data like the content of a file or the buffer to some network message to the caller, then you cannot simply return the address of some array on the stack because that variable will be cleaned up once you return from your function. For returning large data, other approaches have to be used.

Known Uses

The following examples show applications of this pattern:

- Nearly every C program stores something on the stack. In most programs, you'll find storage on the stack as default because it is the easiest solution.

- The auto storage-class specifier of C, which specifies that the variable is an automatic variable and that it goes on the stack, is the default storage-class specifier (and is usually omitted in the code because it is the default anyway).

- The book *Small Memory Software: Patterns for Systems with Limited Memory* by James Noble and Charles Weir (Addison-Wesley, 2000) describes in its Memory Allocation pattern that among the choices of where to put the memory, you should go for the simplest one, which is the stack for C programmers.

Applied to Running Example

Well, that was simple. You now put the memory that you need for storing the text on the stack and provide that memory to your Caesar cipher function:

```
#define MAX_TEXT_SIZE 64

void encryptCaesarText()
{
  char text[MAX_TEXT_SIZE];
  strlcpy(text, "PLAINTEXT", MAX_TEXT_SIZE);
  caesar(text, strnlen(text, MAX_TEXT_SIZE));
  printf("Encrypted text: %s\n", text);
}
```

This was a very easy solution. You did not have to cope with dynamic memory allocation. There is no need to clean up the memory because once the text runs out of scope, it is automatically cleaned up.

Next, you want to encrypt a larger text. That's not easy with your current solution because the memory resides on the stack and you usually don't have a lot of stack memory. Depending on your platform, it could be just a few KB. Still, you want to make it possible to also encrypt larger texts. To avoid coping with dynamic memory, you decide to give Eternal Memory a try.

Eternal Memory

Context

You have large amounts of data with fixed size that you need for a longer time in your program.

Problem

Holding large amounts of data and transporting it between function calls is difficult because you have to make sure that the memory for the data is large enough and that the lifetime extends across your function calls.

Using the stack would be handy because it would do all the memory cleanup work for you. But putting the data on the stack is not a solution for you because it does not allow you to pass large data between functions. It would also be an inefficient way because passing data to a function means copying that data. The alternative of manually allocating the memory at each place in the program where you need it and deallocating it as soon as it is not required anymore would work, but it is cumbersome and error prone. In particular, keeping an overview of the lifetime of all data and knowing where and when the data is being freed is a complicated task.

If you operate in an environment like safety-critical applications, where you must be sure that there is memory available, then neither using memory from the stack nor using dynamic memory is a good option because both could run out of memory and you cannot easily know beforehand. But in other applications there might also be parts of your code for which you want to make sure to not run out of memory. For example, for your error logging code you definitely want to be sure that the required memory is available because otherwise you cannot rely on your logging information, which makes pinpointing bugs difficult.

Solution

Put your data into memory that is available throughout the whole lifetime of your program.

The most common way to do this is to use the static memory. Either mark your variable with the `static` storage-class specifier, or if you want the variable to have larger scope, declare it outside any function (but only do that if you really need the larger scope). Static memory is allocated at startup of your program and is available all through your program's lifetime. The following code gives an example of this:

```
#define ARRAY_SIZE 1024

int global_array[ARRAY_SIZE]; /* variable in static memory, global scope */
static int file_global_array[ARRAY_SIZE]; /* variable in static memory with
                                             scope limited to this file */

void someCode()
{
  static int local_array[ARRAY_SIZE]; /* variable in static memory with
                                         scope limited to this function */
}
```

As an alternative to using static variables, on program startup you could call an initialization function that allocates the memory and by the end of your program call a deinitialization function that deallocates that memory. That way you'd also have the memory available all through the lifetime of your program, but you'd have to cope with allocation and deallocation yourself.

No matter whether you allocate the memory at program startup on your own or whether you use static memory, you have to be careful when accessing this memory. As it is not on the stack, you don't have a separate copy of that memory per thread. In the case of multithreading, you have to use synchronization mechanisms when accessing that memory.

Your data has fixed size. Compared to memory dynamically allocated at runtime, the size of your Eternal Memory cannot be changed at runtime.

Consequences

You don't have to worry about lifetime and the right place for manually deallocating memory. The rules are simple: let the memory live throughout your whole program lifetime. Using static memory even takes the whole burden of allocation and deallocation from you.

You can now store large amounts of data in that memory and even pass it along to other functions. Compared to using Stack First, you can now even provide data to the callers of your function.

However, you have to know at compile time, or startup time at the latest, how much memory you need because you allocate it at program startup. For memory of unknown size or for memory that will be expanded during runtime, Eternal Memory is not the best choice and heap memory should be used instead.

With Eternal Memory, starting the program will take longer because all the memory has to be allocated at that time. But this pays off once you have that memory because there is no allocation necessary during runtime anymore.

Allocating and accessing static memory do not need any complex data structures maintained by your operating system or runtime environment for managing the heap. Thus, the memory is used more efficiently. Another huge advantage of Eternal Memory is that you don't fragment the heap because you don't allocate and deallocate memory all the time. But not doing that has the drawback of blocking memory that you, depending on your application, might not need all the time. A more flexible solution that helps avoid memory fragmentation would be to use a Memory Pool.

One issue with Eternal Memory is that you don't have a copy of it for each of your threads (if you use static variables). So you have to make sure that the memory is not accessed by multiple threads at the same time. Although, in the special case of an Immutable Instance this would not be much of an issue.

Known Uses

The following examples show applications of this pattern:

- The game NetHack uses static variables to store data that is required during the whole lifetime of the game. For example, the information about artifacts found in the game is stored in the static array `artifact_names`.

- The code of the Wireshark network sniffer uses a static buffer in its function `cf_open_error_message` for storing error message information. In general, many programs use static memory or memory allocated at program startup for their error-logging functionality. This is because in case of errors, you want to be sure that at least that part works and does not run out of memory.

- The OpenSSL code uses the static array `OSSL_STORE_str_reasons` to hold error information about error situations that can occur when working with certificates.

Applied to Running Example

Your code pretty much stayed the same. The only thing that changed is that you added the `static` keyword before the variable declaration of `text` and you increased the size of the text:

```
#define MAX_TEXT_SIZE 1024

void encryptCaesarText()
{
  static char text[MAX_TEXT_SIZE];
  strlcpy(text, "LARGETEXTTHATCOULDBETHOUSANDCHARACTERSLONG", MAX_TEXT_SIZE);
  caesar(text, strnlen(text, MAX_TEXT_SIZE));
  printf("Encrypted text: %s\n", text);
}
```

Now your text is not stored on the stack, but instead it resides in the static memory. When doing this you should remember that it also means the variable only exists once and remains its value (even when entering the function multiple times). That could be an issue for multithreaded systems because then you'd have to ensure mutual exclusion when accessing the variable.

You currently don't have a multithreaded system. However, the requirements for your system change: now you want to make it possible to read the text from a file, encrypt it, and show the encrypted text. You don't know how long the text will be, and it could be quite long. So you decide to use dynamic allocation:

```
void encryptCaesarText()
{
  /* open file (omit error handling to keep the code simple) */
  FILE* f = fopen("my-file.txt", "r");

  /* get file length */
  fseek(f, 0, SEEK_END);
  int size = ftell(f);

  /* allocate buffer */
  char* text = malloc(size);

  ...
}
```

But how should that code continue? You allocated the text on the heap. But how would you clean that memory up? As a very first step, you realize that cleaning up that memory could be done by somebody else completely: the operating system. So you go for Lazy Cleanup.

Lazy Cleanup

Context

You want to store some data in your program, and that data is large (and maybe you don't even know its size beforehand). The size of the data does not change often during runtime, and the data is needed throughout almost the whole lifetime of the program. Your program is short-lived (does not run for many days without restart).

Problem

Having dynamic memory is required if you need large amounts of memory and memory where you don't know the required size beforehand. However, handling cleanup of dynamic memory is a hassle and is the source of many programming errors.

In many situations—for example, if you have large data of unknown size—you cannot put the data on the stack or in static memory. So you have to use dynamic memory and cope with allocating it. Now the question arises of how to clean that data up. Cleaning it up is a major source of programming errors. You could accidentally free the memory too early, causing a dangling pointer. You could accidentally free the same memory twice. Both of these programming errors can lead to undefined program behavior, for example, a program crash at some later point in time. Such errors are very difficult to debug, and C programmers spend way too much of their time troubleshooting such situations.

Luckily, most kinds of memory come with some kind of automatic cleanup. The stack memory is automatically cleaned up when returning from a function. The static memory and the heap memory are automatically cleaned up on program termination.

Solution

Allocate dynamic memory and let the operating system cope with deallocation by the end of your program.

When your program ends and the operating system cleans up your process, most modern operating systems also clean up any memory that you allocated and didn't deallocate. Take advantage of that and let the operating system do the entire job of keeping track of which memory still needs cleanup and then actually cleaning it up, as done in the following code:

```
void someCode()
{
  char* memory = malloc(size);
  ...
  /* do something with the memory */
```

```
    ...
    /* don't care about freeing the memory */
}
```

This approach looks very brutal at first sight. You deliberately create memory leaks. However, that's the style of coding you'd also use in other programming languages that have a garbage collector. You could even include some garbage collector library in C to use that style of coding with the benefit of automatic memory cleanup (and the drawback of less predictable timing behavior).

Deliberately having memory leaks might be an option for some applications, particularly those that don't run for a very long time and that don't allocate very often. But for other applications it will not be an option and you'll need Dedicated Ownership of memory and also to cope with its deallocation. An easy way to clean the memory up if you previously had Lazy Cleanup is to use an Allocation Wrapper and to then have one function that by the end of your program cleans up all the allocated memory.

Consequences

The obvious advantage here is that you can benefit from using dynamic memory without having to cope with freeing the memory. That makes life a lot easier for a programmer. Also, you don't waste any processing time on freeing memory and that can speed up the shutdown procedure of your program.

However, this comes at the cost of other running processes that might need the memory that you do not release. Maybe you cannot even allocate any new memory yourself because there is not much left and you didn't free the memory that you could have freed. In particular, if you allocate very often, this becomes a major issue and not cleaning up the memory will not be a good solution for you. Instead, you should Dedicate Ownership and also free the memory.

With this pattern, you accept that you are deliberately creating memory leaks and you do accept it. While that might be OK with you, it might not be OK with other people calling your functions. If you write a library that can be used by others, having memory leaks in that code will not be an option. Also, if you yourself want to stay very clean in some other part of the code and, for example, use a memory debugging tool like *valgrind* to detect memory leaks, you'd have problems with interpreting the results of the tool if some other part of your program is messy and does not free its memory.

This pattern can easily be used as an excuse for not implementing proper memory cleanup, even in cases where you should do that. So you should double check whether you are really in a context where you deliberately do not need to free your memory. If it is likely that in the future your program code evolves and will have to clean up the memory, then it is best not to start with Lazy Cleanup, but instead have Dedicated Ownership for cleaning up the memory properly right from the start.

Known Uses

The following examples show applications of this pattern:

- The Wireshark function `pcap_free_datalinks` does under certain circumstances deliberately not free all memory. The reason is that part of the Wireshark code might have been built with a different compiler and different C runtime libraries. Freeing memory that was allocated by such code might result in a crash. Therefore, the memory is explicitly not freed at all.

- The device drivers of the company B&R's Automation Runtime operating system usually don't have any functionality for deinitializing. All memory they allocate is never freed because these drivers are never unloaded at runtime. If a different driver should be used, the whole system reboots. That makes explicitly freeing the memory unnecessary.

- The code of the NetDRMS data management system, which is used to store images of the sun for scientific processing, does not explicitly free all memory in error situations. For example, if an error occurs, the function `EmptyDir` does not clean up all memory or other resources related to accessing files because such an error would lead to a more severe error and program abort anyway.

- Any C code that uses garbage collection library applies this pattern and conquers its drawbacks of memory leaks with explicit garbage collection.

Applied to Running Example

In your code, you simply omit using any `free` function call. Also, you restructured the code to have the file access functionality in separate functions:

```c
/* Returns the length of the file with the provided 'filename' */
int getFileLength(char* filename)
{
  FILE* f = fopen(filename, "r");
  fseek(f, 0, SEEK_END);
  int file_length = ftell(f);
  fclose(f);
  return file_length;
}

/* Stores the content of the file with the provided 'filename' into the
   provided 'buffer' (which has to be least of size 'file_length'). The
   file must only contain capital letters with no newline in between
   (that's what our caesar function accepts as input). */
void readFileContent(char* filename, char* buffer, int file_length)
{
  FILE* f = fopen(filename, "r");
  fseek(f, 0, SEEK_SET);
  int read_elements = fread(buffer, 1, file_length, f);
```

```
      buffer[read_elements] = '\0';
      fclose(f);
   }

   void encryptCaesarFile()
   {
      char* text;
      int size = getFileLength("my-file.txt");
      if(size>0)
      {
         text = malloc(size);
         readFileContent("my-file.txt", text, size);
         caesar(text, strnlen(text, size));
         printf("Encrypted text: %s\n", text);
         /* you don't free the memory here */
      }
   }
```

You do allocate the memory, but you don't call free to deallocate it. Instead, you let
the pointers to the memory run out of scope and have a memory leak. However, it's
not a problem because your program ends right afterwards anyway, and the operating
system cleans up the memory.

That approach seems quite unrefined, but in a few cases it is completely acceptable. If
you need the memory throughout the lifetime of your program, or if your program is
short-lived and you are sure that your code is not going to evolve or be reused somewhere else, then simply not having to cope with cleaning the memory up can be a
solution that makes life very simple for you. Still, you have to be very careful that
your program does not evolve and become long-lived. In that case, you'd definitely
have to find another approach.

And that is exactly what you'll do next. You want to encrypt more than one file. You
want to encrypt all files from the current directory. You quickly realize that you have
to allocate more often and that not deallocating any of the memory in the meantime
is not an option anymore because you'd use up a lot of memory. This could be a problem for your program or other programs.

The question comes up of where in the code your memory should be deallocated.
Who is responsible for doing that? You definitely need Dedicated Ownership.

Dedicated Ownership

Context

You have large data of previously unknown size in your program and you use
dynamic memory to store it. You don't need that memory for the whole lifetime of
the program and you have to allocate memory of different size often, so you cannot
afford to use Lazy Cleanup.

Problem

The great power of using dynamic memory comes with the great responsibility of having to properly clean that memory up. In larger programs, it becomes difficult to make sure that all dynamic memory is cleaned up properly.

There are many pitfalls when cleaning up dynamic memory. You might clean it up too soon and somebody else afterwards still wants to access that memory (dangling pointer). Or you might accidentally free the memory too often. Both of these programming errors lead to unexpected program behavior, like a crash of the program at some later point in time, and such errors are security issues and could be exploited by an attacker. Also, such errors are extremely difficult to debug.

Yet you do have to clean up the memory, because over time, you'd use up too much memory if you allocate new memory without freeing it. Then your program or other processes would run out of memory.

Solution

Right at the time when you implement memory allocation, clearly define and document where it's going to be cleaned up and who is going to do that.

It should be clearly documented in the code who owns the memory and how long it's going to be valid. Best case, even before writing your first `malloc`, you should have asked yourself where that memory will be freed. You should have also written some comments in the function declarations to make clear if memory buffers are passed along by that function and if so, who is responsible for cleaning it up.

In other programming languages, like C++, you have the option to use code constructs for documenting this. Pointer constructs like `unique_ptr` or `shared_ptr` make it possible to see from the function declarations who is responsible for cleaning the memory up. As there are no such constructs in C, extra care has to be taken to document this responsibility in the form of code comments.

If possible, make the same function responsible for allocation and deallocation, just as it is with Object-Based Error Handling in which you have exactly one point in the code for calling constructor- and destructor-like functions for allocation and deallocation:

```
#define DATA_SIZE 1024
void function()
{
  char* memory = malloc(DATA_SIZE);
  /* work with memory */
  free(memory);
}
```

If the responsibility for allocation and deallocation is spread across the code and if ownership of memory is transferred, it gets complicated. In some cases, this will be necessary, for example, if only the allocating function knows the size of the data and that data is needed in other functions:

```
/* Allocates and returns a buffer that has to be freed by the caller */
char* functionA()
{
  char* memory = malloc(data_size); ❶
  /* fill memory */
  return memory;
}

void functionB()
{
  char* memory = functionA();
  /* work with the memory */
  free(memory); ❷
}
```

❶ The callee allocates some memory.

❷ The caller is responsible for cleaning up the memory.

If possible, avoid putting the responsibility for allocation and deallocation in different functions. But in any case, document who is responsible for cleanup to make that clear.

Other patterns that describe more specific situations related to memory ownership are the Caller-Owned Buffer or the Caller-Owned Instance in which the caller is responsible for allocating and deallocating memory.

Consequences

Finally, you can allocate memory and properly handle its cleanup. That gives you flexibility. You can temporarily use large amounts of memory from the heap and at a later point in time let others use that memory.

But of course that benefit comes at some additional cost. You have to cope with cleaning up the memory and that makes your programming work harder. Even when having Dedicated Ownership, memory-related programming errors can occur and lead to hard-to-debug situations. Also, it takes some time to free the memory. Explicitly documenting where memory will be cleaned helps to prevent some of these errors and in general makes the code easier to understand and maintain. To further avoid memory-related programming errors, you can also use an Allocation Wrapper and Pointer Check.

With the allocation and deallocation of dynamic memory, the problems of heap fragmentation and increased time for allocating and accessing the memory come up. For some applications that might not be an issue at all, but for other applications these topics are very serious. In that case, a Memory Pool can help.

Known Uses

The following examples show applications of this pattern:

- The book *Extreme C* by Kamran Amini (Packt, 2019) suggests that the function that allocated memory should also be responsible for freeing it and that the function or object that owns the memory should be documented as comments. Of course that concept also holds true if you have wrapper functions. Then the function that calls the allocation wrapper should be the one that calls the cleanup wrapper.

- The implementation of the function mexFunction of the numeric computing environment MATLAB clearly documents which memory it owns and will free.

- The NetHack game explicitly documents for the callers of the functions if they have to free some memory. For example, the function nh_compose_ascii_screen shot allocates and returns a string that has to be freed by the caller.

- The Wireshark dissector for "Community ID flow hashes" clearly documents for its functions who is responsible for freeing memory. For example, the function communityid_calc allocates some memory and requires the caller to free it.

Applied to Running Example

The functionality of encryptCaesarFile did not change. The only thing you changed is that you now also call free to deallocate the memory, and you now clearly document in the code comments who is responsible for cleaning up which memory. Also, you implemented the function encryptDirectoryContent that encrypts all files in the current working directory:

```
/* For the provided 'filename', this function reads text from the file and
   prints the Caesar-encrypted text. This function is responsible for
   allocating and deallocating the required buffers for storing the
   file content */
void encryptCaesarFile(char* filename)
{
  char* text;
  int size = getFileLength(filename);
  if(size>0)
  {
    text = malloc(size);
    readFileContent(filename, text, size);
    caesar(text, strnlen(text, size));
```

```
      printf("Encrypted text: %s\n", text);
      free(text);
  }
}

/* For all files in the current directory, this function reads text
   from the file and prints the Caesar-encrypted text. */
void encryptDirectoryContent()
{
  struct dirent *directory_entry;
  DIR *directory = opendir(".");
  while ((directory_entry = readdir(directory)) != NULL)
  {
    encryptCaesarFile(directory_entry->d_name);
  }
  closedir(directory);
}
```

This code prints the Caesar-encrypted content of all files of the current directory. Note that the code only works on UNIX systems and that for reasons of simplicity, no specific error handling is implemented if the files in the directory don't have the expected content.

The memory is now also cleaned up when it is not required anymore. Note that not all the memory that the program requires during its runtime is allocated at the same time. The most memory allocated at any time throughout the program is the memory required for one of the files. That makes the memory footprint of the program significantly smaller, particularly if the directory contains many files.

The preceding code does not cope with error handling. For example, what happens if no more memory is available? The code would simply crash. You want to have some kind of error handling for such situations, but checking the pointers returned from malloc at each and every point where you allocate memory can be cumbersome. What you need is an Allocation Wrapper.

Allocation Wrapper

Context

You allocate dynamic memory at several places in your code, and you want to react to error situations such as running out of memory.

Problem

Each allocation of dynamic memory might fail, so you should check allocations in your code to react accordingly. This is cumbersome because you have many places for such checks in your code.

The malloc function returns NULL if the requested memory is not available. On the one hand, not checking the return value of malloc would cause your program to crash if no memory is available and you access a NULL pointer. On the other hand, checking the return value at each and every place where you allocate makes your code more complicated and thus harder to read and maintain.

If you distribute such checks across your codebase and later on want to change your behavior in case of allocation errors, then you'd have to touch code at many different places. Also, simply adding an error check to existing functions violates the single-responsibility principle, which says that one function should be responsible for only one thing (and not for multiple things like allocation and program logic).

Also, if you want to change the method of allocation later on, maybe to explicitly initialize all allocated memory, then having many calls to allocation functions distributed all over your code makes that very hard.

Solution

Wrap the allocation and deallocation calls, and implement error handling or additional memory management organization in these wrapper functions.

Implement a wrapper function for the malloc and free calls, and for memory allocation and deallocation only call these wrapper functions. In the wrapper function, you can implement error handling at one central point. For example, you can check the allocated pointer (see Pointer Check) and in case of error abort the program as shown in the following code:

```
void* checkedMalloc(size_t size)
{
  void* pointer = malloc(size);
  assert(pointer);
  return pointer;
}

#define DATA_SIZE 1024
void someFunction()
{
  char* memory = checkedMalloc(DATA_SIZE);
  /* work with the memory */
  free(memory);
}
```

As an alternative to aborting the program, you can Log Errors. For logging the debug information, using a macro instead of a wrapper function can make life even easier. You could then without any effort for the caller log the filename, the function name, or the code line number where the error occurred. With that information, it is very easy for the programmer to pinpoint the part of the code where the error occurred. Also, having a macro instead of a wrapper function saves you the additional function call of the wrapper function (but in most cases that doesn't matter, or the compiler would inline the function anyway). With macros for allocation and deallocation you could even build a constructor-like syntax:

```
#define NEW(object, type)                     \
do {                                          \
  object = malloc(sizeof(type));              \
  if(!object)                                 \
  {                                           \
    printf("Malloc Error: %s\n", __func__); \
    assert(false);                            \
  }                                           \
} while (0)

#define DELETE(object) free(object)


typedef struct{
  int x;
  int y;
}MyStruct;

void someFunction()
{
  MyStruct* myObject;
  NEW(myObject, MyStruct);
  /* work with the object */
  DELETE(myObject);
}
```

In addition to handling error situations in the wrapper functions, you could also do other things. For example, you could keep track of which memory your program allocated and store that information along with the code file and code line number in a list (for that you'd also need a wrapper for free, like in the preceding example). That way you can easily print debug information if you want to see which memory is currently allocated (and which of it you might have forgotten to free). But if you are looking for such information, you could also simply use a memory debugging tool like valgrind. Furthermore, by keeping track of which memory you allocated, you could implement a function to free all your memory—this might be an option to make your program cleaner if you previously used Lazy Cleanup.

Having everything in one place will not always be a solution for you. Maybe there are noncritical parts of your application for which you do not want the whole application to abort if an allocation error occurs there. In that case, having multiple Allocation Wrappers could work for you. One wrapper could still assert on error and could be used for the critical allocations that are mandatory for your application to work. Another wrapper for the noncritical part of your application could Return Status Codes on error to make it possible to gracefully handle that error situation.

Consequences

Error handling and other memory handling are now in one central place. At the places in the code where you need to allocate memory, you now simply call the wrapper and there is no need to explicitly handle errors at that point in the code. But that only works for some kinds of error handling. It works very well if you abort the program in case of errors, but if you react to errors by continuing the program with some degraded functionality, then you still have to return some error information from the wrapper and react to it. For that, the Allocation Wrapper does not make life easier. However, in such a scenario, there could still be some logging functionality implemented in the wrapper to improve the situation for you.

The wrapper function brings advantages for testing because you have one central point for changing the behavior of your memory allocation function. In addition, you can mock the wrapper (replace the wrapper calls with some other test function) while still leaving other calls to malloc (maybe from third-party code) untouched.

Separating the error-handling part from the calling code with a wrapper function is good practice because then the caller is not tempted to implement error handling directly inside the code that handles other programing logic. Having several things done in one function (program logic and extensive error handling) would violate the single-responsibility principle.

Having an Allocation Wrapper allows you to consistently handle allocation errors and makes it easier for you if you want to change the error-handling behavior or memory allocation behavior later on. If you decide that you want to log additional information, there is just one place in the code that you'd have to touch. If you decide to later on not directly call malloc but to use a Memory Pool instead, this is a lot easier when having the wrapper.

Known Uses

The following examples show applications of this pattern:

- The book *C Interfaces and Implementations* by David R. Hanson (Addison-Wesley, 1996) uses a wrapper function for allocating memory in an implementation for a Memory Pool. The wrappers simply call assert to abort the program in case of errors.

- GLib provides the functions g_malloc and g_free among other memory-related functions. The benefit of using g_malloc is that in case of error, it aborts the program (Samurai Principle). Because of that, there is no need for the caller to check the return value of each and every function call for allocating memory.

- The GoAccess real-time web log analyzer implements the function xmalloc to wrap malloc calls with some error handling.

- The Allocation Wrapper is an application of the Decorator pattern, which is described in the book *Design Patterns: Elements of Reusable Object-Oriented Software* by Erich Gamma, Richard Helm, Ralph Johnson, and John Vlissides (Prentice Hall, 1997).

Applied to Running Example

Now, instead of directly calling `malloc` and `free` everywhere in your code, you use wrapper functions:

```
/* Allocates memory and asserts if no memory is available */
void* safeMalloc(size_t size)
{
  void* pointer = malloc(size);
  assert(pointer); ❶
  return pointer;
}

/* Deallocates the memory of the provided 'pointer' */
void safeFree(void *pointer)
{
  free(pointer);
}

/* For the provided file 'filename', this function reads text from the file
   and prints the Caesar-encrypted text. This function is responsible for
   allocating and deallocating the required buffers for storing the
   file content */
void encryptCaesarFile(char* filename)
{
  char* text;
  int size = getFileLength(filename);
  if(size>0)
  {
    text = safeMalloc(size);
    readFileContent(filename, text, size);
    caesar(text, strnlen(text, size));
    printf("Encrypted text: %s\n", text);
    safeFree(text);
  }
}
```

❶ If the allocation fails, you adhere to the Samurai Principle and abort the program. For applications like yours, this is a valid option. If there is no way for you to gracefully handle the error, then directly aborting the program is the right and proper choice.

With the Allocation Wrapper you have the advantage that you now have a central point for handling allocation errors. There is no need to write lines of code for checking the pointer after each allocation in your code. You also have a wrapper for freeing the code, which might come in handy in the future if you, for example, decide to keep track of which memory is currently allocated by your application.

After the allocation you now check if the retrieved pointer is valid. After that, you don't check the pointer for validity anymore, and you also trust that the pointers you receive across function boundaries are valid. This is fine as long as no programming errors sneak in, but if you accidentally access invalid pointers, the situation becomes difficult to debug. To improve your code and to be on the safe side, you decide to use a Pointer Check.

Pointer Check

Context

Your program contains many places where you allocate and deallocate memory and many places where you access that memory or other resources with pointers.

Problem

Programming errors that lead to accessing an invalid pointer cause uncontrolled program behavior, and such errors are difficult to debug. However, because your code works with pointers frequently, there is a good chance that you have introduced such programming errors.

C programming requires a lot of struggling with pointers, and the more places you have in the code that work with pointers, the more places you have in the code where you could introduce programming errors. Using a pointer that was already freed or using an uninitialized pointer would lead to error situations that are hard to debug.

Any such error situation is very severe. It leads to uncontrolled program behavior and (if you are lucky) to a program crash. If you are not as lucky, you end up with an error that occurs at a later point in time during program execution and that takes you a week to pinpoint and debug. You want your program to be more robust against such errors. You want to make such errors less severe, and you want to make it easier to find the cause of such error situations if they occur in your running program.

Solution

Explicitly invalidate uninitialized or freed pointers and always check pointers for validity before accessing them.

Right at the variable declaration, set pointer variables explicitly to NULL. Also, right after calling free, set them explicitly to NULL. If you use an Allocation Wrapper that uses a macro for wrapping the free function, you could directly set the pointer to

NULL inside the macro to avoid having additional lines of code for invalidating the pointer at each deallocation.

Have a wrapper function or a macro that checks a pointer for NULL and in case of a NULL pointer aborts the program and Logs Errors to have some debug information. If aborting the program is not an option for you, then in case of NULL pointers you could instead not perform the pointer access and try to handle the error gracefully. This will allow your program to continue with reduced functionality as shown in the following code:

```
void someFunction()
{
  char* pointer = NULL; /* explicitly invalidate the uninitialized pointer */
  pointer = malloc(1024);

  if (pointer != NULL) /* check pointer validity before accessing it */
  {
    /* work with pointer*/
  }

  free(pointer);
  pointer = NULL; /* explicitly invalidate the pointer to freed memory */
}
```

Consequences

Your code is a bit more protected against pointer-related programming errors. Each such error that can be identified and does not lead to undefined program behavior might save you hours and days of debugging effort.

However, this does not come for free. Your code becomes longer and more complicated. The strategy you apply here is like having a belt and suspenders. You do some extra work to be safer. You have additional checks for each pointer access. This makes the code harder to read. For checking the pointer validity before accessing it, you'll have at least one additional line of code. If you do not abort the program but instead continue with degraded functionality, then your program becomes much more difficult to read, maintain, and test.

If you accidentally call free on a pointer multiple times, then your second call would not lead to an error situation because after the first call you invalidated the pointer, and subsequently calling free on a NULL pointer does no harm. Still, you could Log Errors like this to make it possible to pinpoint the root cause for the error.

But even after all that, you are not fully protected against every kind of pointer-related error. For example, you could forget to free some memory and produce a memory leak. Or you could access a pointer that you did not properly initialize, but at least you'd detect that and could react accordingly. A possible drawback here is that if you decide to gracefully degrade your program and continue, you might obscure error situations that are then hard to find later on.

Known Uses

The following examples show applications of this pattern:

- The implementation for C++ smart pointers invalidates the wrapped raw pointer when releasing the smart pointer.
- Cloudy is a program for physical calculations (spectral synthesis). It contains some code for interpolation of data (Gaunt factor). This program checks pointers for validity before accessing them and explicitly sets the pointers to NULL after calling free.
- The libcpp of the GNU Compiler Collection (GCC) invalidates the pointers after freeing them. For example, the pointers in the implementation file *macro.c* do this.
- The function HB_GARBAGE_FUNC of the MySQL database management system sets the pointer ph to NULL to avoid accidentally accessing it or freeing it multiple times later on.

Applied to Running Example

You now have the following code:

```
/* For the provided file 'filename', this function reads text from the file
   and prints the Caesar-encrypted text. This function is responsible for
   allocating and deallocating the required buffers for storing the
   file content */
void encryptCaesarFile(char* filename)
{
  char* text = NULL; ❶
  int size = getFileLength(filename);
  if(size>0)
  {
    text = safeMalloc(size);
    if(text != NULL) ❷
    {
      readFileContent(filename, text, size);
      caesar(text, strnlen(text, size));
      printf("Encrypted text: %s\n", text);
    }
    safeFree(text);
    text = NULL; ❶
  }
}
```

❶ At places where the pointer is not valid, you explicitly set it to NULL—just to be on the safe side.

❷ Before accessing the pointer text, you check whether it is valid. If it is not valid, you don't use the pointer (you don't dereference it).

 Linux Overcommit

Beware that having a valid memory pointer does not always mean that you can safely access that memory. Modern Linux systems work with the *overcommit* principle. This principle provides virtual memory to the program that allocates, but this virtual memory has no direct correspondence to physical memory. Whether the required physical memory is available is checked once you access that memory. If not enough physical memory is available, the Linux kernel shuts down applications that consume a lot of memory (and that might be your application). Overcommit brings the advantage that it becomes less important to check if allocation worked (because it usually does not fail), and you can allocate a lot of memory to be on the safe side, even if you only need a little. But overcommit also comes with the big disadvantage that even with a valid pointer, you can never be sure that your memory access works and will not lead to a crash. Another disadvantage is that you might become lazy with checking allocation return values and with figuring out and allocating only the amount of memory that you actually need.

Next, you also want to show the Caesar-encrypted filename along with the encrypted text. You decide against directly allocating the required memory from the heap because you are afraid of memory fragmentation when repeatedly allocating small memory chunks (for the filenames) and large memory chunks (for the file content). Instead of directly allocating dynamic memory, you implement a Memory Pool.

Memory Pool

Context

You frequently allocate and deallocate dynamic memory from the heap in your program for elements of roughly the same size. You don't know at compile time or startup time exactly where and when in your program these elements are needed.

Problem

Frequently allocating and deallocating objects from the heap leads to memory fragmentation.

When allocating objects, in particular those of strongly varying size, while also deallocating some of them, the heap memory becomes fragmented. Even if the allocations from your code are roughly the same size, they might be mixed with allocations from other programs running in parallel, and you'd end up with allocations of greatly varying size and fragmentation.

The `malloc` function can only succeed if there is enough free consecutive memory available. That means that even if there is enough free memory available, the `malloc` function might fail if the memory is fragmented and no consecutive chunk of memory of the required size is available. Memory fragmentation means that the memory is not being utilized very well.

Fragmentation is a serious issue for long-running systems, like most embedded systems. If a system runs for some years and allocates and deallocates many small chunks, then it will no longer be possible to allocate a larger chunk of memory. This means that you definitely have to tackle the fragmentation issue for such systems if you don't accept that the system has to be rebooted from time to time.

Another issue when using dynamic memory, particularly in combination with embedded systems, is that the allocation of memory from the heap takes some time. Other processes try to use the same heap, and thus the allocation has to be interlocked and its required time becomes very hard to predict.

Solution

Hold a large piece of memory throughout the whole lifetime of your program. At runtime, retrieve fixed-size chunks of that memory pool instead of directly allocating new memory from the heap.

The memory pool can either be placed in static memory or it can be allocated from the heap at program startup and freed at the end of the program. Allocation from the heap has the advantage that, if needed, additional memory can be allocated to increase the size of the memory pool.

Implement functions for retrieving and releasing memory chunks of pre-configured fixed size from that pool. All of your code that needs memory of that size can use these functions (instead of `malloc` and `free`) for acquiring and releasing dynamic memory:

```
#define MAX_ELEMENTS 20;
#define ELEMENT_SIZE 255;
```

```
typedef struct
{
  bool occupied;
  char memory[ELEMENT_SIZE];
}PoolElement;

static PoolElement memory_pool[MAX_ELEMENTS];

/* Returns memory of at least the provided 'size' or NULL
   if no memory chunk from the pool is available */
void* poolTake(size_t size)
{
  if(size <= ELEMENT_SIZE)
  {
    for(int i=0; i<MAX_ELEMENTS; i++)
    {
      if(memory_pool[i].occupied == false)
      {
        memory_pool[i].occupied = true;
        return &(memory_pool[i].memory);
      }
    }
  }
  return NULL;
}

/* Gives the memory chunk ('pointer') back to the pool */
void poolRelease(void* pointer)
{
  for(int i=0; i<MAX_ELEMENTS; i++)
  {
    if(&(memory_pool[i].memory) == pointer)
    {
      memory_pool[i].occupied = false;
      return;
    }
  }
}
```

The preceding code shows a simple implementation of a Memory Pool, and there would be many ways to improve that implementation. For example, free memory slots could be stored in a list to speed up taking such a slot. Also, Mutex or Semaphores could be used to make sure that it works in multithreaded environments.

For the Memory Pool, you have to know which kind of data will be stored because you have to know the size of the memory chunks before runtime. You could also use these chunks to store smaller data, but then you'd waste some of the memory.

As an alternative to having fixed-size memory chunks, you could even implement a Memory Pool that allows retrieving variable-size memory chunks. With that alternative solution, while you'd better utilize your memory, you'd still end up with the same fragmentation problem that you have with the heap memory.

Consequences

You tackled fragmentation. With the pool of fixed-size memory chunks, you can be sure that as soon as you release one chunk, another one will be available. However, you have to know which kinds of elements to store in the pool and their size beforehand. If you decide to also store smaller elements in the pool, you waste memory.

When using a pool of variable size, you don't waste memory for smaller elements, but your memory in the pool gets fragmented. This fragmentation situation is still a bit better compared to directly using the heap because you are the only user of that memory (other processes don't use the same memory). Also, you don't fragment the memory used by other processes. However, the fragmentation problem is still there.

No matter whether you use variable-sized or fixed-sized chunks in your pool, you have performance benefits. Getting memory from the pool is faster compared to allocating it from the heap because no mutual exclusion from other processes trying to get memory is required. Also, accessing the memory from the pool might be a bit faster because all the memory in the pool that your program uses lies closely together, which minimizes time overhead due to paging mechanisms from the operating system. However, initially creating the pool takes some time and will increase the startup time for your program.

Within your pool, you release the memory in order to reuse it somewhere else in your program. However, your program holds the total pool memory the entire time, and that memory will not be available to others. If you don't need all of that memory, you waste it from an overall system perspective.

If the pool is of initially fixed size, then you might have no more pool memory chunks available at runtime, even if there would be enough memory available in the heap. If the pool can increase its size at runtime, then you have the drawback that the time for retrieving memory from the pool can be increased unexpectedly if the pool size has to be increased to retrieve a memory chunk.

Beware of Memory Pools in security- or safety-critical domains. The pool makes your code more difficult to test, and it makes it more difficult for code analysis tools to find bugs related to accessing that memory. For example, it is difficult for tools to detect if by mistake you access memory outside the boundaries of an acquired memory chunk of that pool. Your process also owns the other memory chunks of the pool that are located directly before and after the chunk you intend to access, and that makes it hard for code analysis tools to realize that accessing data across the boundary of a Memory Pool chunk is unintentional. Actually, the OpenSSL Heartbleed bug could have been prevented by code analysis if the affected code was not using a Memory Pool (see David A. Wheeler, "How to Prevent the Next Heartbleed," July 18, 2020 [originally published April 29, 2014], *https://dwheeler.com/essays/heartbleed.html*).

Known Uses

The following examples show applications of this pattern:

- UNIX systems use a pool of fixed size for their process objects.

- The book *C Interfaces and Implementations* by David R. Hanson (Addison-Wesley, 1996) shows an example of a memory pool implementation.

- The Memory Pool pattern is also described in the books *Real-Time Design Patterns: Robust Scalable Architecture for Real-Time Systems* by Bruce P. Douglass (Addison-Wesley, 2002) and *Small Memory Software: Patterns for Systems With Limited Memory* by James Noble and Charles Weir (Addison-Wesley, 2000).

- The Android ION memory manager implements memory pools in its file *ion_system_heap.c.* On release of memory parts, the caller has the option to actually free that part of the memory if it is security-critical.

- The smpl discrete event simulation system described in the book *Simulating Computer Systems: Techniques and Tools* by H. M. MacDougall (MIT Press, 1987) uses a memory pool for events. This is more efficient than allocating and deallocating memory for each event, as processing each event takes only a short time and there is a large number of events in a simulation.

Applied to Running Example

To keep things easy, you decide to implement a Memory Pool with fixed maximum memory chunk size. You do not have to cope with multithreading and simultaneous access to that pool from multiple threads, so you can simply use the exact implementation from the Memory Pool pattern.

You end up with the following final code for your Caesar encryption:

```
#define ELEMENT_SIZE 255
#define MAX_ELEMENTS 10

typedef struct
{
  bool occupied;
  char memory[ELEMENT_SIZE];
}PoolElement;

static PoolElement memory_pool[MAX_ELEMENTS];

void* poolTake(size_t size)
{
  if(size <= ELEMENT_SIZE)
  {
    for(int i=0; i<MAX_ELEMENTS; i++)
    {
```

```
        if(memory_pool[i].occupied == false)
        {
          memory_pool[i].occupied = true;
          return &(memory_pool[i].memory);
        }
      }
    }
    return NULL;
}

void poolRelease(void* pointer)
{
    for(int i=0; i<MAX_ELEMENTS; i++)
    {
      if(&(memory_pool[i].memory) == pointer)
      {
        memory_pool[i].occupied = false;
        return;
      }
    }
}

#define MAX_FILENAME_SIZE ELEMENT_SIZE

/* Prints the Caesar-encrypted 'filename'.This function is responsible for
   allocating and deallocating the required buffers for storing the
   file content.
   Notes: The filename must be all capital letters and we accept that the
   '.' of the filename will also be shifted by the Caesar encryption. */
void encryptCaesarFilename(char* filename)
{
    char* buffer = poolTake(MAX_FILENAME_SIZE);
    if(buffer != NULL)
    {
      strlcpy(buffer, filename, MAX_FILENAME_SIZE);
      caesar(buffer, strnlen(buffer, MAX_FILENAME_SIZE));
      printf("\nEncrypted filename: %s ", buffer);
      poolRelease(buffer);
    }
}

/* For all files in the current directory, this function reads text from the
   file and prints the Caesar-encrypted text. */
void encryptDirectoryContent()
{
    struct dirent *directory_entry;
    DIR *directory = opendir(".");
    while((directory_entry = readdir(directory)) != NULL)
    {
      encryptCaesarFilename(directory_entry->d_name);
      encryptCaesarFile(directory_entry->d_name);
    }
```

```
        closedir(directory);
    }
```

With this final version of your code, you can now perform your Caesar encryption without stumbling across the common pitfalls of dynamic memory handling in C. You make sure that the memory pointers you use are valid, you assert if no memory is available, and you even avoid fragmentation outside of your predefined memory area.

Looking at the code, you realize that it has become very complicated. You simply want to work with some dynamic memory, and you had to implement dozens of lines of code to do that. Keep in mind that most of that code can be reused for any other allocation in your codebase. Still, applying one pattern after another did not come for free. With each pattern you added some additional complexity. However, it is not the aim to apply as many patterns as possible. It is the aim to apply only those patterns that solve your problems. If, for example, fragmentation is not a big issue for you, then please don't use a custom Memory Pool. If you can keep things simpler, then do so and, for example, directly allocate and deallocate the memory using `malloc` or `free`. Or even better, if you have the option, don't use dynamic memory at all.

Summary

This chapter presented patterns on handling memory in C programs. The Stack First pattern tells you to put variables on the stack if possible. Eternal Memory is about using memory that has the same lifetime as your program in order to avoid complicated dynamic allocation and freeing. Lazy Cleanup also makes freeing the memory easier for the programmer by suggesting that you simply not cope with it. Dedicated Ownership, on the other hand, defines where memory is freed and by whom. The Allocation Wrapper provides a central point for handling allocation errors and invalidating pointers, and that makes it possible to implement a Pointer Check when dereferencing variables. If fragmentation or long allocation times become an issue, a Memory Pool helps out.

With these patterns, the burden of making a lot of detailed design decisions on which memory to use and when to clean it up is taken from the programmer. Instead, the programmer can simply rely on the guidance from these patterns and can easily tackle memory management in C programs.

Further Reading

Compared to other advanced C programming topics, there is a lot of literature out there on the topic of memory management. Most of that literature focuses on the basis of the syntax for allocating and freeing memory, but the following books also provide some advanced guidance:

- The book *Small Memory Software: Patterns for Systems With Limited Memory* by James Noble and Charles Weir (Addison-Wesley, 2000) contains a lot of well-elaborated patterns on memory management. For example, the patterns describe the different strategies for allocating memory (at startup or during runtime) and also describe strategies such as memory pools or garbage collectors. All patterns also provide code examples for multiple programming languages.

- The book *Hands-on Design Patterns with C++* by Fedor G. Pikus (Packt, 2019) is as its name says not tailored for C, but the memory management concepts used by C and C++ are similar, so there is also relevant guidance on how to manage memory in C. It contains a chapter that focuses on memory ownership and explains how to use C++ mechanisms (like smart pointers) to make very clear who owns which memory.

- The book *Extreme C* by Kamran Amini (Packt, 2019) covers many C programming topics, like the compilation process, toolchains, unit-testing, concurrency, intra-process communication, and also the basic C syntax. There is also a chapter on heap and stack memory, and it describes platform-specific details on how these memories are represented in the code-, data-, stack-, or heap-segment.

- The book *Real-Time Design Patterns: Robust Scalable Architecture for Real-Time Systems* by Bruce P. Douglass (Addison-Wesley, 2002) contains patterns for real-time systems. Some of the patterns address allocation and cleanup of memory.

Outlook

The next chapter gives guidance on how to transport information in general across interface boundaries. The chapter presents patterns that elaborate on the kinds of mechanisms that C provides for transporting information between functions and which of these mechnisms should be used.

CHAPTER 4

Returning Data from C Functions

Returning data from a function call is a task you are faced with when writing any kind of code that is longer than 10 lines and that you intend to be maintainable. Returning data is a simple task—you simply have to pass the data you want to share between two functions—and in C you only have the option to directly return a value or to return data via emulated "by-reference" parameters. There are not many choices and there is not much guidance to give—right? Wrong! Even the simple task of returning data from C functions is already tricky, and there are many routes you can take to structure your program and your function parameters.

Especially in C, where you have to manage the memory allocation and deallocation on your own, passing complex data between functions becomes tricky because there is no destructor or garbage collector to help you clean up the data. You have to ask yourself: should the data be put on the stack, or should it be allocated? Who should allocate—the caller or the callee?

This chapter provides best practices on how to share data between functions. These patterns help C programming beginners to understand techniques for returning data in C, and they help advanced C programmers to better understand why these different techniques are applied.

Figure 4-1 shows an overview of the patterns discussed in this chapter and their relationships, and Table 4-1 provides a summary of the patterns.

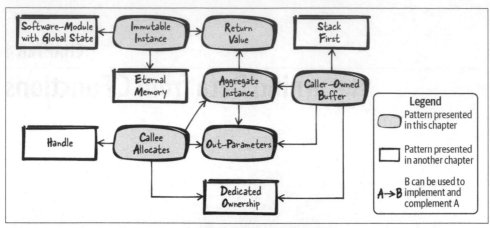

Figure 4-1. Overview of patterns for returning information

Table 4-1. Patterns for returning information

Pattern name	Summary
Return Value	The function parts you want to split are not independent from one another. As usual in procedural programming, some part delivers a result that is then needed by some other part. The function parts that you want to split need to share some data. Therefore, simply use the one C mechanism intended to retrieve information about the result of a function call: the Return Value. The mechanism to return data in C copies the function result and provides the caller access to this copy.
Out-Parameters	C only supports returning a single type from a function call, which makes it complicated to return multiple pieces of information. Therefore, return all the data with a single function call by emulating by-reference arguments with pointers.
Aggregate Instance	C only supports returning a single type from a function call, which makes it complicated to return multiple pieces of information. Therefore, put all data that is related into a newly defined type. Define this Aggregate Instance to contain all the related data that you want to share. Define it in the interface of your component to let the caller directly access all the data stored in the instance.
Immutable Instance	You want to provide information held in large pieces of immutable data from your component to a caller. Therefore, have an instance (for example, a `struct`) containing the data to share in static memory. Provide this data to users who want to access it and make sure that they cannot modify it.
Caller-Owned Buffer	You want to provide complex or large data of known size to the caller, and that data is not immutable (it changes at runtime). Therefore, require the caller to provide a buffer and its size to the function that returns the large, complex data. In the function implementation, copy the required data into the buffer if the buffer size is large enough.
Callee Allocates	You want to provide complex or large data of unknown size to the caller, and that data is not immutable (it changes at runtime). Therefore, allocate a buffer with the required size inside the function that provides the large, complex data. Copy the required data into the buffer and return a pointer to that buffer.

Running Example

You want to implement the functionality to display diagnostic information for an Ethernet driver to the user. First, you simply add this functionality directly into the file with the Ethernet driver implementation and directly access the variables that contain the required information:

```
void ethShow()
{
  printf("%i packets received\n", driver.internal_data.rec);
  printf("%i packets sent\n", driver.internal_data.snd);
}
```

Later on, you realize that the functionality to display diagnostic information for your Ethernet driver will quite likely grow, so you decide to put it into a separate implementation file in order to keep your code clean. Now you need some simple way to transport the information from your Ethernet driver component to your diagnostics component.

One solution would be to use global variables to transport this information, but if you use global variables, then the effort to split the implementation file will have been useless. You split the files because you want to show that these code parts are not tightly coupled—with global variables you would bring that tight coupling back in.

A much better and very simple solution is the following: let your Ethernet component have getter-functions that provide the desired information as a Return Value.

Return Value

Context

You want to split your code into separate functions, as having everything in one function and in one implementation file is bad practice because it gets difficult to read and to debug the code.

Problem

The function parts you want to split are not independent from one another. As usual in procedural programming, some part delivers a result that is then needed by some other part. The function parts that you want to split need to share some data.

You want to have a mechanism for sharing data that makes your code easy to understand. You want to make it explicit in your code that data is shared between functions, and you want to make sure that functions don't communicate over side-channels not clearly visible in the code. Thus, using global variables to return information to a caller is not a good solution for you because global variables can be accessed and modified from any other part of the code. Also, it is not clear from the function signature which exact global variable is used for returning data.

Global variables also have the drawback that they can be used to store state information, which could lead to different results for identical function calls. This makes the code more difficult to understand. Aside from that, code using global variables for returning information would not be reentrant, and it would not be safe to use in a multithreaded environment.

Solution

Simply use the one C mechanism intended to retrieve information about the result of a function call: the Return Value. The mechanism to return data in C copies the function result and provides the caller access to this copy.

Figure 4-2 and the following code show how to implement the Return Value.

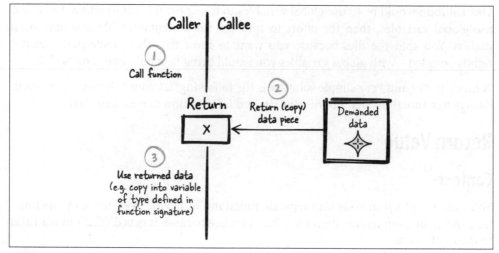

Figure 4-2. Return Value

Caller's code

```
int my_data = getData();
/* use my_data */
```

Callee's code

```
int getData()
{
  int requested_data;
  /* .... */
  return requested_data;
}
```

Consequences

A Return Value allows the caller to retrieve a copy of the function result. No other code apart from the function implementation can modify this value, and, as it is a copy, this value is solely used by the calling function. Compared to using global variables, it is more clearly defined which code influences the data retrieved from the function call.

Also, by not using global variables and using the copy of the function result instead, the function can be reentrant, and it can safely be used in a multithreaded environment.

However, for built-in C types, a function can return only a single object of the type specified in the function signature. It is not possible to define a function with multiple return types. You cannot, for example, have a function that returns three different int objects. If you want to return more information than contained in just one simple, scalar C type, then you have to use an Aggregate Instance or Out-Parameters.

Also, if you want to return data from an array, then the Return Value is not what you want because it does not copy the content of the array, but only the pointer to the array. The caller might then end up with a pointer to data that ran out of scope. For returning arrays, you have to use other mechanisms like a Caller-Owned Buffer or like when the Callee Allocates.

Remember that whenever the simple Return Value mechanism is sufficient, then you should always take this most simple option to return data. You should not go for more powerful, but also more complex, patterns like Out-Parameters, Aggregate Instance, Caller-Owned Buffer, or Callee Allocates.

Known Uses

The following examples show applications of this pattern:

- You can find this pattern everywhere. Any non-void function returns data in this way.
- Every C program has a main function that already provides a return value to its caller (such as the operating system).

Applied to Running Example

Applying Return Value was simple. Now you have a new diagnostic component in an implementation file separate from the Ethernet driver, and this component obtains the diagnostic information from the Ethernet driver as shown in the following code:

Ethernet driver API

```
/* Returns the number of total received packets*/
int ethernetDriverGetTotalReceivedPackets();

/* Returns the number of total sent packets*/
int ethernetDriverGetTotalSentPackets();
```

Caller's code

```
void ethShow()
{
  int received_packets = ethernetDriverGetTotalReceivedPackets();
  int sent_packets = ethernetDriverGetTotalSentPackets();
  printf("%i packets received\n", received_packets);
  printf("%i packets sent\n", sent_packets);
}
```

This code is easy to read, and if you want to add additional information, you can simply add additional functions to obtain this information. And that is exactly what you want to do next. You want to show more information about the sent packets. You want to show the user how many packets were successfully sent and how many failed. Your first attempt is to write the following code:

```
void ethShow()
{
  int received_packets = ethernetDriverGetTotalReceivedPackets();
  int total_sent_packets = ethernetDriverGetTotalSentPackets();
  int successfully_sent_packets = ethernetDriverGetSuccesscullySentPackets();
  int failed_sent_packets = ethernetDriverGetFailedPackets();
  printf("%i packets received\n", received_packets);
  printf("%i packets sent\n", total_sent_packets);
  printf("%i packets successfully sent\n", successfully_sent_packets);
  printf("%i packets failed to send\n", failed_sent_packets);
}
```

With this code, you eventually realize that sometimes, different from what you expected, `successfully_sent_packets` plus `failed_sent_packets` results in a number higher than `total_sent_packets`. This is because your Ethernet driver runs in a separate thread, and between your function calls to obtain the information, the Ethernet driver continues working and updates its packet information. So, if, for example, the Ethernet driver successfully sends a packet between your `ethernetDriverGet` `TotalSentPackets` call and `ethernetDriverGetSuccesscullySentPackets`, then the information that you show to the user is not consistent.

A possible solution would be to make sure that the Ethernet driver is not working while you call the functions to obtain the packet information. You could, for example, use a Mutex or a Semaphore to make sure of this, but for such a simple task like obtaining packet statistics, you'd expect that you are not the one who has to cope with this issue.

As a much easier alternative, you can return multiple pieces of information from one function call by using Out-Parameters.

Out-Parameters

Context

You want to provide data that represents related pieces of information from your component to a caller, and these pieces of information may change between separate function calls.

Problem

C only supports returning a single type from a function call, which makes it complicated to return multiple pieces of information.

Using global variables to transport the data representing your pieces of information is not a good solution because code using global variables for returning information would not be reentrant, and it would not be safe to use in a multithreaded environment. Aside from that, global variables can be accessed and modified from any other part of the code, and when using global variables, it is not clear from the function signature which exact global variables are used for returning the data. Thus, global variables would make your code hard to understand and maintain. Also, using the Return Values of multiple functions is not a good option because the data you want to return is related, so splitting it across multiple function calls makes the code less readable.

Because the pieces of data are related, the caller wants to retrieve a consistent snapshot of all this data. That becomes an issue when using multiple Return Values in a multithreaded environment because the data can change at runtime. In that case, you would have to make sure that the data does not change between the caller's multiple function calls. But you cannot know whether the caller already finished reading all the data or whether there will be another piece of information that the caller wants to retrieve with another function call. Because of that, you cannot make sure that the data is not modified between the caller's function calls. If you are using multiple functions to provide related information, then you don't know the timespan during which the data must not change. Thus, with this approach, you cannot guarantee that the caller will retrieve a consistent snapshot of the information.

Having multiple functions with Return Values also might not be a good solution if a lot of preparation work is required for calculating the related pieces of data. If, for example, you want to return the home and mobile telephone number for a specified person from an address book and you have separate functions to retrieve the numbers, you'd have to search through the address book entry of this person separately for each of the function calls. This requires unnecessary computation time and resources.

Solution

Return all the data with one function call by emulating by-reference arguments with pointers.

C does not support returning multiple types using the Return Value, nor does C natively support by-reference arguments, but by-reference arguments can be emulated as shown in Figure 4-3 and the following code.

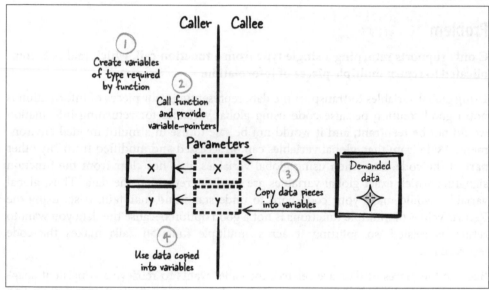

Figure 4-3. Out-Parameters

Caller's code

```
int x,y;
getData(&x,&y);
/* use x,y */
```

Callee's code

```
void getData(int* x, int* y)
{
    *x = 42;
    *y = 78;
}
```

Have a single function with many pointer arguments. In the function implementation, dereference the pointers and copy the data you want to return to the caller into the instance pointed to. In the function implementation, make sure that the data does not change while copying. This can be achieved by mutual exclusion.

Multithreaded Environments

In modern systems, it is common to work in a multithreaded environment. To avoid synchronization issues in such environments, it is best to either have immuatble data or to not share the data or functions (see the video "Thinking Outside the Synchronisation Quadrant" (*https://oreil.ly/SI1ta*) by Kevlin Henney). But this is not possible in all cases, and things become difficult because you have to implement your functions in a way that they can safely be called by multiple threads in arbitrary order or even at the same time.

That requires your functions to be reentrant, which means that the function still works properly if it is interrupted at any time and continued later on. When working on shared resources such as global variables, you have to make sure to protect these resources from simultaneous acccss by other threads. This can be done with synchronization primitives such as Mutex or Semaphores.

This book does not focus on such synchronization primitives or how to use them, but the book *Real-Time Design Patterns: Robust Scalable Architecture for Real-Time Systems* by Bruce P. Douglass (Addison-Wesley, 2002) does; it also provides C patterns on concurrency and resource management.

Consequences

Now all data that represents related pieces of information are returned in one single function call and can be kept consistent (for example, by copying data protected by Mutex or Semaphores). The function is reentrant and can safely be used in a multithreaded environment.

For each additional data item, an additional pointer is passed to the function. This has the drawback that if you want to return a lot of data, the function's parameter list becomes longer and longer. Having many parameters for one function is a code smell because it makes the code unreadable. That is why multiple Out-Parameters are rarely used for a function and instead, to clean up the code, related pieces of information are returned with an Aggregate Instance.

Also, for each piece of data, the caller has to pass a pointer to the function. This means that for each piece of data, an additional pointer has to be put onto the stack. If the caller's stack memory is very limited, that might become an issue.

Out-Parameters have the disadvantage that when only looking at the function signature, they cannot clearly be identified as Out-Parameters. From the function signature, callers can only guess whenever they see a pointer that it might be an Out-Parameter. But such a pointer parameter could also be an input for the function. Thus, it has to be clearly described in the API documentation which parameters are for input and which are for output.

For simple, scalar C types the caller can simply pass the pointer to a variable as a function argument. For the function implementation all the information to interpret the pointer is specified because of the specified pointer type. To return data with complex types, like arrays, either a Caller-Owned Buffer has to be provided, or the Callee Allocates and additional information about the data, like its size, has to be communicated.

Known Uses

The following examples show applications of this pattern:

- The Windows RegQueryInfoKey function returns information about a registry key via the function's Out-Parameters. The caller provides unsigned long pointers, and the function writes, among other pieces of information, the number of subkeys and the size of the key's value into the unsigned long variables being pointed to.

- Apple's Cocoa API for C programs uses an additional NSError parameter to store errors occurring during the function calls.

- The function userAuthenticate of the real-time operating system VxWorks uses Return Values to return information, in this case whether a provided password is correct for a provided login name. Additionally, the function takes an Out-Parameter to return the user ID associated with the provided login name.

Applied to Running Example

By applying Out-Parameters you'll get the following code:

Ethernet driver API

```
/* Returns driver status information via out-parameters.
   total_sent_packets    --> number of packets tried to send (success and fail)
   successfully_sent_packets --> number of packets successfully sent
   failed_sent_packets   --> number of packets failed to send */
void ethernetDriverGetStatistics(int* total_sent_packets,
     int* successfully_sent_packets, int* failed_sent_packets); ❶
```

❶ To retrieve information about sent packets, you have only one function call to the Ethernet driver, and the Ethernet driver can make sure that the data delivered within this call is consistent.

Caller's code

```
void ethShow()
{
  int total_sent_packets, successfully_sent_packets, failed_sent_packets;
  ethernetDriverGetStatistics(&total_sent_packets, &successfully_sent_packets,
                              &failed_sent_packets);
  printf("%i packets sent\n", total_sent_packets);
  printf("%i packets successfully sent\n", successfully_sent_packets);
  printf("%i packets failed to send\n", failed_sent_packets);

  int received_packets = ethernetDriverGetTotalReceivedPackets();
  printf("%i packets received\n", received_packets);
}
```

You consider also retrieving the received_packets in the same function call with the sent packets, but you realize that the one function call becomes more and more complicated. Having one function call with three Out-Parameters is already complicated to write and read. When calling the functions, the parameter order could easily be mixed up. Adding a fourth parameter wouldn't make the code better.

To make the code more readable, an Aggregate Instance can be used.

Aggregate Instance

Context

You want to provide data that represents related pieces of information from your component to a caller, and these pieces of information may change between separate function calls.

Problem

C only supports returning a single type from a function call, which makes it complicated to return multiple pieces of information.

Using global variables to transport the data representing your pieces of information is not a good solution because code using global variables for returning information would not be reentrant, and it would not be safe to use in a multithreaded environment. Aside from that, global variables can be accessed and modified from any other part of the code, and when using global variables, it is not clear from the function signature which exact global variables are used for returning the data. Thus, global variables would make your code hard to understand and maintain. Also, using the Return Values of multiple functions is not a good option because the data you want to return is related, so splitting it across multiple function calls makes the code less readable.

Having a single function with many Out-Parameters is also not a good idea because if you have many such Out-Parameters, it gets easy to mix them up and your code becomes unreadable. Also, you want to show that the parameters are closely related, and you might even need the same set of parameters to be provided to or returned by other functions. When explicitly doing that with function parameters, you'd have to modify each such function in case additional parameters are added later on.

Because the pieces of data are related, the caller wants to retrieve a consistent snapshot of all this data. That becomes an issue when using multiple Return Values in a multithreaded environment because the data can change at runtime. In that case, you would have to make sure that the data does not change between the caller's multiple function calls. But you cannot know whether the caller already finished reading all the data or whether there will be another piece of information that the caller wants to retrieve with another function call. Because of that, you cannot make sure that the data is not modified between the caller's function calls. If you are using multiple functions to provide related information, then you don't know the timespan during which the data must not change. Thus, with this approach, you cannot guarantee that the caller will retrieve a consistent snapshot of the information.

Having multiple functions with Return Values also might not be a good solution if a lot of preparation work is required for calculating the related pieces of data. If, for example, you want to return the home and mobile telephone number for a specified person from an address book and you have separate functions to retrieve the numbers, you'd have to search through the address book entry of this person separately for each of the function calls. This requires unnecessary computation time and resources.

Solution

Put all data that is related into a newly defined type. Define this Aggregate Instance to contain all the related data that you want to share. Define it in the interface of your component to let the caller directly access all the data stored in the instance.

To implement this, define a `struct` in your header file and define all types to be returned from the called function as members of this `struct`. In the function implementation, copy the data to be returned into the `struct` members as shown in Figure 4-4. In the function implementation, make sure that the data does not change while copying. This can be achieved by mutual exclusion via Mutex or Semaphores.

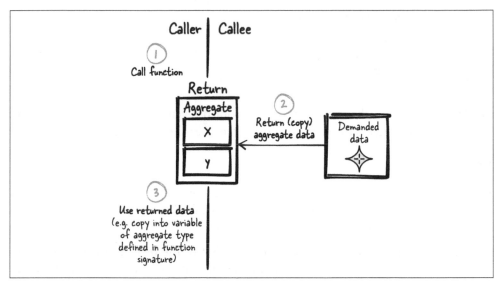

Figure 4-4. Aggregate Instance

To actually return the struct to the caller, there are two main options:

- Pass the whole struct as a Return Value. C allows not only built-in types to be passed as a Return Value of functions but also user-defined types such as a struct.

- Pass a pointer to the struct using an Out-Parameter. However, when only passing pointers, the issue arises of who provides and owns the memory being pointed to. That issue is addressed in Caller-Owned Buffer and Callee Allocates. Instead of passing a pointer and letting the caller directly access the Aggregate Instance, you could consider hiding the struct from the caller by using a Handle.

The following code shows the variant with passing the whole struct:

Caller's code

```
struct AggregateInstance my_instance;
my_instance = getData();
/* use my_instance.x
   use my_instance.y, ... */
```

Callee's code

```
struct AggregateInstance
{
  int x;
  int y;
};
```

```
struct AggregateInstance getData()
{
  struct AggregateInstance inst;
  /* fill inst.x and inst.y */
  return inst;  ❶
}
```

❶ When returning, the content of `inst` is copied (even though it is a `struct`), and
   the caller can access the copied content even after `inst` runs out of scope.

Consequences

Now the caller can retrieve multiple data that represent related pieces of information
via the Aggregate Instance with a single function call. The function is reentrant and
can safely be used in a multithreaded environment.

This provides the caller with a consistent snapshot of the related pieces of information. It also makes the caller's code clean because they don't have to call multiple functions or one function with many Out-Parameters.

When passing data between functions without pointers by using Return Values, all
this data is put on the stack. When passing one `struct` to 10 nested functions, this
`struct` is on the stack 10 times. In some cases this is not a problem, but in other cases
it is—especially if the `struct` is too large and you don't want to waste stack memory
by copying the whole `struct` onto the stack every time. Because of this, quite often
instead of directly passing or returning a `struct`, a pointer to that `struct` is passed or
returned.

When passing pointers to the `struct`, or if the `struct` contains pointers, you have to
keep in mind that C does not perform the work of doing a deep copy for you. C only
copies the pointer values and does not copy the instances they point to. That might
not be what you want, so you have to keep in mind that as soon as pointers come into
play, you have to deal with providing and cleaning up the memory being pointed to.
This issue is addressed in Caller-Owned Buffer and Callee Allocates.

Known Uses

The following examples show applications of this pattern:

- The article "Patterns of Argument Passing" (*https://oreil.ly/VlCgm*) by Uwe Zdun
  describes this pattern, including C++ examples, as Context Object, and the book
  Refactoring: Improving the Design of Existing Code by Martin Fowler (Addison-
  Wesley, 1999) describes it as Parameter Object.

- The code of the game NetHack stores monster-attributes in Aggregate Instances
  and provides a function for retrieving this information.

- The implementation of the text editor sam copies `structs` when passing them to functions and when returning them from functions in order to keep the code simpler.

Applied to Running Example

With the Aggregate Instance, you'll get the following code:

Ethernet driver API

```
struct EthernetDriverStat{
  int received_packets;        /* Number of received packets */
  int total_sent_packets;      /* Number of sent packets (success and fail)*/
  int successfully_sent_packets;/* Number of successfully sent packets */
  int failed_sent_packets;     /* Number of packets failed to send */
};

/* Returns statistics information of the Ethernet driver */
struct EthernetDriverStat ethernetDriverGetStatistics();
```

Caller's code

```
void ethShow()
{
  struct EthernetDriverStat eth_stat = ethernetDriverGetStatistics();
  printf("%i packets received\n", eth_stat.received_packets);
  printf("%i packets sent\n", eth_stat.total_sent_packets);
  printf("%i packets successfully sent\n",eth_stat.successfully_sent_packets);
  printf("%i packets failed to send\n", eth_stat.failed_sent_packets);
}
```

Now you have one single call to the Ethernet driver, and the Ethernet driver can make sure that the data delivered within this call is consistent. Also, your code looks cleaned up because the data that belongs together is now collected in a single `struct`.

Next, you want to show more information about the Ethernet driver to your user. You want to show the user to which Ethernet interface the packet statistics information belongs to, and thus you want to show the driver name including a textual description of the driver. Both are contained in a string stored in the Ethernet driver component. The string is quite long and you don't exactly know how long it is. Luckily, the string does not change during runtime, so you can access an Immutable Instance.

Immutable Instance

Context

Your component contains a lot of data, and another component wants to access this data.

Problem

You want to provide information held in large pieces of immutable data from your component to a caller.

Copying the data for each and every caller would be a waste of memory, so providing all the data by returning an Aggregate Instance or by copying all the data into Out-Parameters is not an option due to stack memory limitations.

Usually, simply returning a pointer to such data is tricky. You'd have the problem that with a pointer, such data can be modified, and as soon as multiple callers read and write the same data, you have to come up with mechanisms to ensure that the data you want to access is consistent and up-to-date. Luckily, in your situation the data you want to provide to the caller is fixed at compile time or at boot time and does not change at runtime.

Solution

Have an instance (for example, a struct) containing the data to share in static memory. Provide this data to users who want to access it and make sure that they cannot modify it.

Write the data to be contained in the instance at compile time or at boot time and do not change it at runtime anymore. You can either directly write the data hardcoded in your program, or you can initialize it at program startup (see "Software-Module with Global State" on page 127 for initialization variants and "Eternal Memory" on page 65 for storage variants). As shown in Figure 4-5, even if multiple callers (and multiple threads) access the instance at the same time, they don't have to worry about each other because the instance does not change and is thus always in a consistent state and contains the required information.

Implement a function that returns a pointer to the data. Alternatively, you could even directly make the variable containing the data global and put it into your API because the data does not change at runtime anyway. But still, the getter-function is better because compared to global variables, it makes writing unit tests easier, and in case of future behavior changes of your code (if your data is not immutable anymore), you'd not have to change your interface.

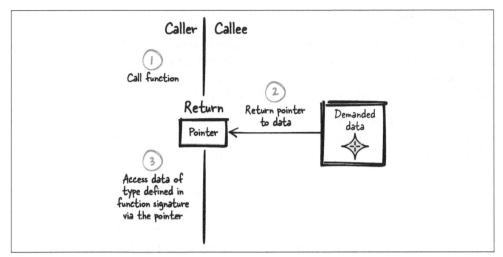

Figure 4-5. Immutable Instance

To make sure that the caller does not modify the data, when returning a pointer to the data, make the data being pointed to const as shown in the following code:

Caller's code

```
const struct ImmutableInstance* my_instance;
my_instance = getData(); ❶
/* use my_instance->x,
   use my_instance->y, ... */
```

❶ The caller obtains a reference but doesn't get ownership of the memory.

Callee API

```
struct ImmutableInstance
{
  int x;
  int y;
};
```

Callee Implementation

```
static struct ImmutableInstance inst = {12, 42};
const struct ImmutableInstance* getData()
{
  return &inst;
}
```

Consequences

The caller can call one simple function to get access to even complex or large data and does not have to care about where this data is stored. The caller does not have to provide buffers in which this data can be stored, does not have to clean up memory, and does not have to care about the lifetime of the data—it simply always exists.

The caller can read all data via the retrieved pointer. The simple function for retrieving the pointer is reentrant and can safely be used in multithreaded environments. Also the data can safely be accessed in multithreaded environments because it does not change at runtime, and multiple threads that only read the data are no problem.

However, the data cannot be changed at runtime without taking further measures. If it is necessary for the caller to be able to change the data, then something like copy-on-write can be implemented. If the data in general can change at runtime, then an Immutable Instance isn't an option and instead, for sharing complex and large data, a Caller-Owned Buffer has to be used or the Callee Allocates.

Known Uses

The following examples show applications of this pattern:

- In his article "Patterns in Java: Patterns of Value" (*https://oreil.ly/cVY9N*), Kevlin Henney describes the similar Immutable Object pattern in detail and provides C++ code examples.

- The code of the game NetHack stores immutable monster-attributes in an Immutable Instance and provides a function for retrieving this information.

Applied to Running Example

Usually, returning a pointer to access data stored within a component is tricky. This is because if multiple callers access (and maybe write) this data, then a plain pointer isn't the solution for you because you never know if the pointer you have is still valid and if the data contained in this pointer is consistent. But in this case we are lucky because we have an Immutable Instance. The driver name and description are both information that is determined at compile time and does not change afterwards. Thus, we can simply retrieve a constant pointer to this data:

Ethernet driver API

```
struct EthernetDriverInfo{
  char name[64];
  char description[1024];
};

/* Returns the driver name and description */
const struct EthernetDriverInfo* ethernetDriverGetInfo();
```

Caller's code

```
void ethShow()
{
  struct EthernetDriverStat eth_stat = ethernetDriverGetStatistics();
  printf("%i packets received\n", eth_stat.received_packets);
  printf("%i packets sent\n", eth_stat.total_sent_packets);
  printf("%i packets successfully sent\n",eth_stat.successfully_sent_packets);
  printf("%i packets failed to send\n", eth_stat.failed_sent_packets);

  const struct EthernetDriverInfo* eth_info = ethernetDriverGetInfo();
  printf("Driver name: %s\n", eth_info->name);
  printf("Driver description: %s\n", eth_info->description);
}
```

As a next step, in addition to the name and description of the Ethernet interface, you also want to show the user the currently configured IP address and subnet mask. The addresses are stored as a string in the Ethernet driver. Both addresses are information that might change during runtime, so you cannot simply return a pointer to an Immutable Instance.

While it would be possible to have the Ethernet driver pack these strings into an Aggregate Instance and simply return this instance (arrays in a struct are copied when returning the struct), such a solution is rather uncommon for large amounts of data because it consumes a lot of stack memory. Usually, pointers are used instead.

Using pointers is the exact solution you are looking for: use a Caller-Owned Buffer.

Caller-Owned Buffer

Context

You have large data that you want to share between different components.

Problem

You want to provide complex or large data of known size to the caller, and that data is not immutable (it changes at runtime).

Because the data changes at runtime (maybe because you provide the callers with functions to write the data), you cannot simply provide the caller with a pointer to static data (as is the case with an Immutable Instance). If you simply provide the callers with such a pointer, you'd run into the problem that the data one caller reads might be inconsistent (partially overwritten) because, in a multithreaded environment, another caller might simultaneously write that data.

Simply copying all the data into an Aggregate Instance and passing it via the Return Value to the caller is not an option because, as the data is large, it cannot be passed via the stack, which only has very limited memory.

When instead only returning a pointer to the Aggregate Instance, there would be no problem with stack memory limitations anymore, but you have to keep in mind that C does not do the work of performing a deep copy for you. C only returns the pointer. You have to make sure that the data (stored in an Aggregate Instance or in an array) being pointed to is still valid after the function call. For example, you cannot store the data in auto-variables within your function and provide a pointer to these variables because after the function call, the variables run out of scope.

Now the question arises of where the data should be stored. It has to be clarified whether the caller or the callee should provide the required memory and which one is then responsible for managing and cleaning up the memory.

Solution

Require the caller to provide a buffer and its size to the function that returns the large, complex data. In the function implementation, copy the required data into the buffer if the buffer size is large enough.

Make sure that the data does not change while copying. This can be achieved by mutual exclusion via Mutex or Semaphores. The caller then has a snapshot of the data in the buffer, is the sole owner of this snapshot, and thus can consistently access this snapshot even if the original data changes in the meantime.

The caller can provide the buffer and its size each as a separate function parameter, or the caller can pack the buffer and its size into an Aggregate Instance and pass a pointer to the Aggregate Instance to the function.

As the caller has to provide the buffer and its size to the function, the caller has to know the size beforehand. To let the caller know what size the buffer has to be, the size requirement has to be present in the API. This can be implemented by defining the size as a macro or by defining a `struct` containing a buffer of the required size in the API.

Figure 4-6 and the following code show the concept of a Caller-Owned Buffer.

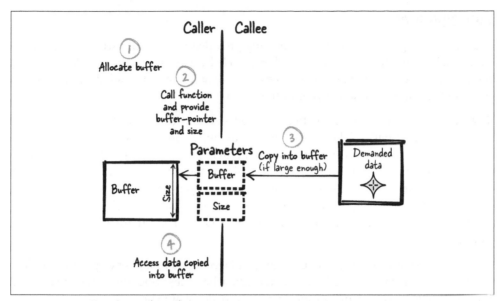

Figure 4-6. Caller-Owned Buffer

Caller's code

```
struct Buffer buffer;

getData(&buffer);
/* use buffer.data */
```

Callee's API

```
#define BUFFER_SIZE 256
struct Buffer
{
  char data[BUFFER_SIZE];
};

void getData(struct Buffer* buffer);
```

Callee's implementation

```
void getData(struct Buffer* buffer)
{
  memcpy(buffer->data, some_data, BUFFER_SIZE);
}
```

Consequences

The large, complex data can be consistently provided to the caller with a single function call. The function is reentrant and can safely be used in a multithreaded environment. Also, the caller can safely access the data in multithreaded environments because the caller is the sole owner of the buffer.

The caller provides a buffer of the expected size and can even decide the kind of memory for that buffer. The caller can put the buffer on the stack (see "Stack First" on page 62) and benefit from the advantage that stack memory will be cleaned up after the variable runs out of scope. Alternatively, the caller can put the memory on the heap to determine the lifetime of the variable or to not waste stack memory. Also, the calling function might only have a reference to a buffer obtained by its calling function. In this case this buffer can simply be passed on and there is no need to have multiple buffers.

The time-intensive operation of allocating and freeing memory is not performed during the function call. The caller can determine when these operations take place, and thus the function call becomes quicker and more deterministic.

From the API it is absolutely clear that the caller has Dedicated Ownership of the buffer. The caller has to provide the buffer and clean it up afterwards. If the caller allocated the buffer, then the caller is the one responsible for freeing it afterwards.

The caller has to know the size of the buffer beforehand and because this size is known, the function can safely operate in the buffer. But in some cases the caller might not know the exact size required, and it would be better if instead the Callee Allocates.

Known Uses

The following examples show applications of this pattern:

- The NetHack code uses this pattern to provide the information about a savegame to the component that then actually stores the game progress on the disk.
- The B&R Automation Runtime operating system uses this pattern for a function to retrieve the IP address.
- The C stdlib function `fgets` reads input from a stream and stores it in a provided buffer.

Applied to Running Example

You now provide a Caller-Owned Buffer to the Ethernet driver function, and the function copies its data into this buffer. You have to know beforehand how large the buffer has to be. In the case of obtaining the IP address string, this is not a problem

---

because the string has a fixed size. So you can simply put the buffer for the IP address on the stack and provide this stack variable to the Ethernet driver. Alternatively, it would have been possible to allocate the buffer on the heap, but in this case that is not required because the size of the IP address is known and the size of the data is small enough to fit on the stack:

Ethernet driver API

```
struct IpAddress{
  char address[16];
  char subnet[16];
};

/* Stores the IP information into 'ip', which has to be provided
   by the caller*/
void ethernetDriverGetIp(struct IpAddress* ip);
```

Caller's code

```
void ethShow()
{
  struct EthernetDriverStat eth_stat = ethernetDriverGetStatistics();
  printf("%i packets received\n", eth_stat.received_packets);
  printf("%i packets sent\n", eth_stat.total_sent_packets);
  printf("%i packets successfully sent\n",eth_stat.successfully_sent_packets);
  printf("%i packets failed to send\n", eth_stat.failed_sent_packets);

  const struct EthernetDriverInfo* eth_info = ethernetDriverGetInfo();
  printf("Driver name: %s\n", eth_info->name);
  printf("Driver description: %s\n", eth_info->description);

  struct IpAddress ip;
  ethernetDriverGetIp(&ip);
  printf("IP address: %s\n", ip.address);
}
```

Next, you want to extend your diagnostic component to also print a dump of the last received packet. This is now a piece of information that is too large to put on the stack, and because Ethernet packets have variable size, you cannot know beforehand how large the buffer for the packet has to be. Therefore, Caller-Owned Buffer isn't an option for you.

You could, of course, simply have functions EthernetDriverGetPacketSize() and EthernetDriverGetPacket(buffer), but here again you'd have the problem that you'd have to call two functions. Between the two function calls the Ethernet driver could receive another packet, which would make your data inconsistent. Also, this solution is not very elegant because you'd have to call two different functions to achieve one purpose. Instead, it is much easier if the Callee Allocates.

Callee Allocates

Context

You have large data that you want to share between different components.

Problem

You want to provide complex or large data of unknown size to the caller, and that data is not immutable (it changes at runtime).

The data changes at runtime (maybe because you provide the callers with functions to write the data), so you cannot simply provide the caller with a pointer to static data (as is the case with an Immutable Instance). If you simply provide the callers with such a pointer, you'd run into the problem that the data one caller reads might be inconsistent (partially overwritten) because, in a multithreaded environment, another caller might simultaneously write that data.

Simply copying all the data into an Aggregate Instance and passing it via the Return Value to the caller is not an option. With the Return Value you can only pass data of known size, and because the data is large, it cannot be passed via the stack, which only has very limited memory.

When instead only returning a pointer to the Aggregate Instance, there would be no problem with stack memory limitations anymore, but you have to keep in mind that C does not do the work of performing a deep copy for you. C only returns the pointer. You have to make sure that the data (stored in an Aggregate Instance or in an array) being pointed to is still valid after the function call. For example, you cannot store the data in auto-variables within your function and provide a pointer to these variables because after the function call, the variables run out of scope and are being cleaned up.

Now the problem arises of where the data should be stored. It has to be clarified whether the caller or the callee should provide the required memory and which one is then responsible for managing and cleaning up the memory.

The amount of data you want to provide is not fixed at compile time. For example, you want to return a string of previously unknown size. That makes using a Caller-Owned Buffer impractical because the caller does not know the size of the buffer beforehand. The caller could beforehand ask for the required buffer size (for example, with a getRequiredBufferSize() function), but that is also impractical because in order to retrieve one piece of data, the caller would have to make multiple function calls. Also, the data you want to provide could potentially change between those function calls, and then the caller would again provide a buffer of the wrong size.

Solution

Allocate a buffer with the required size inside the function that provides the large, complex data. Copy the required data into the buffer and return a pointer to that buffer.

Provide the pointer to the buffer and its size to the caller as Out-Parameters. After the function call, the caller can operate on the buffer, knows its size, and has the sole ownership of the buffer. The caller determines its lifetime and thus is responsible for cleaning it up as shown in Figure 4-7 and the following code.

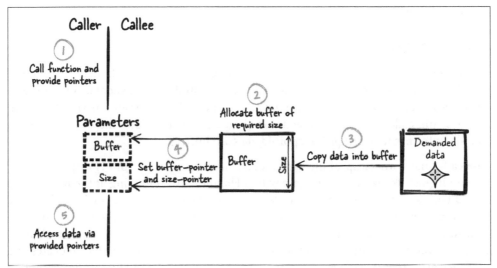

Figure 4-7. Callee Allocates

Caller's code

```
char* buffer;
int size;
getData(&buffer, &size);
/* use buffer */
free(buffer);
```

Callee's code

```
void getData(char** buffer, int* size)
{
  *size = data_size;
  *buffer = malloc(data_size);
  /* write data to buffer */ ❶
}
```

❶ When copying the data into that buffer, make sure that it does not change in the meantime. This can be achieved by mutual exclusion via Mutex or Semaphores.

Alternatively, the pointer to the buffer and the size can be put into an Aggregate Instance provided as a Return Value. To make it clearer for the caller that there is a pointer in the Aggregate Instance that has to be freed, the API can provide an additional function for cleaning it up. When also providing a function to clean up, the API already looks very similar to an API with a Handle, which would bring the additional benefit of flexibility while maintaining API compatibility.

No matter whether the called function provides the buffer via an Aggregate Instance or via Out-Parameters, it has to be made clear to the caller that the caller owns the buffer and is responsible for freeing it. That Dedicated Ownership has to be well documented in the API.

Consequences

The caller can retrieve the buffer of previously unknown size with a single function call. The function is reentrant, can safely be used in multithreaded environments, and provides the caller with consistent information about the buffer and its size. Knowing the size, the caller can safely operate on the data. For example, the caller can even handle unterminated strings transported via such buffers.

The caller has ownership of the buffer, determines its lifetime, and is responsible for freeing it (just like would be the case with a Handle). From looking at the interface, it has to be made very clear that the caller has to do this. One way of making this clear is to document it in the API. Another approach is to have an explicit cleanup function to make it more obvious that something has to be cleaned up. Such a cleanup function has the additional advantage that the same component that allocates the memory also frees it. This is important if the two involved components are compiled with different compilers or if they run on different platforms—in such cases the functions for allocating and freeing memory could differ between the components, which makes it mandatory that the same component that allocates also frees.

The caller cannot determine which kind of memory should be used for the buffer—that would have been possible with a Caller-Owned Buffer. Now the caller must use the kind of memory that is allocated inside the function call.

Allocating takes time, which means that compared to Caller-Owned Buffer, the function call becomes slower and less deterministic.

Known Uses

The following examples show applications of this pattern:

- The malloc function does exactly that. It allocates some memory and provides it to the caller.

- The `strdup` function takes a string as input, allocates the duplicated string, and returns it.
- The `getifaddrs` Linux function provides information about configured IP addresses. The data holding this information is stored in a buffer allocated by the function.
- The NetHack code uses this pattern to retrieve buffers.

Applied to Running Example

The following final code of your diagnostic component retrieves the packet data in a buffer that the Callee Allocates:

Ethernet driver API

```
struct Packet
{
  char data[1500]; /* maximum 1500 byte per packet */
  int size;        /* actual size of data in the packet */
};

/* Returns a pointer to a packet that has to be freed by the caller */
struct Packet* ethernetDriverGetPacket();
```

Caller's code

```
void ethShow()
{
  struct EthernetDriverStat eth_stat = ethernetDriverGetStatistics();
  printf("%i packets received\n", eth_stat.received_packets);
  printf("%i packets sent\n", eth_stat.total_sent_packets);
  printf("%i packets successfully sent\n",eth_stat.successfully_sent_packets);
  printf("%i packets failed to send\n", eth_stat.failed_sent_packets);

  const struct EthernetDriverInfo* eth_info = ethernetDriverGetInfo();
  printf("Driver name: %s\n", eth_info->name);
  printf("Driver description: %s\n", eth_info->description);

  struct IpAddress ip;
  ethernetDriverGetIp(&ip);
  printf("IP address: %s\n", ip.address);

  struct Packet* packet = ethernetDriverGetPacket();
  printf("Packet Dump:");
  fwrite(packet->data, 1, packet->size, stdout);
  free(packet);
}
```

With this final version of the diagnostic component, we can see all the presented ways of how to retrieve information from another function. Mixing all these ways in one piece of code might not be what you actually want to do because it gets a bit confusing to have one piece of data on the stack and another piece of data on the heap. As soon as you allocate buffers, you don't want to mix different approaches, so using Caller-Owned Buffer and Callee Allocates in a single function might not be what you want to do. Instead, pick the one approach that suits all your needs and stick to that within one function or component. This makes your code more uniform and easier to understand.

However, if you have to obtain just a single piece of data from another component and you have the choice to use the easier alternatives to retrieve data (the patterns covered earlier in this chapter), then always do that to keep your code simple. For example, if you have the option of putting buffers on the stack, then do that, because it saves you the effort to free the buffer.

Summary

This chapter showed different ways of how to return data from functions and how to handle buffers in C. The simplest way is to use Return Value to return a single piece of data, but if multiple pieces of related data have to be returned, then instead use Out-Parameters or, even better, Aggregate Instance. If the data to be returned does not change at runtime, Immutable Instance can be used. When returning data in a buffer, Caller-Owned Buffer can be used if the size of the buffer is known beforehand, and Callee Allocates can be used if the size is unknown beforehand.

With the patterns from this chapter, a C programmer has some basic tools and guidance on how to transport data between functions and how to cope with returning, allocating, and freeing buffers.

Outlook

The next chapter covers how larger programs are organized into software-modules and how lifetime and ownership of data is handled by these software-modules. These patterns give an overview of the building blocks that are used to construct larger pieces of C code.

CHAPTER 5

Data Lifetime and Ownership

If we have a look at procedural programming languages like C, there are no native object-oriented mechanisms. This makes life harder to some extent, because most design guidance is tailored for object-oriented software (like the Gang of Four design patterns).

This chapter discusses patterns for how to structure your C program with object-like elements. For these object-like elements, the patterns put special focus on who is responsible for creating and destroying them—in other words, they put special focus on lifetime and ownership. This topic is especially important for C because C has no automatic destructor and no garbage collection mechanism, and thus special attention has to be paid to cleanup of resources.

However, what is an "object-like element" and what is the meaning of it for C? The term *object* is well defined for object-oriented programming languages, but for non-object-oriented programming languages it is not clear what the term object means. For C, a simple definition for object is the following:

> "An object is a named region of storage."
>
> —Kernighan and Ritchie

Usually such an object describes a related set of data that has an identity and properties and that is used to store representations of things found in the real world. In object-oriented programming, an object additionally has the capability of polymorphism and inheritance. The object-like elements described throughout this book do not address polymorphism or inheritance, and therefore we'll not use the term object anymore. Instead, we'll consider such an object-like element simply as an instance of a data structure and will furthermore call it *instance*.

Such instances do not stand by themselves, but instead they usually come with related pieces of code that make it possible to operate on the instances. This code is usually put together into a set of header files for its interface and a set of implementation files for its implementation. Throughout this chapter, the sum of all this related code that, similar to object-oriented classes, often defines the operations that can be performed on an instance, will be called *software-module*.

When programming C, the described instances of data are usually implemented as abstract data types (for example, by having an instance of a `struct` with functions accessing the `struct` members). An example of such an instance is the C stdlib `FILE` `struct` that stores information like the file pointer or the position in the file. The corresponding software-module is the *stdio.h* API and its implementation of functions like `fopen` and `fclose`, which provide access to the `FILE` instances.

Figure 5-1 shows an overview of the patterns discussed in this chapter and their relationships, and Table 5-1 provides a summary of the patterns.

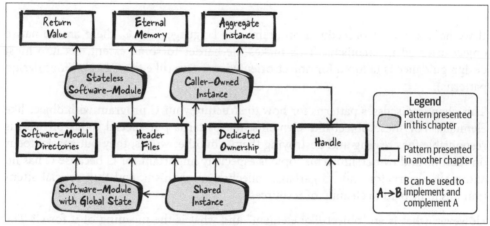

Figure 5-1. Overview of patterns for lifetime and ownership

Table 5-1. Patterns for lifetime and ownership

Pattern name	Summary
Stateless Software-Module	You want to provide logically related functionality to your caller and make that functionality as easy as possible for the caller to use. Therefore, keep your functions simple and don't build up state information in your implementation. Put all related functions into one header file and provide the caller this interface to your software-module.
Software-Module with Global State	You want to structure your logically related code that requires common state information and make that functionality as easy as possible for the caller to use. Therefore, have one global instance to let your related functions share common resources. Put all functions that operate on the instance into one header file and provide the caller this interface to your software-module.

Pattern name	Summary
Caller-Owned Instance	You want to provide multiple callers or threads access to functionality with functions that depend on one another, and the interaction of the caller with your functions builds up state information. Therefore, require the caller to pass an instance, which is used to store resource and state information, along to your functions. Provide explicit functions to create and destroy these instances, so that the caller can determine their lifetime.
Shared Instance	You want to provide multiple callers or threads access to functionality with functions that depend on one another, and the interaction of the caller with your functions builds up state information, which your callers want to share. Therefore, require the caller to pass an instance, which is used to store resource and state information, along to your functions. Use the same instance for multiple callers and keep the ownership of that instance in your software-module.

As a running example, in this chapter you want to implement a device driver for your Ethernet network interface card. The Ethernet network interface card is installed on the operating system your software runs on, so you can use the POSIX socket functions to send and receive network data. You want to build some abstraction for your user because you want to provide an easier way to send and receive data compared to socket functions, and because you want to add some additional features to your Ethernet driver. Thus you want to implement something that encapsulates all the socket details. To achieve this, start with a simple Stateless Software-Module.

Stateless Software-Module

Context

You want to provide functions with related functionality to a caller. The functions don't operate on common data shared between the functions, and they don't require preparation of resources like memory that has to be initialized prior to the function call.

Problem

You want to provide logically related functionality to your caller and make that functionality as easy as possible for the caller to use.

You want to make it simple for the caller to access your functionality. The caller should not have to deal with initialization and cleanup aspects of the provided functions, and the caller should not be confronted with implementation details.

You don't necessarily need the functions to be very flexible regarding future changes while maintaining backwards compatibility—instead the functions should provide an easy-to-use abstraction for accessing the implemented functionality.

You have many options for organizing the header and implementation files, and going through and evaluating each of these options becomes a lot of effort if you have to do it for each and every functionality that you implement.

Solution

Keep your functions simple and don't build up state information in your implementation. Put all related functions into one header file and provide the caller this interface to your software-module.

No communication or sharing of internal or external state information takes place between the functions, and state information is not stored between function calls. This means the functions calculate a result or perform an action that does not depend on other function calls in the API (the header file) or previous function calls. The only communication that takes place is between the caller and the called function (for example, in the form of Return Values).

If a function requires any resources, such as heap memory, then the resources have to be handled transparently for the caller. They have to be acquired, implicitly initialized before they are used, and released within the function call. This makes it possible to call the functions completely independent from one another.

Still, the functions are related and because of this they are put together into one API. Being related means that the functions are usually applied together by a caller (interface segregation principle) and that if they change, they change for the same reason (common closure principle). These principles are described in the book *Clean Architecture* by Robert C. Martin (Prentice Hall, 2018).

Put the declarations of the related functions into one Header File, and put the implementations of the functions into one or more implementation files, but into the same Software-Module Directory. The functions are related because they logically belong together, but they do not share a common state or influence one another's state, so there is no need to share information between the functions via global variables or to encapsulate this information by passing instances between the functions. That's why each single function implementation could be put into a separate implementation file.

The following code shows an example for a simple Stateless Software-Module:

Caller's code

```
int result = sum(10, 20);
```

API (header file)

```
/* Returns the sum of the two parameters */
int sum(int summand1, int summand2);
```

Implementation

```
int sum(int summand1, int summand2)
{
  /* calculate result only depending on parameters and
     not requiring any state information */
  return summand1 + summand2;
}
```

The caller calls sum and retrieves a copy of the function result. If you call the function twice with the same input parameters, the function would deliver the exact same result because no state information is maintained in the Stateless Software-Module. As in this special case, no other function that holds state information is called either.

Figure 5-2 shows an overview of the Stateless Software-Module.

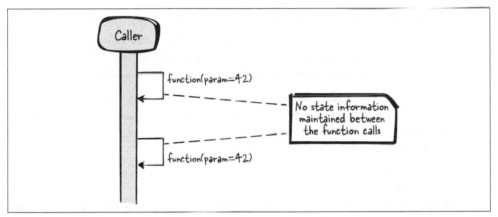

Figure 5-2. Stateless Software-Module

Consequences

You have a very simple interface, and the caller does not have to cope with initializing or cleaning up anything for your software-module. The caller can simply call one of the functions independently of previous function calls and other parts of the program, for example, other threads that concurrently access the software-module. Having no state information makes it much easier to understand what a function does.

The caller does not have to cope with questions about ownership because there is nothing to own—the functions have no state. The resources required by the function are allocated and cleaned up within the function call and are thus transparent to the caller.

But not all functionality can be provided with such a simple interface. If the functions within an API share state information or data (for example, one has to allocate resources required by another), then a different approach, like a Software-Module with Global State or a Caller-Owned Instance, has to be taken in order to share this information.

Known Uses

These types of related functions gathered into one API are found each time that the function within the API does not require shared information or state information. The following examples show applications of this pattern:

- The `sin` and `cos` functions from *math.h* are provided in the same header file and calculate their results solely based on the function input. They do not maintain state information, and each call with the same input produces the same output.

- The *string.h* functions `strcpy` or `strcat` do not depend on each other. They don't share information, but they belong together and are thus part of a single API.

- The Windows header file *VersionHelpers.h* provides information about which Microsoft Windows version is currently running. Functions like `IsWindows 7OrGreater` or `IsWindowsServer` provide related information, but the functions still don't share information and are independent from one another.

- The Linux header file *parser.h* comes with functions like `match_int` or `match_hex`. These functions try to parse an integer or a hexadecimal value from a substring. The functions are independent from one another, but they still belong together in the same API.

- The source code of the NetHack game also has many applications of this pattern. For example, the *vision.h* header file includes functions to calculate if the player is able to see specific items on the game map. The functions `couldsee(x,y)` and `cansee(x,y)` calculate if the player has a clear line of sight to the item and if the player also faces that item. Both functions are independent from each other and don't share state information.

- The pattern Header Files present a variant of this pattern with more focus on API flexibility.

- The pattern called Per-Request Instance from the book *Remoting Patterns* by Markus Voelter et al. (Wiley, 2007) explains that a server in a distributed object middleware should activate a new servant for each invocation, and that it should, after the servant handles the request, return the result and deactivate the servant. Such a call to a server maintains no state information and is similar to calls in Stateless Software-Modules, but with the difference that Stateless Software-Modules don't deal with remote entities.

Applied to Running Example

Your first device driver has the following code:

API (header file)

```
void sendByte(char data, char* destination_ip);
char receiveByte();
```

Implementation

```
void sendByte(char data, char* destination_ip)
{
  /* open socket to destination_ip, send data via this socket and close
     the socket */
}

char receiveByte()
{
  /* open socket for receiving data, wait some time and return
     the received data */
}
```

The user of your Ethernet driver does not have to cope with implementation details like how to access sockets and can simply use the provided API. Both of the functions in this API can be called at any time independently from each other and the caller can obtain data provided by the functions without having to cope with ownership and freeing resources. Using this API is simple but also very limited.

Next, you want to provide additional functionality for your driver. You want to make it possible for the user to see whether the Ethernet communication works, and thus you want to provide statistics showing the number of sent or received bytes. With a simple Stateless Software-Module, you cannot achieve this, because you have no retained memory for storing state information from one function call to another.

To achieve this, you need a Software-Module with Global State.

Software-Module with Global State

Context

You want to provide functions with related functionality to a caller. The functions operate on common data shared between them, and they might require preparation of resources like memory that has to be initialized prior to using your functionality, but the functions do not require any caller-dependent state information.

Problem

You want to structure your logically related code that requires common state information and make that functionality as easy as possible to use for the caller.

You want to make it simple for the caller to access your functionality. The caller should not have to deal with initialization and cleanup aspects of the functions, and the caller should not be confronted with implementation details. The caller should not necessarily realize that the functions access common data.

You don't necessarily need the functions to be very flexible regarding future changes while maintaining backwards compatibility—instead the functions should provide an easy-to-use abstraction for accessing the implemented functionality.

Solution

Have one global instance to let your related function implementations share common resources. Put all functions that operate on this instance into one header file and provide the caller this interface to your software-module.

Put the function declaration in one Header File, and put all the implementations for your software-module into one implementation file in a Software-Module Directory. In this implementation file, have a global instance (a file-global static `struct` or several file-global static variables—see Eternal Memory) that holds the common shared resources that should be available for your function implementations. Your function implementations can then access these shared resources similar to how private variables work in object-oriented programming languages.

The initialization and lifetime of the resources are transparently managed in the software-module and are independent from the lifetime of its callers. If the resources have to be initialized, then you can initialize them at startup time, or you can use lazy acquisition to initialize the resources right before they are needed.

The caller does not realize from the function call syntax that the functions operate on common resources, so you should document this for the caller. Within your software-module, the access to these file-global resources might have to be protected by synchronization primitives such as a Mutex to make it possible to have multiple callers from different threads. Make this synchronization within your function implementation, so that the caller does not have to deal with synchronization aspects.

The following code shows an example of a simple Software-Module with Global State:

Caller's code

```
int result;
result = addNext(10);
result = addNext(20);
```

API (header file)

```
/* Adds the parameter 'value' to the values accumulated
   with previous calls of this function. */
int addNext(int value);
```

Implementation

```
static int sum = 0;

int addNext(int value)
{
  /* calculation of the result depending on the parameter
     and on state information from previous function calls */
  sum = sum + value;
  return sum;
}
```

The caller calls addNext and retrieves a copy of the result. When calling the function twice with same the input parameters, the function might deliver different results because the function maintains state information.

Figure 5-3 shows an overview of the Software-Module with Global State.

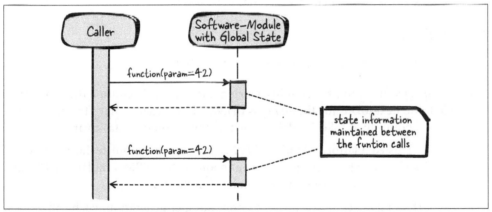

Figure 5-3. Software-Module with Global State

Consequences

Now your functions can share information or resources, even though the caller is not required to pass parameters containing this shared information, and the caller is not responsible for allocating and cleaning up resources. To achieve this sharing of information in your software-module, you implemented the C version of a Singleton. Beware of the Singleton—many have commented on the disadvantages of this pattern, and often it is instead called an antipattern.

Still, in C such Software-Modules with Global State are widespread, because it is quite easy to write the keyword static before a variable, and as soon as you do that, you have your Singleton. In some cases that is OK. If your implementation files are short, having file-global variables is quite similar to having private variables in object-oriented programming. If your functions do not require state information or do not operate in multithreaded environments, then you might be just fine. However if multithreading and state information become an issue and your implementation file becomes longer and longer, then you are in trouble and the Software-Module with Global State is not a good solution anymore.

If your Software-Module with Global State requires initialization, then you either have to initialize it during an initialization phase like at system startup, or you have to use lazy acquisition to initialize short before the first use of resources. However, this has the drawback that the duration for your function calls varies, because additional initialization code is implicitly called at the very first call. In any case, the resource acquisition is performed transparently to the caller. The resources are owned by your software-module, and thus the caller is not burdened with ownership of resources and does not have to explicitly acquire or release the resources.

However, not all functionality can be provided with such a simple interface. If the functions within an API share caller-specific state information, then a different approach, like a Caller-Owned Instance, has to be taken.

Known Uses

The following examples show applications of this pattern:

- The *string.h* function strtok splits a string into tokens. Each time the function is called, the next token for the string is delivered. In order to have the state information about which token to deliver next, the function uses static variables.

- With a Trusted Platform Module (TPM) one can accumulate hash values of loaded software. The corresponding function in the TPM-Emulator v0.7 code uses static variables to store this accumulated hash value.

- The math library uses a state for its random number generation. Each call of rand calculates a new pseudorandom number based on the number calculated with the previous rand call. srand has to be called first in order to set the seed (the initial static information) for the pseudorandom number generator called with rand.

- An Immutable Instance can be seen as part of a Software-Module with Global State with the special case that the instance is not modified at runtime.

- The source code of the NetHack game stores information about items (swords, shields) in a static list defined at compile time and provides functions to access this shared information.

- The pattern called Static Instance from the book *Remoting Patterns* by Markus Voelter et al. (Wiley, 2007) suggests providing remote objects with lifetime decoupled from the lifetime of the caller. The remote objects can, for example, be initialized at startup time and then be provided to a caller when requested. Software-Module with Global State presents the same idea of having static data, but it is not meant to have multiple instances for different callers.

Applied to Running Example

Now you have the following code for your Ethernet driver:

API (header file)

```
void sendByte(char data, char* destination_ip);
char receiveByte();
int getNumberOfSentBytes();
int getNumberOfReceivedBytes();
```

Implementation

```
static int number_of_sent_bytes = 0;
static int number_of_received_bytes = 0;

void sendByte(char data, char* destination_ip)
{
  number_of_sent_bytes++;
  /* socket stuff */
}

char receiveByte()
{
  number_of_received_bytes++;
  /* socket stuff */
}

int getNumberOfSentBytes()
{
  return number_of_sent_bytes;
}

int getNumberOfReceivedBytes()
{
  return number_of_received_bytes;
}
```

The API looks very similar to an API of a Stateless Software-Module, but behind this API now lies functionality to retain information between the function calls, which is needed for the counters for sent and received bytes. As long as there is only one user (one thread) who uses this API, everything is just fine. However, if there are multiple threads, then with static variables you always run into the problem that race conditions occur if you don't implement mutual exclusion for the access to the static variables.

All right—now you want the Ethernet driver to be more efficient, and you want to send more data. You could simply call your sendByte function frequently to do this, but in your Ethernet driver implementation that means that for each sendByte call, you establish a socket connection, send the data, and close the socket connection again. Establishing and closing the socket connection takes most of the communication time.

This is quite inefficient and you'd prefer to open your socket connection once, then send all the data by calling your sendByte function several times, and then close the socket connection. But now your sendByte function requires a preparation and a teardown phase. This state cannot be stored in a Software-Module with Global State because as soon as you have more than one caller (that is, more than one thread), you'd run into the problem or multiple callers wanting to simultaneously send data— maybe even to different destinations.

To achieve that, provide each of these callers with a Caller-Owned Instance.

Caller-Owned Instance

Context

You want to provide functions with related functionality to a caller. The functions operate on common data shared between them, they might require preparation of resources like memory that has to be initialized prior to using your functionality, and they share caller-specific state information among one another.

Problem

You want to provide multiple callers or threads access to functionality with functions that depend on one another, and the interaction of the caller with your functions builds up state information.

Maybe one function has to be called before another because it influences a state stored in your software-module that is then needed by the other function. This can be achieved with a Software-Module with Global State, but it only works as long as there is only one caller. In a multithreaded environment with multiple callers, you cannot have one central software-module holding all caller-dependent state information.

Still, you want to hide implementation details from the caller, and you want to make it as simple as possible for the caller to access your functionality. It has to be clearly defined if the caller is responsible for allocating and cleaning up resources.

Solution

Require the caller to pass an instance, which is used to store resource and state information, along to your functions. Provide explicit functions to create and destroy these instances, so that the caller can determine their lifetime.

To implement such an instance that can be accessed from multiple functions, pass a `struct` pointer along with all functions that require sharing resources or state information. The functions can now use the `struct` members, which are similar to private variables in object-oriented languages, to store and read resource and state information.

The `struct` can be declared in the API to let the caller conveniently access its members directly. Alternatively, the `struct` can be declared in the implementation, and only a pointer to the `struct` can be declared in the API (as suggested by Handle). The caller does not know the `struct` members (they are like private variables) and can only operate with functions on the `struct`.

Because the instance has to be manipulated by multiple functions and you do not know when the caller finished calling functions, the lifetime of the instance has to be determined by the caller. Therefore, Dedicate Ownership to the caller and provide explicit functions for creating and destroying the instance. The caller has an aggregate relationship to the instance.

Aggregation Versus Association

If an instance is semantically related to another instance, then those instances are associated. A stronger type of association is an aggregation, in which one instance has ownership of the other.

The following code shows an example of a simple Caller-Owned Instance:

Caller's code

```
struct INSTANCE* inst;
inst = createInstance();
operateOnInstance(inst);
/* access inst->x or inst->y */
destroyInstance(inst);
```

API (header file)

```
struct INSTANCE
{
  int x;
  int y;
};

/* Creates an instance which is required for working
   with the function 'operateOnInstance' */
struct INSTANCE* createInstance();

/* Operates on the data stored in the instance */
void operateOnInstance(struct INSTANCE* inst);

/* Cleans up an instance created with 'createInstance' */
void destroyInstance(struct INSTANCE* inst);
```

Implementation

```
struct INSTANCE* createInstance()
{
  struct INSTANCE* inst;
  inst = malloc(sizeof(struct INSTANCE));
  return inst;
}

void operateOnInstance(struct INSTANCE* inst)
{
  /* work with inst->x and inst->y */
}

void destroyInstance(struct INSTANCE* inst)
{
  free(inst);
}
```

The function `operateOnInstance` works on resources created with the previous function call `createInstance`. The resource or state information between the two function calls is transported by the caller, who has to provide the INSTANCE for each function call and who also has to clean up all the resources by calling `destroy Instance`.

Figure 5-4 shows an overview of the Caller-Owned Instance.

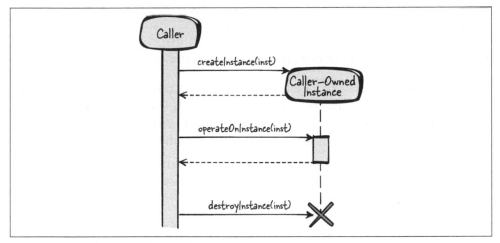

Figure 5-4. Caller-Owned Instance

Consequences

The functions in your API are more powerful now because they can share state information and operate on shared data while still being available for multiple callers (that is, multiple threads). Each created Caller-Owned Instance has its own private variables, and even if more than one such Caller-Owned Instance is created (for example, by multiple callers in a multithreaded environment), it is not a problem.

However, to achieve this, your API becomes more complicated. You have to make explicit `create()` and `destroy()` calls for managing the instance's lifetime, because C does not support constructors and destructors. This makes handling with instances much more difficult because the caller obtains ownership and is responsible for cleaning up the instance. As this has to be done manually with the `destroy()` call, and not via an automatic destructor like in object-oriented programing languages, this is a common pitfall for memory leaks. This issue is addressed by Object-Based Error Handling, which suggests that the caller should also have a dedicated cleanup function to make this task more explicit.

Also, compared to a Stateless Software-Module, calling each of the functions becomes a bit more complicated. Each function takes an additional parameter referencing the instance, and the functions cannot be called in arbitrary order—the caller has to know which one has to be called first. This is made explicit through the function signatures.

Known Uses

The following examples show applications of this pattern:

- An example of the use of a Caller-Owned Instance is the doubly linked list provided with the glibc library. The caller creates a list with g_list_alloc and can then insert items into this list with g_list_insert. When finished working with the list, the caller is responsible for cleaning it up with g_list_free.

- This pattern is described by Robert Strandh in the article "Modular C" (*https://oreil.ly/UVodl*). It describes how to write modular C programs. The article states the importance of identifying abstract data types—which can be manipulated or accessed with functions—in the application.

- The Windows API to create menus in the menu bar has a function to create a menu instance (CreateMenu), functions to operate on menus (like InsertMenu Item), and a function to destroy the menu instance (DestroyMenu). All these functions have one parameter to pass the Handle to the menu instance.

- Apache's software-module to handle HTTP requests provides functions to create all required request information (ap_sub_req_lookup_uri), to process it (ap_run_sub_req), and to destroy it (ap_destroy_sub_req). These functions take a struct pointer to the request instance in order to share request information.

- The source code of the NetHack game uses a struct instance to represent monsters and provides functions to create and destroy a monster. The NetHack code also provides functions to obtian information from monsters (is_starting_pet, is_vampshifter).

- The pattern called Client-Dependent Instance, from the book *Remoting Patterns* by Markus Voelter et al. (Wiley, 2007), suggests for distributed object middlewares, providing remote objects whose lifetime is controlled by the clients. The server creates new instances for clients and the client can then work with these instances, pass them along, or destroy them.

Applied to Running Example

Now you have the following code for your Ethernet driver:

API (header file)

```
struct Sender
{
  char destination_ip[16];
  int socket;
};

struct Sender* createSender(char* destination_ip);
```

```
    void sendByte(struct Sender* s, char data);
    void destroySender(struct Sender* s);
```

Implementation

```
    struct Sender* createSender(char* destination_ip)
    {
      struct Sender* s = malloc(sizeof(struct Sender));
      /* create socket to destination_ip and store it in Sender s*/
      return s;
    }

    void sendByte(struct Sender* s, char data)
    {
      number_of_sent_bytes++;
      /* send data via socket stored in Sender s */
    }

    void destroySender(struct Sender* s)
    {
      /* close socket stored in Sender s */
      free(s);
    }
```

A caller can first create a sender, then send all the data, and then destroy the sender. Thus, the caller can make sure that the socket connection does not have to be established again for each sendByte() call. The caller has ownership of the created sender, has full control over how long the sender lives, and is responsible for cleaning it up:

Caller's code

```
    struct Sender* s = createSender("192.168.0.1");
    char* dataToSend = "Hello World!";
    char* pointer = dataToSend;
    while(*pointer != '\0')
    {
      sendByte(s, *pointer);
      pointer++;
    }
    destroySender(s);
```

Next, let's assume that you are not the only user of this API. There might be multiple threads using your API. As long as one thread creates a sender for sending to IP address X and another thread creates a sender for sending to Y, we are just fine, and the Ethernet driver creates independent sockets for both threads.

However, let's say the two threads want to send data to the same recipient. Now the Ethernet driver is in trouble because on one specific port, it can only open one socket per destination IP. A solution to this problem would be to not allow two different threads to send to the same destination—the second thread creating the sender could simply receive an error. But it is also possible to allow both threads to send data using the same sender.

To achieve this, simply construct a Shared Instance.

Shared Instance

Context

You want to provide functions with related functionality to a caller. The functions operate on shared common data, and they might require preparation of resources like memory that has to be initialized prior to using your functionality. There are multiple contexts in which the functionality can be called, and these contexts are shared between the callers.

Problem

You want to provide multiple callers or threads access to functionality with functions that depend on one another, and the interaction of the caller with your functions builds up state information, which your callers want to share.

Storing the state information in a Software-Module with Global State is not an option because there are multiple callers who want to build up different state information. Storing the state information per caller in a Caller-Owned Instance is not an option because either some of your callers want to access and operate on the same instance, or because you don't want to create new instances for every caller in order to keep resource costs low.

Still, you want to hide implementation details from the caller, and you want to make it as simple as possible for the caller to access your functionality. It has to be clearly defined if the caller is responsible for allocating and cleaning up resources.

Solution

Require the caller to pass an instance, which is used to store resource and state information, along to your functions. Use the same instance for multiple callers and keep the ownership of that instance in your software-module.

Just like with the Caller-Owned Instance, provide a `struct` pointer or a Handle that the caller then passes along the function calls. When creating the instance, the caller now also has to provide an identifier (for example, a unique name) to specify the kind of instance to create. With this identifier you can know if such an instance already exists. If it exists, you don't create a new instance, but instead return the `struct` pointer or Handle to the instance that you already created and returned to other callers.

To know if an instance already exists, you have to hold a list of already created instances in your software-module. This can be done by implementing a Software-Module with Global State to hold the list. In addition to whether an instance was already created or not, you can store the information of who currently accesses which instances or at least how many callers currently access an instance. This additional information is required because when everybody is finished accessing an instance, it is your duty to clean it up because you are the one who has Dedicated Ownership of it.

You also have to check whether your functions can be called simultaneously by different callers on the same instance. In some easier cases, there might be no data whose access has to be mutually excluded by different callers because it is only read. In such cases an Immutable Instance, which does not allow the caller to change the instance, could be implemented. But in other cases, you have to implement mutual exclusion in your functions for resources shared through the instance.

The following code shows an example of a simple Shared Instance:

Caller1's code

```
struct INSTANCE* inst = openInstance(INSTANCE_TYPE_B);
/* operate on the same instance as caller2 */
operateOnInstance(inst);
closeInstance(inst);
```

Caller2's code

```
struct INSTANCE* inst = openInstance(INSTANCE_TYPE_B);
/* operate on the same instance as caller1 */
operateOnInstance(inst);
closeInstance(inst);
```

API (header file)

```
struct INSTANCE
{
  int x;
  int y;
};

/* to be used as IDs for the function openInstance */
#define INSTANCE_TYPE_A 1
#define INSTANCE_TYPE_B 2
#define INSTANCE_TYPE_C 3

/* Retrieve an instance identified by the parameter 'id'. That instance is
   created if no instance of that 'id' was yet retrieved from any
   other caller. */
struct INSTANCE* openInstance(int id);
```

```
/* Operates on the data stored in the instance. */
void operateOnInstance(struct INSTANCE* inst);

/* Releases an instance which was retrieved with 'openInstance'.
   If all callers release an instance, it gets destroyed. */
void closeInstance(struct INSTANCE* inst);
```

Implementation

```
#define MAX_INSTANCES 4

struct INSTANCELIST
{
  struct INSTANCE* inst;
  int count;
};

static struct INSTANCELIST list[MAX_INSTANCES];

struct INSTANCE* openInstance(int id)
{
  if(list[id].count == 0)
  {
    list[id].inst = malloc(sizeof(struct INSTANCE));
  }
  list[id].count++;
  return list[id].inst;
}

void operateOnInstance(struct INSTANCE* inst)
{
  /* work with inst->x and inst->y */
}

static int getInstanceId(struct INSTANCE* inst)
{
  int i;
  for(i=0; i<MAX_INSTANCES; i++)
  {
    if(inst == list[i].inst)
    {
      break;
    }
  }
  return i;
}

void closeInstance(struct INSTANCE* inst)
{
  int id = getInstanceId(inst);
  list[id].count--;
  if(list[id].count == 0)
```

```
    {
        free(inst);
    }
}
```

The caller retrieves an INSTANCE by calling openInstance. The INSTANCE might be created by this function call, or it might have already been created by a previous function call and might also be used by another caller. The caller can then pass the INSTANCE along to the operateOnInstance function calls, to provide this function with the required resource or state information from the INSTANCE. When finished, the caller has to call closeInstance so that the resources can be cleaned up, if no other caller operates on the INSTANCE anymore.

Figure 5-5 shows an overview of the Shared Instance.

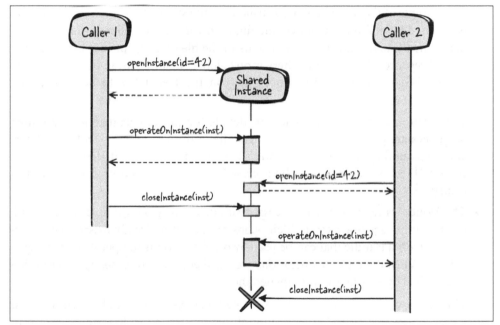

Figure 5-5. Shared Instance

Consequences

Multiple callers now have simultaneous access to a single instance. This quite often implies that you have to cope with mutual exclusion within your implementation in order not to burden the user with such issues. This implies that the duration for a function call varies because the caller never knows if another caller currently uses the same resources and blocks them.

Your software-module, not the caller, has ownership of the instance, and your software-module is responsible for cleaning up resources. The caller is still responsible for releasing the resources so that your software-module knows when to clean everything up—as with the Caller-Owned Instance, this is a pitfall for memory leaks.

Because the software-module has ownership of the instances, it can also clean up the instances without requiring the callers to initiate cleanup. For example, if the software-module receives a shutdown signal from the operating system, it can clean up all instances because it has ownership of them.

Known Uses

The following examples show applications of this pattern:

- An example of the use of a Shared Instance is the *stdio.h* file-functions. A file can be opened by multiple callers via the function `fopen`. The caller retrieves a Handle to the file and can read from or write to the file (`fread`, `fprintf`). The file is a shared resource. For example, there is one global cursor position in the file for all callers. When a caller finishes operating on the file, it has to be closed with `fclose`.

- This pattern and its implementation details for object-oriented programming languages are presented as Counting Handle in the article "C++ Patterns: Reference Accounting" (*https://oreil.ly/inThj*) by Kevlin Henney. It describes how a shared object on the heap can be accessed and how its lifetime can be handled transparently.

- The Windows registry can be accessed simultaneously by multiple threads with the function `RegCreateKey` (which opens the key, if it already exists). The function delivers a Handle that can be used by other functions to operate on the registry key. When the registry operations are finished, the `RegCloseKey` function has to be called by everybody who opened the key.

- The Windows functionality to access Mutex (`CreateMutex`) can be used to access a shared resource (the Mutex) from multiple threads. With the Mutex, interprocess synchronization can be implemented. When finished working with the Mutex, each caller has to close it by using the function `CloseHandle`.

- The B&R Automation Runtime operating system allows multiple callers to access device drivers simultaneously. A caller uses the function `DmDeviceOpen` to select one of the available devices. The device driver framework checks if the selected driver is available and then provides a Handle to the caller. If multiple callers operate on the same driver, they share the Handle. The callers can then simultaneously interact with the driver (send or read data, interact via IO-controls, etc.), and after this interaction they tell the device driver framework that they are finished by calling `DmDeviceClose`.

Applied to Running Example

The driver now additionally implements the following functions:

API (header file)

```
struct Sender* openSender(char* destination_ip);
void sendByte(struct Sender* s, char data);
void closeSender(struct Sender* s);
```

Implementation

```
struct Sender* openSender(char* destination_ip)
{
  struct Sender* s;
  if(isInSenderList(destination_ip))
  {
    s = getSenderFromList(destination_ip);
  }
  else
  {
    s = createSender(destination_ip);
  }
  increaseNumberOfCallers(s);
  return s;
}

void sendByte(struct Sender* s, char data)
{
  number_of_sent_bytes++;
  /* send data via socket stored in Sender s */
}

void closeSender(struct Sender* s)
{
  decreaseNumberOfCallers(s);
  if(numberOfCallers(s) == 0)
  {
    /* close socket stored in Sender s */
    free(s);
  }
}
```

The API of the running example did not change a lot—instead of having create/destroy functions, your driver now provides open/close functions. By calling such a function, the caller retrieves the Handle for the sender and indicates to the driver that this caller is now operating a sender, but the driver does not necessarily create this sender at that point in time. That might have already been done by an earlier call to the driver (maybe performed by a different thread). Also, a close call might not actually destroy the sender. The ownership of this sender remains in the driver implementation, which can decide when to destroy the senders (for example, when all callers close the sender, or if some termination signal is received).

The fact that you now have a Shared Instance instead of a Caller-Owned Instance is mostly transparent to the caller. But the driver implementation changed—it has to remember if a specific sender was already created and provide this shared instance instead of creating a new one. When opening a sender, the caller does not know whether this sender will be newly created or whether an existing sender is retrieved. Depending on this, the duration of the function call might vary.

The presented running driver example showed different kinds of ownership and data lifetime in a single example. We saw how a simple Ethernet driver evolved by adding functionality. First, a Stateless Software-Module was sufficient because the driver did not require any state information. Next, such state information was required, and it was realized by having a Software-Module with Global State in the driver. Then, the need for more performant send functions and for multiple callers for these send functions came up and was first implemented by the Caller-Owned Instance and in a next step by the Shared Instance.

Summary

The patterns in this chapter showed different ways of structuring your C programs and how long different instances in your program live. Table 5-2 gives an overview of the patterns and compares their consequences.

Table 5-2. Comparing patterns on lifetime and ownership

	Stateless Software-Module	Software-Module with Global State	Caller-Owned Instance	Shared Instance
Resource sharing between functions	Not possible	Single set of resources	Set of resources per instance (= per caller)	Set of resources per instance (shared by multiple callers)
Resource ownership	Nothing to own	The software-module owns the static data	The caller owns the instance	The software-module owns instances and provides references
Resource lifetime	No resources live longer than a function call	Static data lives forever in the software-module	Instances live until callers destroy them	Instances live until the software-module destroys them
Resource initialization	Nothing to initialize	At compile time or at startup	By the caller when creating an instance	By the software-module when the first caller opens an instance

With these patterns, a C programmer has some basic guidance about the design options for organizing programs into software-modules and the design options regarding ownership and lifetime when constructing instances.

Further Reading

The patterns in this chapter cover how to provide access to instances and who has ownership of these instances. A very similar topic is covered by a subset of the patterns from the book *Remoting Patterns* by Markus Voelter et al. (Wiley, 2007). The book presents patterns for building distributed object middleware, and three of these patterns focus on lifetime and ownership of objects created by remote servers. Compared to that, the patterns presented in this chapter focus on a different context. They are not patterns for remote systems, but for local procedural programs. They focus on C programming, but can also be used for other procedural programming languages. Still, some of the underlying ideas in the patterns are very similar to those in *Remoting Patterns*.

Outlook

The next chapter presents different kinds of interfaces for software-modules with a special focus on how to make the interface flexible. The patterns elaboarate on the trade-off between simplicity and flexibility.

CHAPTER 6

Flexible APIs

Designing interfaces with the right level of flexibility and the right level of abstraction is one of the most important things when writing software, because interfaces represent a contract that often cannot be changed once the system is in operation. Because of this it is important to put stable declarations into the interface and to abstract implementation details, which should have the flexibility to change at a later point in time.

For object-oriented programming languages, you'll find much guidance on how to design interfaces (for example, in the form of design patterns), but there is not much guidance of this kind for procedural programming languages like C. There are the SOLID design principles (see nearby sidebar) that tell you in general how to design good software. However, for the C programming language, detailed design guidance on how to design interfaces is hard to find, and that's where the patterns from this chapter come in.

SOLID

The SOLID principles tell us how to implement good, flexible, and maintainable software.

Single-responsibility principle
> The code has one responsibility and one reason to be changed in the future.

Open-closed principle
> Code should be open for behavior changes without requiring changes to the existing code.

Liskow substitution principle
> Codes that implement the same interface should be interchangable for the caller.

Figure 6-1 shows the four patterns covered in this chapter, as well as related patterns, and Table 6-1 contains a short description of the four patterns. Keep in mind that not all of the patterns should always be applied in all possible contexts. Generally it is advisable to design a system to not be more complex than it has to be. This means that some of the presented patterns should only be applied if the gained flexibility is already required by your API or will likely be required in the future. If it is not likely to be required, then the pattern should perhaps not be applied to keep the API as simple as possible.

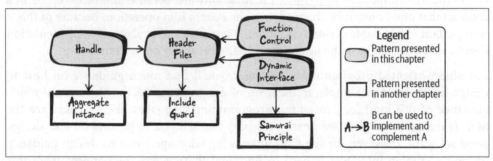

Figure 6-1. Overview of patterns for flexible APIs

Table 6-1. Patterns for flexible APIs

Pattern name	Summary
Header Files	You want a functionality that you implement to be accessible to code from other implementation files, but you want to hide your implementation details from the caller. Therefore, provide function declarations in your API for any functionality you want to provide to your user. Hide any internal functions, internal data, and your function definitions (the implementations) in your implementation file and don't provide this implementation file to the user.
Handle	You have to share state information or operate on shared resources in your function implementations, but you don't want your caller to see or even access all that state information and shared resources. Therefore, have a function to create the context on which the caller operates and return an abstract pointer to internal data for that context. Require the caller to pass that pointer to all your functions, which can then use the internal data to store state information and resources.

Pattern name	Summary
Dynamic Interface	It should be possible to call implementations with slightly deviating behaviors, but it should not be necessary to duplicate any code, not even the control logic implementation and interface declaration. Therefore, define a common interface for the deviating functionalities in your API and require the caller to provide a callback function for that functionality, which you then call in your function implementation.
Function Control	You want to call implementations with slightly deviating behaviors, but you don't want to duplicate any code, not even the control logic implementation or the interface declaration. Therefore, add a parameter to your function that passes meta-information about the function call and that specifies the actual functionality to be performed.

As a running example, in this chapter you want to implement a device driver for your Ethernet network interface card. The firmware of this card provides several registers with which you can send or receive data and with which you can configure the card. You want to build some abstraction of these hardware details, and you want to make sure that a user of your API is not affected if you change some parts of your implementation. To achieve this, you build an API consisting of Header Files.

Header Files

Context

You write a larger piece of software in C. You split that software up into several functions, and you implement these functions in several files because you want to make your program modular and easy to maintain.

Problem

You want a functionality that you implement to be accessible to code from other implementation files, but you want to hide your implementation details from the caller.

Unlike many object-oriented languages, C does not provide any built-in support for defining APIs, abstracting functionality, or enforcing that the caller can only access this abstraction. C only provides a mechanism to include files into other files.

The caller of your code could use that mechanism to simply include your implementation file. But then the caller could access all internal data in that file, such as variables or functions with file scope that you only intend to use internally. Once the caller uses this internal functionality, it might not be easy to change it later on, so the code becomes tightly coupled in places where you might not want that to happen. If the caller includes the implementation file, the names of the internal variables and functions might clash with names used by the caller.

Solution

Provide function declarations in your API for any functionality you want to provide to your user. Hide any internal functions, internal data, and your function definitions (the implementations) in your implementation file and don't provide this implementation file to the user.

In C, it is a common convention that anybody who uses functions of your software only uses functions defined in your header file (*.h* file) and does not use other functions in your implementation (your *.c* files). In some cases, this abstraction can be partially enforced (for example, you cannot use a `static` function from another file), but the C language does not support such enforcements to the full extent. Therefore, the convention of not accessing other implementation files is even more important than the enforcement mechanisms.

Within the header file, make sure to include all related artifacts needed by your functions in the header file. It should not be neccessary for your caller to include other header files in order to be able to use the functionality from your header file. If you have common declarations (like data types or `#defines`) that are needed in multiple header files, then put these declarations into a separate header file and include it in the other header files that need the declarations. To ensure that the header files are not included multiple times in a compilation unit, protect them with Include Guards.

Only put functions into the same header file if they are related. If the functions operate on the same Handle or perform an operation in the same domain (like math calculations), then that is an indicator to put them into the same header file. In general, if you can think of a relevant use case that requires all of the functions, then you should put them into the same header file.

Clearly document the behavior of your API in the header file. The user should not be required to have a look at the implementation in order to understand how the functions provided in the API work.

The following code shows an example of a Header File:

API (h-file)

```
/* Sorts the numbers of the 'array' in ascending order.
   'length' defines the number of elements in the 'array'. */
void sort(int* array, int length);
```

Implementation (c-file)

```
void sort(int* array, int length)
{
  /* here goes the implementation*/
}
```

Consequences

You have a very clear separation between the things relevant for your caller (the *.h file) and the implementation details that the caller does not have to care about (the *.c file). Thus, you abstracted some functionality for the caller.

Having many header files will influence your build times. On the one hand this enables you to split your implementations into separate files, and your toolchain will be able to have an incremental build that only rebuilds files that changed. On the other hand, a complete rebuild will have slightly increased build times compared to having all the code in one file, because all the files have to be opened and read for the build.

If you discover that your functions require more interaction between one another or that they have to be called in different contexts that require different internal state information, then you have to think about how to realize that with your API. A Handle can help in such cases.

The caller of your functions now relies on the abstraction and might rely on the fact that the behavior of these functions does not change. The API might have to be kept stable. To add new functionality, you can always add new functions to the API. But in some cases you might want to extend existing functions, and to be able to cope with such future changes, you have to consider how to make your functions flexible while keeping them stable. Handles, Dynamic Interfaces, or Function Controls can help in such cases.

Known Uses

The following examples show applications of this pattern:

- Pretty much every C program that is larger than a simple "Hello World" program contains header files.
- Using a header file in C is analogous to using interfaces in Java or abstract classes in C++.
- The Pimpl Idiom describes how to hide private implementation details and not put them into the header file. You can find a description of that idiom in the Portland Pattern Repository.

Applied to Running Example

Your first device driver API looks like the following:

```
void sendByte(char byte);
char receiveByte();
void setIpAddress(char* ip);
void setMacAddress(char* mac);
```

The user of your API does not have to cope with implementation details like how you access Ethernet registers, and you are free to change these details without affecting the user.

Now your requirements for your driver change. Your system has a second, identical Ethernet network interface card, and it should be possible to operate both of them. Here are two straightforward options to achieve this:

- You copy your code and have one piece of code for each network interface card. In the copied code, you only modify the address of the exact interface to be accessed. However, such code duplication is never a good idea and makes maintenance of your code much more difficult.

- You add a parameter to address the network interface card (for example, a device name string) to each function. But it's quite likely that more than just one parameter will have to be shared between the functions, and passing each of them to every function makes the usage of your API cumbersome.

A better idea to support multiple Ethernet network interface cards is to introduce Handles to your API.

Handle

Context

You want to provide a set of functions to your caller, and these functions operate on shared resources or they share state information.

Problem

You have to share state information or operate on shared resources in your function implementations, but you don't want your caller to see or even access all that state information and shared resources.

That state information and shared resources should remain invisible to your caller because later on you might want to change it or add to it without requiring any changes to your caller's code.

In object-oriented programming languages, such data on which functions can operate is realized by class member variables. These class member variables can be made private if the caller should not be able to access them. However, C does not natively support classes and private member variables.

Simply having a Software-Module with Global State holding static global variables in your implementation file for storing shared data between your functions is not an option for you, because it should be possible to call your functions in multiple contexts. The function calls for each of your callers should be able to build up their state information. And even though that information should remain invisible to your callers, you need a way to identify which information belongs to which specific caller and how to access that information in your function implementations.

Solution

Have a function to create the context on which the caller operates and return an abstract pointer to internal data for that context. Require the caller to pass that pointer to all your functions, which can then use the internal data to store state information and resources.

Your functions know how to interpret this abstract pointer, which is an opaque data type also called Handle. However, the data structure that you point to should not be part of the API. The API only provides the functionality to relay hidden data to the functions.

The Handle can be implemented as a pointer to an Aggregate Instance like a `struct`. The `struct` should contain all required state information or other variables—it usually holds variables similar to those you would declare as member variables for objects in object-oriented programming. The `struct` should be hidden in your implementation. The API only contains the definition of a pointer to the `struct` as shown in the following code:

API

```
typedef struct SORT_STRUCT* SORT_HANDLE;

SORT_HANDLE prepareSort(int* array, int length);
void sort(SORT_HANDLE context);
```

Implementation

```
struct SORT_STRUCT
{
  int* array;
  int length;
  /* other parameters like sort order */
};

SORT_HANDLE prepareSort(int* array, int length)
{
  struct SORT_STRUCT* context = malloc(sizeof(struct SORT_STRUCT));
  context->array = array;
  context->length = length;

  /* fill context with required data or state information */
```

```
    return context;
}

void sort(SORT_HANDLE context)
{
    /* operate on context data */
}
```

Have one function in your API for creating a Handle. That function returns the Handle to the caller. The caller can then call other functions of your API that require the Handle. In most cases, you also need a function to delete the Handle by cleaning up all the allocated resources.

Consequences

You can now share state information and resources between your functions without requiring the caller to worry about it and without giving the caller the opportunity to make the code depend on these internals.

Multiple instances of data are supported. You can call the function that creates the Handle multiple times to obtain multiple contexts, and then you can work with these contexts independently from one another.

If your functions that operate on the Handle are changed at a later point in time and have to share different or additional data, the members of the struct can simply be changed without requiring any changes to the caller's code.

The declarations of your functions explicitly show that they are tightly coupled, because they all require the Handle. This makes it, on one hand, easy to see which functions should go into the same Header File, and on the other hand, makes it very easy for the caller to spot which functions should be applied together.

With the Handle, you now require the caller to provide one additional parameter to all function calls, and each additional parameter makes the code harder to read.

Known Uses

The following examples show applications of this pattern:

- The C standard library contains the definition of FILE in *stdio.h*. This FILE is defined in most implementations as a pointer to a struct, and the struct is not part of the header file. The FILE handle is created by the function fopen, and several other functions can then be called for an opened file (fwrite, fread, etc.).

- The struct AES_KEY in the OpenSSL code is used to exchange the context between several functions related to AES encryption (AES_set_decrypt_key, AES_ set_ encrypt_key). The struct and its members are not hidden in the implementation, but instead they are part of the header file because some parts of other OpenSSL code need to know the size of the struct.

- The code for the logging functionality of the Subversion project operates on a Handle. The struct logger_t is defined in the implementation file of the logging functionality, and a pointer to this struct is defined in the corresponding header file.

- This pattern is described in *C Interfaces and Implementations* by David R. Hanson (Addison-Wesley, 1996) as Opaque Pointer Type and in *Patterns in C* by Adam Tornhill (Leanpub, 2014) as "First Class Abstract Data Type Pattern."

Applied to Running Example

You can now support as many Ethernet interface cards as you want. Each created instance of your driver produces its own data-context that is then passed to the functions via the Handle. Now you have the following code for your device driver API:

```
/* the INTERNAL_DRIVER_STRUCT contains data shared by the functions (like
   how to select the interface card the driver is responsible for) */
typedef struct INTERNAL_DRIVER_STRUCT* DRIVER_HANDLE;

/* 'initArg' contains information for the implementation to identify
   the exact interface for the driver instance */
DRIVER_HANDLE driverCreate(void* initArg);
void driverDestroy(DRIVER_HANDLE h);
void sendByte(DRIVER_HANDLE h, char byte);
char receiveByte(DRIVER_HANDLE h);
void setIpAddress(DRIVER_HANDLE h, char* ip);
void setMacAddress(DRIVER_HANDLE h, char* mac);
```

Your requirements have changed again. Now you have to support multiple different Ethernet network interface cards, for example, from different vendors. The cards provide similar functionality, but they differ in the details of how the registers have to be accessed, and thus different implementations for the drivers are needed. Two straightforward options to support this would be as follows:

- You have two separate driver APIs. This approach has the drawback that it is cumbersome for the users to build mechanisms for selecting the driver at runtime. Also, having two separate APIs duplicates code because the two device drivers at minimum share a common control flow (for example, for creating or destroying the driver).

- You add functions like sendByteDriverA and sendByteDriverB to your API. However, you usually want your API to be rather minimal because having all driver functions in a single API can be confusing for the API user. Also, the user's code depends on all function signatures included via your API, and if code depends on something, that something should be rather minimal (as stated by the interface segregation principle).

A better idea to support different Ethernet network interface cards is to provide a Dynamic Interface.

Dynamic Interface

Context

You or your caller want to implement multiple functionalities that follow a similar control logic, but that deviate in their behavior.

Problem

It should be possible to call implementations with slightly deviating behaviors, but it should not be necessary to duplicate any code, not even the control logic implementation and interface declaration.

You want to be able to add additional implementation behaviors to the declared interface later on, without requiring callers who use the existing implementation behaviors to change anything in their code.

Maybe you do not only want to provide differing behaviors to your caller without duplicating your own code, but you also want to provide the callers a mechanism to bring in their own implementation behaviors.

Solution

Define a common interface for the deviating functionalities in your API and require the caller to provide a callback function for that functionality, which you then call in your function implementation.

To implement such an interface in C, define function signatures in your API. The caller then implements functions according to these signatures and attaches them via function pointers. They can either be attached and stored permanently inside your software-module or they can be attached with each function call as shown in the following code:

API

```
/* The compare function should return true if x is smaller than y, else false */
typedef bool (*COMPARE_FP)(int x, int y);

void sort(COMPARE_FP compare, int* array, int length);
```

Implementation

```
void sort(COMPARE_FP compare, int* array, int length)
{
```

```
    int i, j;
    for(i=0; i<length; i++)
    {
      for(j=i; j<length; j++)
      {
        /* call provided user function */
        if(compare(array[i], array[j]))
        {
          swap(&array[i], &array[j]);
        }
      }
    }
  }
```

Caller

```
#define ARRAY_SIZE 4

bool compareFunction(int x, int y)
{
  return x<y;
}

void sortData()
{
  int array[ARRAY_SIZE] = {3, 5, 6, 1};
  sort(compareFunction, array, ARRAY_SIZE);
}
```

Make sure to clearly document, next to the definition of the function signature, what behavior the function implementations should have. Also, document the behavior in case no such function implementation is attached to your function call. Maybe then you'd abort the program (Samurai Principle) or maybe you'd provide some default functionalty as fallback.

Consequences

The caller can use different implementations and there is still no code duplication. Neither the control logic, the interface, nor the interface documentation is duplicated.

Implementations can be added by the caller at a later point in time without changing the API. This means that the role of the API designer and the implementation provider can be completely separated.

In your code, you now execute the caller's code. Thus, you must trust that the caller knows what the function has to do. In case of bugs in your caller's code, it might still happen that your code will initially be suspected because, after all, the faulty behavior occurs in the context of your code.

Using function pointers implies that you have a platform-specific and programming-language-specific interface. You can use this pattern only if the caller's code is also written in C. You cannot add marshaling functionality to this interface and provide it to a caller who is, for example, writing applications with Java code.

Known Uses

The following examples show applications of this pattern

- James Grenning describes this pattern and a variant as Dynamic Interface and Per-Type Dynamic Interface in the article "SOLID Design for Embedded C" (*https://oreil.ly/kGZVG*).

- The presented solution is a C-version of the Strategy design pattern. You can find alternative C implementations of that pattern in the books *Patterns in C* by Adam Tornhill (Leanpub, 2014) and *C Interfaces and Implementations* by David R. Hanson (Addison-Wesley, 1996).

- Device driver frameworks often use function pointers where the driver inserts its function at startup. The device drivers in the Linux kernel usually work that way.

- The function `svn_sort__hash` of the source code of the Subversion project sorts a list according to some key value. The function takes the function pointer `comparison_func` as a parameter. The `comparison_func` has to return information, namely, which of two provided key values is greater than the other.

- The OpenSSL function `OPENSSL_LH_new` creates a hash table. The caller has to provide a function pointer to a hash function that is used as a callback when operating on the hash table.

- The Wireshark code contains the function pointer `proto_tree_foreach_func` that is provided as a function parameter when traversing tree structures. The function pointer is used to decide which actions to perform on the tree elements.

Applied to Running Example

Your driver API now supports multiple different Ethernet network interface cards. The specific drivers for these network interface cards have to implement the send and receive functions and provide them in a separate header file. The API user can then include and attach these specific send and receive functions to the API.

You have the benefit that users of your API can bring in their own driver implementation. Thus, you as the API designer are independent from the provider of the driver implementation. Integrating new drivers does not require any API changes, which means it does not require any work from you as the API designer. All that is possible with the following API:

```
typedef struct INTERNAL_DRIVER_STRUCT* DRIVER_HANDLE;
typedef void (*DriverSend_FP)(char byte);      /* this is the          */
typedef char (*DriverReceive_FP)();            /* interface definition */
```

```
struct DriverFunctions
{
  DriverSend_FP fpSend;
  DriverReceive_FP fpReceive;
};

DRIVER_HANDLE driverCreate(void* initArg, struct DriverFunctions f);
void driverDestroy(DRIVER_HANDLE h);
void sendByte(DRIVER_HANDLE h, char byte);    /* internally calls fpSend   */
char receiveByte(DRIVER_HANDLE h);            /* internally calls fpReceive */
void setIpAddress(DRIVER_HANDLE h, char* ip);
void setMacAddress(DRIVER_HANDLE h, char* mac);
```

Again, the requirements changed. Now you don't just have to support Ethernet network interface cards, but also other interface cards (like USB interface cards). From the view of the API, these interfaces have some similar functionalities (the send and receive data functions), but they also have some completely different functionalities (for example, a USB interface has no IP address to set, but might require other configurations).

A straightforward solution for this would be to provide two different APIs for the different driver types. But this would duplicate code for the send/receive and create/destroy functions.

A better solution to support different kinds of device drivers in a single abstract API is to introduce Function Control.

Function Control

Context

You want to implement multiple functionalities that follow a similar control logic, but that deviate in their behavior.

Problem

You want to call implementations with slightly deviating behaviors, but you don't want to duplicate any code, not even the control logic implementation or the interface declaration.

The caller should be able to use specific existing behaviors that you implemented. It should even be possible for you to add new behaviors later on without touching the existing implementations and without requiring changes to the existing caller's code.

Having a Dynamic Interface is not an option for you because you do not want to offer the callers the flexibility of attaching their own implementation. That might be because the interface should be easier to use for the caller. Or it might be because you cannot easily attach the implementations of your caller, which is the case if your caller, for example, uses another programming language to access your functionality.

Solution

Add a parameter to your function that passes meta-information about the function call and that specifies the actual functionality to be performed.

Compared to a Dynamic Interface, you do not require the caller to provide the implementation, but instead the caller selects from existing implementations.

To implement this pattern, you apply data-based abstraction by adding an additional parameter (for example, an `enum` or `#define` integer value) that specifies the function's behavior. The parameter is then evaluated in the implementation, and depending on the value of the parameter, different implementations are called:

API

```
#define QUICK_SORT 1
#define MERGE_SORT 2
#define RADIX_SORT 3

void sort(int algo, int* array, int length);
```

Implementation

```
void sort(int algo, int* array, int length)
{
  switch(algo)
  {
    case QUICK_SORT: ❶
      quicksort(array, length);
    break;
    case MERGE_SORT:
      mergesort(array, length);
    break;
    case RADIX_SORT:
      radixsort(array, length);
    break;
  }
}
```

❶ When adding new functionality at a later point in time, you can simply add a new `enum` or `#define` value and select the corresponding new implementation.

Consequences

The caller can use different implementations and there is still no code duplication. Neither the control logic, the interface, nor the interface documentation is duplicated.

It is easy to add new functionality at a later time. Existing implementations do not have to be touched to do that, and the existing caller's code is not affected by the change.

Compared to Dynamic Interface, this pattern is easier for selecting functionalities across different programs or platforms (for example, remote procedure calls) because no program-specific pointers are passed via the API.

When providing the selection of different implementation behaviors in one function, you might be tempted to pack multiple functionalities that do not closely belong together into a single function. This violates the single-responsibility principle.

Known Uses

The following examples show applications of this pattern:

- Device drivers often use Function Control to pass specific functionalities that do not fit into common init/read/write functions. For device drivers this pattern is commonly known as I/O-Control. That concept is described in the book *Making Embedded Systems: Design Patterns for Great Software* by Elecia White (O'Reilly, 2011).

- Some Linux syscalls were extended to have flags that extend the syscalls' functionality depending on the value of the flag without breaking old code.

- The concept of data-driven APIs in general is described in the book *API Design for C++* by Martin Reddy (Morgan Kaufmann, 2011).

- The OpenSSL code uses the function CTerr to log errors. This function takes an enum parameter to specify how and where the error should be logged.

- The POSIX socket function ioctl takes a numeric parameter cmd that determines which actual action will be performed on a socket. The allowed values for the parameter are defined and documented in a header file, and since the first release of that header file, many additional values and thus function behaviors were added.

- The function svn_fs_ioctl of the Subversion project performs some filesystem-specific input or output operations. The function takes the struct svn_fs_ioctl_code_t as a parameter. This struct contains a numeric value that determines which kind of operation should be performed.

Applied to Running Example

The following code shows the final version of your device driver API:

Driver.h

```
typedef struct INTERNAL_DRIVER_STRUCT* DRIVER_HANDLE;
typedef void (*DriverSend_FP)(char byte);
typedef char (*DriverReceive_FP)();
typedef void (*DriverIOCTL_FP)(int ioctl, void* context);

struct DriverFunctions
{
  DriverSend_FP fpSend;
  DriverReceive_FP fpReceive;
  DriverIOCTL_FP fpIOCTL;
};

DRIVER_HANDLE driverCreate(void* initArg, struct DriverFunctions f);
void driverDestroy(DRIVER_HANDLE h);
void sendByte(DRIVER_HANDLE h, char byte);
char receiveByte(DRIVER_HANDLE h);
void driverIOCTL(DRIVER_HANDLE h, int ioctl, void* context);
/* the parameter "context" is required to pass information like the
   value of the IP address to configure to the implementation */
```

EthIOCTL.h

```
#define SET_IP_ADDRESS  1
#define SET_MAC_ADDRESS 2
```

UsbIOCTL.h

```
#define SET_USB_PROTOCOL_TYPE   3
```

Users who want to use the Ethernet- or USB-specific functions (for example, the application actually sending or receiving data via the interface) have to know which driver type they operate on in order to call the right I/O-control and also have to include the *EthIOCTL.h* or *UsbIOCTL.h* files.

Figure 6-2 shows the include-relationships of the source code files of this final version of our device driver API. Note that the *EthApplication.c* code does not depend on USB-specific header files. If, for example, an additional USB-IOCTL is added, the *EthApplication.c* shown in the code does not even need to be recompiled, because none of the files it depends on are changed.

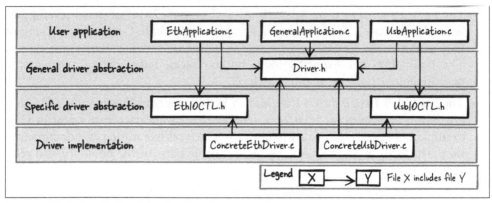

Figure 6-2. File relationships for function control

Keep in mind that of all the code snippets presented in this chapter, this last, most flexible code snippet of the device drivers might not always be what you are looking for. You buy increased flexibility with complexity of your interface, and while you have to make your code as flexible as needed, you should also always try to keep it as simple as possible.

Summary

This chapter discussed four API patterns for C and showed their application in a running example of how to design a device driver. Header Files tells you the basic concept of hiding implementation details in c-files while providing a well-defined interface in your h-files. The pattern Handle is about the well-known concept of passing opaque data types between functions to share state information. Dynamic Interface makes it possible to not duplicate program logic by allowing the injection of caller-specific code via a callback function. Function Control uses an additional function parameter that specifies the actual action that should be performed by the function call. These patterns showed basic C design options to make an interface more flexible by introducing abstractions.

Further Reading

If you're ready for more, here are some resources that can help you further your knowledge of designing APIs.

- The article "SOLID Design for Embedded C" (*https://oreil.ly/07SUX*) by James Grenning covers the five SOLID design principles in general and presents ways to implement flexibility for C interfaces. What makes this article unique is that it is the only article that covers the topic of interfaces specifically for C and also includes detailed code snippets.

- The book *Patterns in C* by Adam Tornhill (Leanpub, 2014) presents several patterns that include C code snippets. The patterns include C versions of Gang of Four patterns like Strategy or Observer as well as C-specific patterns and idioms. The book does not explicitly focus on interfaces, but some of the patterns describe interactions on an interface level.

- The book *API Design for C++* by Martin Reddy (Morgan Kaufmann, 2011) covers design principles for interfaces, object-oriented interface patterns with C++ examples, and interface quality issues with interfaces like testing and documentation. The book addresses C++ design, but some parts of the book are also relevant for C.

- The book *C Interfaces and Implementations* by David R. Hanson (Addison-Wesley, 1996) presents interface design, including C code for specific components implemented in C.

Outlook

The next chapter goes into detail on how to find the right level of abstraction and the right interface for one very specific kind of application: it describes how to design and implement iterators.

CHAPTER 7

Flexible Iterator Interfaces

Iterating over a set of elements is a common operation in any program. Some programming languages provide native constructs to iterate over elements, and object-oriented programming languages have guidance in the form of design patterns on how to implement generic iteration functionality. However, there is very little guidance of this kind for procedural programming languages like C.

The verb "iterate" means to do the same thing multiple times. In programming, it usually means to run the same program code on multiple data elements. Such an operation is often required, which is why it is natively supported in C for arrays, as shown in the following code:

```
for (i=0; i<MAX_ARRAY_SIZE; i++)
{
  doSomethingWith(my_array[i]);
}
```

If you want to iterate over a different data structure, like a red-black tree, for example, then you have to implement your own iteration function. You might equip this function with data structure–specific iteration options, like whether to traverse the tree depth-first or breadth-first. There is literature available on how to implement such specific data structures and how the iteration interfaces for these data structures look. If you use such a data structure-specific interface for iteration and your underlying data structure changes, you'd have to adapt your iteration function and all your code that calls this function. In some cases this is just fine, and even required, because you want to perform some special kind of iteration specific to the underlying data structure—perhaps to optimize the performance of your code.

In other cases, if you have to provide an iteration interface across component boundaries, having such an abstraction that leaks implementation details isn't an option because it might require interface changes in the future. For example, if you sell your customers a component providing iteration functions, and your customers write code using these functions, then they likely expect their code to work without any modification if you provide them with a newer version of your component that maybe uses a different data structure. In that case, you'd even put some extra effort into your implementation to make sure that the interface to the customers stays compatible so that they do not have to change (or maybe not even recompile) their code.

That is where we start in this chapter. I'll show you three patterns on how you, the iterator implementer, can provide stable iterator interfaces to the user (the customer). The patterns do not describe the specific kinds of iterators for specific kinds of data structures. Instead, the patterns assume that within your implementation you already have functions to retrieve the elements from your underlying data structure. The patterns show the options you have to abstract these functions in order to provide a stable iteration interface.

Figure 7-1 shows an overview of the patterns covered in this chapter and their relationships, and Table 7-1 provides a summary of the patterns.

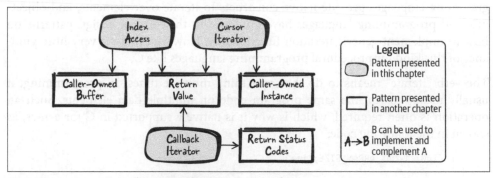

Figure 7-1. Overview of patterns for iterator interfaces

Table 7-1. Patterns for iterator interfaces

Pattern name	Summary
Index Access	You want to make it possible for the user to iterate elements in your data structure in a convenient way, and it should be possible to change internals of the data structure without resulting in changes to the user's code. Therefore, provide a function that takes an index to address the element in your underlying data structure and return the content of this element. The user calls this function in a loop to iterate over all elements.
Cursor Iterator	You want to provide an iteration interface to your user that is robust in case the elements change during the iteration and that enables you to change the underlying data structure at a later point without requiring any changes to the user's code. Therefore, create an iterator instance that points to an element in the underlying data structure. An iteration function takes this iterator instance as argument, retrieves the element the iterator currently points to, and modifies the iteration instance to point to the next element. The user then iteratively calls this function to retrieve one element at a time.

Pattern name	Summary
Callback Iterator	You want to provide a robust iteration interface that does not require the user to implement a loop in the code for iterating over all elements and and that enables you to change the underlying data structure at a later point without requiring any changes to the user's code. Therefore, use your existing data structure–specific operations to iterate over all your elements within your implementation and call some provided user-function on each element during this iteration. This user-function gets the element content as a parameter and can then perform its operations on this element. The user calls just one function to trigger the iteration, and the whole iteration takes place inside your implementation.

Running Example

You implemented an access control component for your application with an underlying data structure in which you have a function to randomly access any of the elements. More specifically, in the following code you have a struct array that holds account information like login names and passwords:

```
struct ACCOUNT
{
  char loginname[MAX_NAME_LENGTH];
  char password[MAX_PWD_LENGTH];
};
struct ACCOUNT accountData[MAX_USERS];
```

The next code shows how users can access this struct to read specific information like the login names:

```
void accessData()
{
  char* loginname;

  loginname = accountData[0].loginname;
  /* do something with loginname */

  loginname = accountData[1].loginname;
  /* do something with loginname */
}
```

Of course, you could simply not worry about abstracting access to your data structure and let other programmers directly retrieve a pointer to this struct to loop over the struct elements and access any information in the struct. But that would be a bad idea because there might be information in your data structure that you do not want to provide to the client. If you have to keep your interface to the client stable over time, you won't be able to remove information you once revealed to the client, because your client might use that information and you don't want to break the client's code.

To avoid this problem, a much better idea is to let the user only access the required information. A simple solution is to provide Index Access.

Index Access

Context

You have a set of elements stored in a data structure that can be randomly accessed. For example, you have an array or a database with functions to randomly retrieve single elements. A user wants to iterate these elements.

Problem

You want to make it possible for the user to iterate elements in your data structure in a convenient way, and it should be possible to change internals of the data structure without resulting in changes to the user's code.

The user might be somebody who writes code that is not versioned and released with your codebase, so you have to make sure that future versions of your implementation also work with the user code written against the current version of your code. Thus, the user should not be able to access any internal implementation details, such as the underlying data structure you use to hold your elements, because you might want to change that at a later point.

Solution

Provide a function that takes an index to address the element in your underlying data structure and return the content of this element. The user calls this function in a loop to iterate over all elements as shown in Figure 7-2.

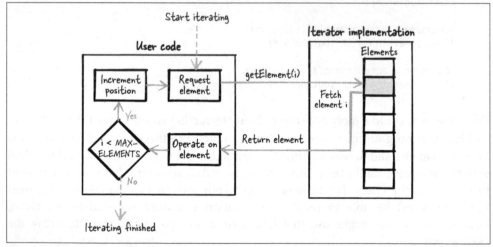

Figure 7-2. Index-accessed iteration

The equivalent to this approach would be that in an array, the user would simply use an index to retrieve the value of one array element or to iterate over all elements. But when you have a function that takes such an index, more complex underlying data structures are also possible to iterate without requiring the user's knowledge.

In order to achieve this, provide the users only the data they are interested in and do not reveal all elements of your underlying data structure. For example, do not return a pointer to the whole `struct` element, return a pointer only to the `struct` member the user is interested in:

Caller's code

```
void* element;

element = getElement(1);
/* operate on element 1 */

element = getElement(2);
/* operate on element 2 */
```

Iterator API

```
#define MAX_ELEMENTS 42

/* Retrieve one single element identified by the provided 'index' */
void* getElement(int index);
```

Consequences

Users can retrieve the elements by using the index to conveniently loop over the elements in their code. They do not have to deal with the internal data structure from which this data was gathered. If something in the implementation changes (for example, the retrieved `struct` member is renamed), users need not recompile their code.

Other changes to the underlying data structure might turn out to be more difficult. If, for example, the underlying data structure changes from an array (randomly accessible) to a linked list (sequentially accessible), then you'd have to iterate the list each time until you get to the requested index. That would not be efficient at all, and to make sure to also allow such changes in the underlying data structure, it would be better to use a Cursor Iterator or Callback Iterator instead.

If the user retrieves only basic data types that can be returned as Return Value of a C function, then the user implicitly retrieves a copy of this element. If the corresponding element in the underlying data structure changes in the meantime, then this would not affect the user. But if the user retrieves a more complex data type (like a string), then compared to simply providing direct access to the underlying data structure, you have with Index Access the advantage that you can copy the current data element in a thread-safe way and provide it to the user, for example with a Caller-Owned Buffer. If you are not operating in a multithreaded environment, you could simply return a pointer for complex data types.

When accessing a set of elements, the user often wants to iterate over all elements. If somebody else adds or removes an element in the underlying data in the meantime, then the user's understanding of the index to access the elements might become invalid, and they might unintentionally retrieve an element twice during the iteration. A straightforward solution to this would be to simply copy all elements the user is interested in into an array and provide this exclusive array to the user, who can then conveniently loop over this array. The user would have Dedicated Ownership of that copy and could even modify the elements. But if that is not explicitly required, copying all the elements might not be worth it. A much more convenient solution, where the user does not have to worry about changes to the underlying data order during iteration, is to provide a Callback Iterator instead.

Known Uses

The following examples show applications of this pattern:

- James Noble describes the External Iterator pattern in his article "Iterators and Encapsulation" (*https://oreil.ly/fganK*). This is an object-oriented version of the concept described in this pattern.

- The book *Data Structures and Problem Solving Using Java* by Mark Allen Weiss (Addison-Wesley, 2006) describes this approach and calls it access with an array-like interface.

- The function `service_response_time_get_column_name` of the Wireshark code returns the name of columns for a statistics table. The name to be returned is addressed with an index parameter provided by the user. The column names cannot change at runtime, and therefore even in multithreaded environments this way of accessing the data or iterating over column names is safe.

- The Subversion project contains code that is used to build up a table of strings. These strings can be accessed with the function `svn_fs_x__string_table_get`. This function takes an index as parameter that is used to address the string to be retrieved. The retrieved string is copied into a provided buffer.

- The OpenSSL function `TXT_DB_get_by_index` retrieves a string selected with an index from a text database and stores it in a provided buffer.

Applied to Running Example

Now you have a clean abstraction for reading the login names, and you don't reveal internal implementation details to the user:

```
char* getLoginName(int index)
{
  return accountData[index].loginname;
}
```

Users do not have to deal with accessing the underlying `struct` array. This has the advantage that access to the required data is easier for them and that they cannot use any information that is not intended for them. For example, they cannot access sub-elements of your `struct` that you might want to change in the future and that can only be changed if nobody accesses this data because you do not want to break the users' code.

Someone using this interface, such as someone who wants to write a function that checks if there is any login name starting with the letter "X," writes the following code:

```
bool anyoneWithX()
{
  int i;
  for(i=0; i<MAX_USERS; i++)
  {
    char* loginName = getLoginName(i);
    if(loginName[0] == 'X')
    {
      return true;
    }
  }
  return false;
}
```

You are happy with your implementation until the data structure that you use to store the login names changes, because you need a more convenient way to insert and delete account data, which is quite difficult when storing the data in a plain array. Now the login names are no longer stored in a single plain array but in an underlying data structure that offers you an operation to get from one element to the next without offering an operation to randomly access elements. More specifically, you have a linked list that can be accessed, as shown in the following code:

```
struct ACCOUNT_NODE
{
  char loginname[MAX_NAME_LENGTH];
  char password[MAX_PWD_LENGTH];
  struct ACCOUNT_NODE* next;
};

struct ACCOUNT_NODE* accountList;

struct ACCOUNT_NODE* getFirst()
{
  return accountList;
}
```

```
struct ACCOUNT_NODE* getNext(struct ACCOUNT_NODE* current)
{
  return current->next;
}

void accessData()
{
  struct ACCOUNT_NODE* account = getFirst();
  char* loginname = account->loginname;
  account = getNext(account);
  loginname = account->loginname;
  ...
}
```

That makes the situation difficult with your current interface, which provides one randomly index-accessed login name at a time. To further support this, you'd have to emulate the index by calling the `getNext` function and counting until you reach the indexed element. That is quite inefficient. All that hassle is only necessary because you designed the interface in a way that turned out to be not flexible enough.

To make things easier, provide a Cursor Iterator to access the login names.

Cursor Iterator

Context

You have a set of elements stored in a data structure that can be accessed randomly or sequentially. For example, you have an array, a linked list, a hash map, or a tree data structure. A user wants to iterate these elements.

Problem

You want to provide an iteration interface to your user that is robust in case the elements change during the iteration and that enables you to change the underlying data structure at a later point without requiring any changes to the user's code.

The user might be somebody who writes code that is not versioned and released with your codebase, so you have to make sure that future versions of your implementation also work with the user code written against the current version of your code. Thus, the user should not be able to access any internal implementation details, such as the underlying data structure you use to hold your elements, because you might want to change that at a later point.

Aside from that, when operating in multithreaded environments, you want to provide the user a robust and clearly defined behavior if the element's content changes while

---

the user iterates over it. Even for complex data like strings, the user should not have to worry about other threads changing that data while the user wants to read it.

You don't care if you have to make an extra implementation effort to achieve all this, because many users will use your code, and if you can take implementation effort away from the user by implementing it in your code, then the overall effort will be decreased.

Solution

Create an iterator instance that points to an element in the underlying data structure. An iteration function takes this iterator instance as argument, retrieves the element the iterator currently points to, and modifies the iteration instance to point to the next element. The user then iteratively calls this function to retrieve one element at a time as shown in Figure 7-3.

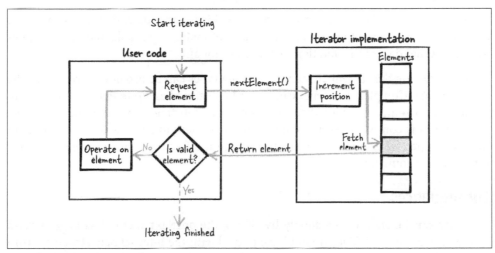

Figure 7-3. Iteration with a Cursor Iterator

The iterator interface requires two functions to create and destroy the iterator instance and one function to perform the actual iteration and to retrieve the current element. Having explicit create/destroy functions makes it possible to have an instance in which you store your internal iteration data (position, data of the current element). The user then has to pass this instance to all your iteration function calls as shown in the following code:

Caller's code

```
void* element;
ITERATOR* it = createIterator();

while(element = getNext(it))
```

```
{
    /* operate on element */
}

destroyIterator(it);
```

Iterator API

```
/* Creates an iterator and moves it to the first element */
ITERATOR* createIterator();

/* Returns the element currently pointed to and sets the iterator to the
   next element. Returns NULL if the element does not exist. */
void* getNext(ITERATOR* iterator);

/* Cleans up an iterator created with the function createIterator() */
void destroyIterator(ITERATOR* iterator),
```

If you do not want the user to be able to access this internal data, then you can hide it and provide the user with a Handle instead. That makes it possible that even changes to this internal data of the iteration instance do not affect the user.

When retrieving the current element, basic data types can be provided direcetly as the Return Value. Complex data types can either be returned as a reference or copied into the iterator instance. Copying them into the iterator instance gives you the advantage that the data is consistent, even if the data in the underlying data structure changes in the meantime (for example, because it is being modified by someone else in a multi-threaded environment).

Consequences

The user can iterate the data simply by calling the getNext method as long as valid elements are retrieved. They do not have to deal with the internal data structure from which this data was gathered, nor do they have to worry about an element index or about the maximum number of elements. But not being able to index the elements also means that the user cannot randomly access the elements (which could be done with Index Access).

Even if the underlying data structure changes, for example, from a linked list to a randomly accessible data structure like an array, then that change can be hidden in the iterator implementation and the user need not change or recompile code.

No matter which kind of data the user retrieves—simple or complex data types—they need not be afraid that the retrieved element will become invalid if the underlying element is changed or removed in the meantime. To make this possible, the user now has to explicitly call functions to create and destroy the iterator instance. Compared to Index Access, more function calls are necessary.

When accessing a set of elements, the user often wants to iterate over all elements. If somebody else adds an element to the underlying data in the meantime, then the user might miss this element during the iteration. If this is a problem for you and you want to make sure that the elements do not change at all during the iteration, then it is easier to use a Callback Iterator.

Known Uses

The following examples show applications of this pattern:

- James Noble describes an object-oriented version of this iterator as the Magic Cookie pattern in his article "Iterators and Encapsulation." (*https://oreil.ly/ NVnbw*)

- The article "Interruptible Iterators" (*https://oreil.ly/BzFJJ*) by Jed Liu et al. describes the presented concept as *cursor object*.

- This kind of iteration is used for file access. For example, the `getline` C function iterates over the lines in a file, and the iterator position is stored in the `FILE` pointer.

- The OpenSSL code provides the functions `ENGINE_get_first` and `ENGINE_ get_next` to iterate a list of encryption engines. Each of these calls takes the pointer to an `ENGINE struct` as a parameter. This `struct` stores the current position in the iteration.

- The Wireshark code contains the functions `proto_get_first_protocol` and `proto_get_next_protocol`. These functions make it possible for a user to iterate over a list of network protocols. The functions take a `void` pointer as out-parameter to store and pass along state information.

- The code of the Subversion project for generating diffs between files contains the function `datasource_get_next_token`. This function is to be called in a loop in order to get the next diff token from a provided datasource object that stores the iteration position.

Applied to Running Example

You now have the following function to retrieve the login names:

```
struct ITERATOR
{
  char buffer[MAX_NAME_LENGTH];
  struct ACCOUNT_NODE* element;
};

struct ITERATOR* createIterator()
{
```

```
    struct ITERATOR* iterator = malloc(sizeof(struct ITERATOR));
    iterator->element = getFirst();
    return iterator;
}

char* getNextLoginName(struct ITERATOR* iterator)
{
    if(iterator->element != NULL)
    {
        strcpy(iterator->buffer, iterator->element->loginname);
        iterator->element = getNext(iterator->element);
        return iterator->buffer;
    }
    else
    {
        return NULL;
    }
}

void destroyIterator(struct ITERATOR* iterator)
{
    free(iterator);
}
```

The following code shows how this interface is used:

```
bool anyoneWithX()
{
    char* loginName;
    struct ITERATOR* iterator = createIterator();
    while(loginName = getNextLoginName(iterator)) ❶
    {
        if(loginName[0] == 'X')
        {
            destroyIterator(iterator); ❷
            return true;
        }
    }
    destroyIterator(iterator); ❷
    return false;
}
```

❶ The application does not have to deal with the index and the maximum number
   of elements anymore

❷ In this case, the required cleanup code for destroying the iterator leads to code
   duplication.

Next, you don't just want to implement the anyoneWithX function, but you also want
to implement an additional function that, for example, tells you how many login
names start with the letter "Y." You could simply copy the code, modify the body of

the `while` loop, and count the occurrences of "Y" but with this approach you'll end up with duplicated code because both of your functions will contain the same code for creating and destroying the iterator and for performing the loop operation. To avoid this code duplication, you can use a Callback Iterator instead.

Callback Iterator

Context

You have a set of elements stored in a data structure that can be accessed randomly or sequentially. For example, you have an array, a linked list, a hash map, or a tree data structure. A user wants to iterate these elements.

Problem

You want to provide a robust iteration interface that does not require the user to implement a loop in the code for iterating over all elements and that enables you to change the underlying data structure at a later point without requiring any changes to the user's code.

The user might be somebody who writes code that is not versioned and released with your codebase, so you have to make sure that future versions of your implementation also work with the user code written against the current version of your code. Thus, the user should not be able to access any internal implementation details, such as the underlying data structure you use to hold your elements, because you might want to change that at a later point.

Aside from that, when operating in multithreaded environments, you want to provide the user a robust and clearly defined behavior if the element's content changes while the user iterates over it. Even for complex data like strings, the user should not have to worry about other threads changing that data while the user wants to read it. Also, you want to make sure that the user iterates over each element exactly once. That should hold even if other threads try to create new elements or delete existing elements during the iteration.

You don't care if you have to make an extra implementation effort to achieve all this, because many users will use your code, and if you can take implementation effort away from the user by implementing it in your code, then the overall effort will be decreased.

You want to make access to your elements as easy as possible. In particular, the user shouldn't have to cope with iteration details like mappings between index and element or the number of available elements. Also, they shouldn't have to implement loops in their code because that would lead to duplications in the user code, so Index Access or a Cursor Iterator isn't an option for you.

Solution

Use your existing data structure-specific operations to iterate over all your elements within your implementation, and call some provided user-function on each element during this iteration. This user-function gets the element content as a parameter and can then perform its operations on this element. The user calls just one function to trigger the iteration, and the whole iteration takes place inside your implementation as shown in Figure 7-4.

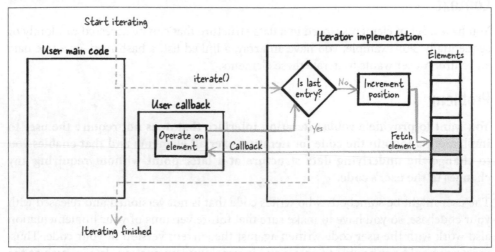

Figure 7-4. Iteration with a Callback Iterator

To realize this, you have to declare a function pointer in your interface. The declared function takes an element that should be iterated over as parameter. The user implements such a function and passes it to your iteration function. Within your implementation you iterate over all elements, and you'll call the user's function for each element with the current element as parameter.

You can add an additional `void*` parameter to your iteration function and to the function pointer declaration. In the implementation of your iteration function, you simply pass that parameter to the user's function. That makes it possible for the user to pass some context information to the function:

Caller's code

```
void myCallback(void* element, void* arg)
{
    /* operate on element */
}

void doIteration()
{
```

```
    iterate(myCallback, NULL);
}
```

Iterator API

```
/* Callback for the iteration to be implemented by the caller. */
typedef void (*FP_CALLBACK)(void* element, void* arg);

/* Iterates over all elements and calls callback(element, arg)
   on each element. */
void iterate(FP_CALLBACK callback, void* arg);
```

Sometimes the user does not want to iterate over all elements but wants to find one specific element. To make that use case more efficient, you can add a break condition to your iteration function. For example, you can declare the function pointer for the user function that operates on the elements of return type bool, and if the user function returns the Return Value true, you stop the iteration. Then the user can signal as soon as the desired element is found and save the time it would take for iterating all the rest of the elements.

When implementing the iteration function for multithreaded environments, make sure to cover the situation when during the iteration, the current element is changed, new elements are added, or elements are deleted by other threads. In case of such changes, you could Return Status Codes to the user who currently iterates, or you could prevent such changes during an iteration by locking write access to the elements in the meantime.

Because the implementation can ensure that the data is not changed during the iteration, it is not necessary to copy the elements on which the user operates. The user simply retrieves a pointer to this data and works with the original data.

Consequences

The user code for iterating over all elements is now just a single line of code. All the implementation details, like an element index and the maximum number of elements, are hidden inside the iterator implementation. The user does not even have to implement a loop to iterate over the elements. They also do not have to create or destroy an iterator instance, nor do they have to cope with the internal data structure from which the elements are gathered. Even if you change the type of underlying data structure in your implementation, they need not even recompile the code.

If the underlying elements change during an iteration, then the iterator implementation can react accordingly, which ensures that the user iterates over a consistent set of data while not having to cope with locking functionality in the user code. All this is possible because the control flow does not jump between the user code and the iterator-code. The control flow stays inside the iterator implementation, and thus the iterator implementation can detect if elements are changed during the iteration and react accordingly.

The user can iterate over all elements, but the iteration loop is implemented inside the iterator implementation, so the user cannot randomly access elements as with Index Access.

In the callback, your implementation runs user code on each element. To some extent this means that you have to trust that the user's code does the right thing. For example, if your iterator implementation locks all elements during the iteration, then you expect the user code to quickly do something with the retrieved element and to not perform any time-consuming operations, because during this iteration, all other calls accessing this data will be locked.

Using callbacks implies that you have a platform- and programming language–specific interface, because you call the code implemented by your caller, and you can only do that if that code uses the same calling conventions (i.e., the same way of providing function parameters and returning data). That means, for implementing an iterator in C, you can only use this pattern if the user code is also written in C. You cannot provide a C Callback Iterator, for example, to a user writing code with Java (which could with some effort be done with any of the other iterator patterns).

When reading the code, the program flow with callbacks is more difficult to follow. For example, compared to having a simple `while` loop directly in the code, it might be more difficult to find out that the program iterates over elements when seeing only one line of user code with a callback parameter. Thus, it is critical to give the iteration function a name that makes it clear that this function performs an iteration.

Known Uses

The following examples show applications of this pattern:

- James Noble describes an object-oriented version of this iterator as the Internal Iterator pattern in his article "Iterators and Encapsulation" (*https://oreil.ly/u8B7I*).

- The function `svn_iter_apr_hash` of the Subversion project iterates over all elements in a hash table that is provided to the function as a parameter. For each element of the hash table, a function pointer, which has to be provided by the caller, is called, and if that call returns `SVN_ERR_ITER_BREAK`, the iteration is stopped.

- The OpenSSL function `ossl_provider_forall_loaded` iterates over a set of OpenSSL provider objects. The function takes a function pointer as a parameter, and that function pointer is called for each provider object. A `void*` parameter can be provided to the iteration call, and this parameter is then provided for each call in the iteration so that users can pass their own context.

- The Wireshark function `conversation_table_iterate_tables` iterates through a list of "conversation" objects. Each such object stores information about sniffed network data. The function takes a function pointer and a void* as parameters. For each conversation object, the function pointer is called with the void* as context.

Applied to Running Example

You now provide the following function for accessing the login names:

```
typedef void (*FP_CALLBACK)(char* loginName, void* arg);

void iterateLoginNames(FP_CALLBACK callback, void* arg)
{
  struct ACCOUNT_NODE* account = getFirst(accountList);
  while(account != NULL)
  {
    callback(account->loginname, arg);
    account = getNext(account);
  }
}
```

The following code shows how to use this interface:

```
void findX(char* loginName, void* arg)
{
  bool* found = (bool*) arg;
  if(loginName[0] == 'X')
  {
    *found = true;
  }
}

void countY(char* loginName, void* arg)
{
  int* count = (int*) arg;
  if(loginName[0] == 'Y')
  {
    (*count)++;
  }
}

bool anyoneWithX()
{
  bool found=false;
  iterateLoginNames(findX, &found); ❶
  return found;
}

int numberOfUsersWithY()
{
  int count=0;
```

```
    iterateLoginNames(countY, &count); ❶
    return count;
}
```

❶ The application no longer contains an explicit loop statement.

As a possible enhancement, the callback function could have a return value that determines whether the iteration is continued or stopped. With such a return value, the iteration could, for example, be stopped once the findX function iterates over the first user starting with "X."

Summary

This chapter showed you three different ways to implement interfaces that provide iteration functionality. Table 7-2 gives an overview of the three patterns and compares their consequences.

Table 7-2. Comparison of the iterator patterns

	Index Access	Cursor Iterator	Callback Iterator
Element access	Allows random access	Only sequential access	Only sequential access
Data structure changes	Underlying data structure can only easily be changed to another random-access data structure	Underlying data structure can easily be changed	Underlying data structure can easily be changed
Info leaked through interface	Amount of elements; usage of a random-access data structure	Iterator position (user can stop and continue the iteration at a later point)	-
Code duplication	Loop in user code; index increment in user code	Loop in user code	-
Robustness	Difficult to implement robust iteration behavior	Difficult to implement robust iteration behavior	easy to implement robust iteration behavior because control flow stays within the iteration code, and insert/delete/modify operations can simply be locked during the iteration (but would block other iterations during that time)
Platforms	Interface can be used across different languages and platforms	Interface can be used across different languages and platforms	Can only be used with the same language and platform (with the same calling convention) as the implementation

Further Reading

If you're ready for more, here are some resources that can help you further your knowledge of iterator interface design.

- The most closely related work regarding iterators in C is an online version of university class notes (*https://oreil.ly/2fuPK*) by James Aspnes. The class notes describe different C iterator designs, discuss their advantages and disadvantages, and provide source code examples.

- There is more guidance on iterators for other programming languages, but many of the concepts can also be applied to C. For example, the article "Iterators and Encapsulation" (*https://oreil.ly/GWR0F*) by James Noble describes eight patterns on how to design object-oriented iterators, the book *Data Structures and Problem Solving Using Java* by Mark Allen Weiss (Addison-Wesley, 2006) describes different iterator designs for Java, and the book *Higher-Order Perl* by Mark Jason Dominus (Morgan Kaufmann, 2005) describes different iterator designs for Perl.

- The article "Loop Patterns" (*https://oreil.ly/JsEKb*) by Owen Astrachan and Eugene Wallingford contains patterns that describe best practices for implementing loops and that include C++ and Java code snippets. Most of the ideas are also relevant for C.

- The book *C Interfaces and Implementations* by David R. Hanson (Addison-Wesley, 1996) describes C implementations and their interfaces for several common data structures like linked lists or hash tables. These interfaces of course also contain functions that traverse these data structures.

Outlook

The next chapter focuses on how to organize the code files in large programs. Once you apply the patterns from the previous chapters to define your interfaces and to program their implementations, you end up with many files. Their file organization has to be tackled to implement modular, large scale programs.

CHAPTER 8

Organizing Files in Modular Programs

Any programmer who implements a larger piece of software and wants to make that software maintainable confronts the question of how to make the software modular. The most important part of that question that is related to dependencies between software-modules is answered, for example, by the SOLID design principles described in the book *Clean Code: A Handbook of Agile Software Craftsmanship* by Robert C. Martin (Prentice Hall, 2008) or by the design patterns described in the book *Design Patterns: Elements of Reusable Object-Oriented Software* by the Gang of Four (Prentice Hall, 1997).

However, making software modular also raises the question of how to organize the source files in a way that allows someone to make the software modular. That question has not yet been answered very well, which results in bad file structures in codebases. It is difficult to make such codebases modular later on, because you don't know which files you should separate into different software-modules or into different codebases. Also, as a programmer, it is difficult to find the files containing APIs that you are supposed to use, and thus you might bring in dependencies to APIs that you are not supposed to use. This is an issue for C in particular because C does not support any mechanism to mark APIs for internal use only and restrict access to them.

There are such mechanisms in other programming languages, and there is advice on how to structure files. For example, the Java programming language comes with the concept of *packages*. Java provides a default way for the developer to organize the classes for these packages and thus the files within the package. For other programming languages, such as C, there is no such advice on how to structure files. Developers have to come up with their own approach for how to structure the header files containing the C function declarations and the implementation files containing the C function definitions.

This chapter shows how to tackle this problem by providing guidance for C programmers on how to structure implementation files, in particular, how to structure header files (APIs) in order to allow the development of large, modular C programs.

Figure 8-1 shows an overview of the patterns covered in this chapter, and Table 8-1 provides a short description of these patterns.

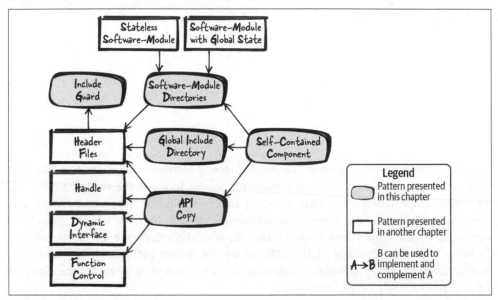

Figure 8-1. Overview of patterns for how to organize your code files

Table 8-1. Patterns for how to organize your code files

Pattern name	Summary
Include Guard	It's easy to include a header file multiple times, but including the same header file leads to compile errors if types or certain macros are part of it, because during compilation they get redefined. Therefore, protect the content of your header files against multiple inclusion so that the developer using the header files does not have to care whether it is included multiple times. Use an interlocked #ifdef statement or a #pragma once statement to achieve this.
Software-Module Directories	Splitting code into different files increases the number of files in your codebase. Having all files in one directory makes it difficult to keep an overview of all the files, particularly for large codebases. Therefore, put header files and implementation files that belong to a tightly coupled functionality into one directory. Name that directory after the functionality that is provided via the header files.
Global Include Directory	To include files from other software-modules, you have to use relative paths like *../othersoftwaremodule/file.h*. You have to know the exact location of the other header file. Therefore, have one global directory in your codebase that contains all software-module APIs. Add this directory to the global include paths in your toolchain.

Pattern name	Summary
Self-Contained Components	From the directory structure it is not possible to see the dependencies in the code. Any software-module can simply include the header files from any other software-module, so it's impossible to check dependencies in the code via the compiler. Therefore, identify software-modules that contain similar functionality and that should be deployed together. Put these software-modules into a common directory and have a designated subdirectory for their header files that are relevant for the caller.
API Copy	You want to develop, version, and deploy the parts of your codebase independently from one another. However, to do that, you need clearly defined interfaces between the code parts and the ability to separate that code into different repositories. Therefore, to use the functionality of another component, copy its API. Build that other component separately and copy the build artifacts and its public header files. Put these files into a directory inside your component and configure that directory as a global include path.

Running Example

Imagine you want to implement a piece of software that prints the hash value for some file content. You start with the following code for a simple hash function:

main.c

```c
#include <stdio.h>

static unsigned int adler32hash(const char* buffer, int length)
{
  unsigned int s1=1;
  unsigned int s2=0;
  int i=0;

  for(i=0; i<length; i++)
  {
    s1=(s1+buffer[i]) % 65521;
    s2=(s1+s2) % 65521;
  }
  return (s2<<16) | s1;
}

int main(int argc, char* argv[])
{
  char* buffer = "Some Text";
  unsigned int hash = adler32hash(buffer, 100);
  printf("Hash value: %u", hash);
  return 0;
}
```

The preceding code simply prints the hash output of a fixed string to the console output. Next, you want to extend that code. You want to read the content of a file and print the hash of the file content. You could simply add all this code to the *main.c* file, but that would make the file very long, and it would make the code more unmaintainable the more it grows.

Instead, it is much better to have separate implementation files and access their functionality with Header Files. You now have the following code for reading the content of a file and printing the hash of the file content. To make it easier to see which parts of the code changed, the implementations that did not change are skipped:

main.c

```
#include <stdio.h>
#include <stdlib.h>
#include "hash.h"
#include "filereader.h"

int main(int argc, char* argv[])
{
  char* buffer = malloc(100);
  getFileContent(buffer, 100);
  unsigned int hash = adler32hash(buffer, 100);
  printf("Hash value: %u", hash);
  return 0;
}
```

hash.h

```
/* Returns the hash value of the provided "buffer" of size "length".
   The hash is calculated according to the Adler32 algorithm. */
unsigned int adler32hash(const char* buffer, int length);
```

hash.c

```
#include "hash.h"

unsigned int adler32hash(const char* buffer,  int length)
{
  /* no changes here */
}
```

filereader.h

```
/* Reads the content of a file and stores it in the  provided "buffer"
   if is is long enough according to its provided "length" */
void getFileContent(char* buffer, int length);
```

filereader.c

```
#include <stdio.h>
#include "filereader.h"

void getFileContent(char* buffer, int length)
{
```

```
    FILE* file = fopen("SomeFile", "rb");
    fread(buffer, length, 1, file);
    fclose(file);
}
```

Organizing the code in separate files made the code more modular because dependencies in the code can now be made explicit as all related functionality is put into the same file. Your codebase files are currently all stored in the same directory, as shown in Figure 8-2.

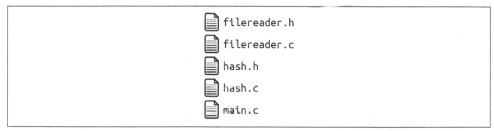

Figure 8-2. File overview

Now that you have separate header files, you can include these header files in your implementation files. However, you'll soon end up with the problem that you get a build error if the header files are included multiple times. To help out with this issue, you can install Include Guards.

Include Guard

Context

You split your implementation into multiple files. Inside the implementation you include header files to get forward declarations of other code that you want to call or use.

Problem

It's easy to include a header file multiple times, but including the same header file leads to compile errors if types or certain macros are part of it, because during compilation they get redefined.

In C, during compilation, the #include directive lets the C preprocessor fully copy the included file into your compilation unit. If, for example, a struct is defined in the header file and that header file is included multiple times, then that struct definition is copied multiple times and is present multiple times in the compilation unit, which then leads to a compile error.

To avoid this, you could try to not include files more than once. However, when including a header file, you usually don't have the overview of whether other additional header files are included inside that header file. Thus, it is easy to include files multiple times.

Solution

Protect the content of your header files against multiple inclusion so that the developer using the header files does not have to care whether it is included multiple times. Use an interlocked `#ifdef` statement or a `#pragma once` statement to achieve this.

The following code shows how to use the Include Guard:

somecode.h

```
#ifndef SOMECODE_H
#define SOMECODE_H
/* put the content of your headerfile here */
#endif
```

othercode.h

```
#pragma once
/* put the content of your headerfile here */
```

During the build procedure, the interlocked `#ifdef` statement or the `#pragma once` statement protects the content of the header file against being compiled multiple times in a compilation unit.

The `#pragma once` statement is not defined in the C standard, but it is supported by most C preprocessors. Still, you have to keep in mind that you could have a problem with this statement when switching to a different toolchain with a different C preprocessor.

While the interlocked `#ifdef` statement works with all C preprocessors, it brings the difficulty that you have to use a unique name for the defined macro. Usually, a name scheme that relates to the name of the header file is used but that could lead to outdated names if you rename a file and forget to change the Include Guard. Also, you could run into problems when using third-party code, because the names of your Include Guards might collide. A way to avoid these problems is to not use the name of the header file, but instead use some other unique name like the current timestamp or a UUID.

Consequences

As a developer who includes header files, you now don't have to care whether that file might be included multiple times. This makes life a lot easier, especially when you have nested #include statements, because it is difficult to know exactly which files are already included.

You have to either take the nonstandard #pragma once statement, or you have to come up with a unique naming scheme for your interlocked #ifdef statement. While filenames work as unique names most of the time, there could still be problems with similar names in third-party code that you use. Also, there could be inconsistent names of the #define statements when renaming your own files, but some IDEs help out here. They already create an Include Guard when creating a new header file or adapt the name of the #define when renaming the header file.

The interlocked #ifdef statements prevent compilation errors when you have a file included multiple times, but they don't prevent opening and copying the included file multiple times into the compilation unit. That is an unnecessary part of the compilation time and could be optimized. One approach to optimize would be to have an additional Include Guard around each of your #include statements, but this makes including the files more cumbersome. Also, this is unnecessary for most modern compilers because they optimize compilation by themselves (for example, by caching the header file content or remembering which files are already included).

Known Uses

The following examples show applications of this pattern:

- Pretty much every C code that consists of more than one file applies this pattern.
- The book *Large-Scale C++ Software Design* by John Lakos (Addison-Wesley, 1996) describes optimizing the performance of Include Guards by having an additional guard around each #include statement.
- The Portland Pattern Repository describes the Include Guard pattern and also describes a pattern to optimize compilation time by having an additional guard around each #include statement.

Applied to Running Example

The Include Guard in the following code ensure that even if a header file is included multiple times, no build error occurs:

hash.h

```
#ifndef HASH_H
#define HASH_H
/* Returns the hash value of the provided "buffer" of size "length".
   The hash is calculated according to the Adler32 algorithm. */
unsigned int adler32hash(const char* buffer, int length);
#endif
```

filereader.h

```
#ifndef FILEREADER_H
#define FILEREADER_H
/* Reads the content of a file and stores it in the provided "buffer"
   if is is long enough according to its provided "length" */
void getFileContent(char* buffer, int length);
#endif
```

As the next feature of your code, you want to also print the hash value calculated by another kind of hash function. Simply adding another *hash.c* file for the other hash function is not possible because filenames have to be unique. It would be an option to give another name to the new file. However, even if you do that, you are still not happy with the situation because more and more files are now in one directory, which makes it difficult to get an overview of the files and to see which files are related. To improve the situation, you could use Software-Module Directories.

Software-Module Directories

Context

You split your source code into different implementation files, and you utilize header files to use functionality from other implementation files. More and more files are being added to your codebase.

Problem

Splitting code into different files increases the number of files in your codebase. Having all files in one directory makes it difficult to keep an overview of all the files, particularly for large codebases.

Putting the files into different directories raises the question of which files you want to put into which directory. It should be easy to find files that belong together, and it should be easy to know where to put files if additional files have to be added later.

Solution

Put header files and implementation files that belong to a tightly coupled functionality into one directory. Name that directory after the functionality that is provided via the header files.

The directory and its content is furthermore called a *software-module*. Quite often, a software-module contains all code that provides operations on an instance addressed with Handles. In that case, the software-module is the non-object-oriented equivalent to an object-oriented class. Having all files for a software-module in one directory is the equivalent to having all files for a class in one directory.

The software-module could contain a single header file and a single implementation file or multiple such files. The main criteria for putting the files into one directory is high cohesion between the files within the directory and low coupling to other Software-Module Directories.

When you have header files used only inside the software-module and header files used outside the software-module, name the files in a way that makes clear which header files are not to be used outside the software-module (for example, by giving them the postfix *internal* as shown in Figure 8-3 and the following code):

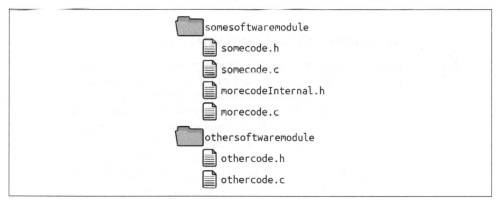

Figure 8-3. File overview

somecode.c

```
#include "somecode.h"
#include "morecode.h"
#include "../othersoftwaremodule/othercode.h"
...
```

morecode.c

```
#include "morecode.h"
...
```

othercode.c

```
#include "othercode.h"
...
```

The preceding code excerpt shows how the files are being included, but it does not show the implementation. Note that files from the same software-module can easily be included. In order to include header files of other software-modules, it is necessary to know the path to these software-modules.

When your files are distributed across different directories, you have to make sure that your toolchain is configured in a way to compile all these files. Maybe your IDE automatically compiles all files in subdirectories of your codebase, but you might have to adapt build settings or manipulate Makefiles to compile the files from the new directories.

Configuring Include Directories and Files to Compile

Modern C programming IDEs usually provide a carefree environment where the C programmer can focus on programming and does not necessarily have to get in touch with the build procedure. These IDEs provide build settings that allow you to easily configure which directories contain the implementation files to be built and which directories contain your include files. This allows the C programmer to focus on programming and not on writing Makefiles and compiler commands. This chapter assumes you have such an IDE and doesn't focus on Makefiles and their syntax.

Consequences

Splitting code files into different directories makes it possible to have the same filenames in different directories. This comes in handy when using third-party code, because otherwise those filenames might clash with the filenames in your own codebase.

However, having similar filenames, even when they are in different directories, is not recommended. For header files in particular, it is advisable to have unique filenames to make sure that the file that will be included does not depend on the search order of your include paths. To make filenames unique, you can use a short and unique prefix for all files of your software-module.

Putting all files that are related to a software-module into one directory makes it easier to find files that are related, because you only have to know the name of the software-module. The number of files inside a software-module is usually low enough to be able to quickly spot files in that directory.

Most code dependencies are local to each software-module, so you now have the highly dependent files within the same directory. This makes it much easier for programmers trying to understand some part of the code to see which other files are also relevant. Any implementation files outside the software-module directory are usually not relevant for understanding the functionality of that software-module.

Known Uses

The following examples show applications of this pattern:

- The Git source code structures some of its code in directories, and other code then includes these headers by using relative paths. For example, *kwset.c* includes *compat/obstack.h*.

- The Netdata real-time performance monitoring and visualization system organizes its code files into directories like *database* or *registry*, which contain a handful of files each. To include files from another directory, relative include paths are used.

- The network mapper Nmap organizes its software-modules into directories like *ncat* or *ndiff*. Header files from other software-modules are included using relative paths.

Applied to Running Example

The code pretty much stayed the same. Only a new header file and a new implementation file for the new hash function were added. The location of the files changed, as you can see from the include paths. In addition to putting the files into separate directories, their names were also changed to make the filenames unique.

main.c

```
#include <stdio.h>
#include <stdlib.h>
#include "adler/adlerhash.h"
#include "bernstein/bernsteinhash.h"
#include "filereader/filereader.h"
```

```
int main(int argc, char* argv[])
{
    char* buffer = malloc(100);
    getFileContent(buffer, 100);

    unsigned int hash = adler32hash(buffer, 100);
    printf("Adler32 hash value: %u", hash);

    unsigned int hash = bernsteinHash(buffer, 100);
    printf("Bernstein hash value: %u", hash);

    return 0;
}
```

bernstein/bernsteinhash.h

```
#ifndef BERNSTEINHASH_H
#define BERNSTEINHASH_H
/* Returns the hash value of the provided "buffer" of size "length".
   The hash is calculated according to the D.J. Bernstein algorithm. */
unsigned int bernsteinHash(const char* buffer, int length);
#endif
```

bernstein/bernsteinhash.c

```
#include "bernsteinhash.h"

unsigned int bernsteinHash(const char* buffer, int length)
{
    unsigned int hash = 5381;
    int i;
    for(i=0; i<length; i++)
    {
        hash = 33 * hash ^ buffer[i];
    }
    return hash;
}
```

Splitting the code files into separate directories is very common. It makes it easier to find a file and makes it possible to have files with similar filenames. Still, instead of having similar filenames it might even be better to have unique filenames, for example, by having a unique filename prefix per software-module. Without these prefixes, you'll end up with the directory structure and filenames shown in Figure 8-4.

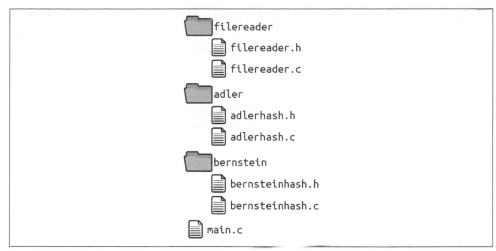

Figure 8-4. File overview

All files that belong together are now in the same directory. The files are well structured into directories, and the header files from other directories can be accessed with relative paths.

However, relative paths bring the problem that if you want to rename one of the directories, you also have to touch other source files to fix their include paths. This is a dependency you don't want, and you can get rid of it by having a Global Include Directory.

Global Include Directory

Context

You have header files, and you have structured your code into Software-Module Directories.

Problem

To include files from other software-modules, you have to use relative paths like *../othersoftwaremodule/file.h*. You have to know the exact location of the other header file.

If the path to the other header file changes, you have to change your code that includes that header file. If, for example, the other software-module is renamed, you have to change your code. So you have a dependency on the name and location of the other software-module.

As a developer, you want to clearly see which header files belong to the API of a software-module that you are supposed to use and which header files are internal header files that nobody outside the software-module should use.

Solution

Have one global directory in your codebase that contains all software-module APIs. Add this directory to the global include paths in your toolchain.

Leave all implementation files and all header files that are only used by one software-module in the directory of that software-module. If a header file is used by other code as well, then put it in the global directory, which is commonly named */include*, as shown in Figure 8-5 and in the following code.

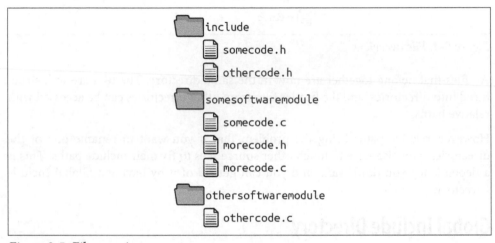

Figure 8-5. File overview

The configured global include path is */include*.

somecode.c

```
#include <somecode.h>
#include <othercode.h>
#include "morecode.h"
...
```

morecode.c

```
#include "morecode.h"
...
```

othercode.c

```
#include <othercode.h>
...
```

The preceding code excerpt shows how the files are being included. Note that there are no more relative paths. To make it clearer in this code which files are included from the global include path, all these files are included with angle brackets in the #include statement.

#include Syntax

For all of the included files, the syntax with the quotation marks could be used as well (#include "stdio.h"). Most C preprocessors would look up these include files by relative path first, not find them there, and then look them up in the global directories configured on your system and used by the toolchain. In C, you usually use the syntax with the angle brackets (#include <stdio.h>), which only searches the global directories, when including files from outside of your codebase. But that syntax could also be used for files in your own codebase if they are not included by a relative path.

The global include path has to be configured in the build settings of your toolchain, or if you manually write Makefiles and compiler commands, you have to add the include path there.

If the number of header files in this directory grows large, or if there are very specific header files that are used by only a few software-modules, you should consider splitting your codebase into Self-Contained Components.

Consequences

It is very clear which header files are supposed to be used by other software-modules and which header files are internal and are supposed to be used within this software-module only.

Now there is no more need to use relative directories in order to include files from other software-modules. But the code from other software-modules is not inside a single directory anymore and is instead split over your codebase.

Putting all APIs into one directory might lead to many files inside this directory, which would make it difficult to find files that belong together. You have to be careful not to end up with all your header files of the whole codebase in that one include directory. That would mitigate the benefits of having Software-Module Directories. And what would you do if software-module A is the only one that needs the interfaces of software-module B? With the proposed solution, you'd put the interfaces of software-module B into the Global Include Directory. However, if nobody else needs these interfaces, then you might not want them to be available for everyone in your codebase. To avoid that problem, use Self-Contained Components.

Known Uses

The following examples show applications of this pattern:

- The OpenSSL code has an /include directory that contains all header files that are used in multiple software-modules.

- The code of the game NetHack has all its header files in the directory /include. The implementations are not organized into software-modules, but instead they are all in one single /src directory.

- The OpenZFS code for Linux has one global directory called /include that contains all header files. This directory is configured as an include path in the Makefiles that are in the directories of the implementation files.

Applied to Running Example

The location of the header files changed in your codebase. You moved them to a Global Include Directory that you configured in your toolchain. Now you can simply include the files without searching through relative filepaths. Note that because of this, angle brackets instead of quotation marks are now used for the #include statements:

main.c

```
#include <stdio.h>
#include <stdlib.h>
#include <adlerhash.h>
#include <bernsteinhash.h>
#include <filereader.h>

int main(int argc, char* argv[])
{
  char* buffer = malloc(100);
  getFileContent(buffer, 100);

  unsigned int hash = adler32hash(buffer, 100);
  printf("Adler32 hash value: %u", hash);

  hash = bernsteinHash(buffer, 100);
  printf("Bernstein hash value: %u", hash);

  return 0;
}
```

In your code, you now have the file organization and the global include path */include* configured in your toolchain as shown in Figure 8-6.

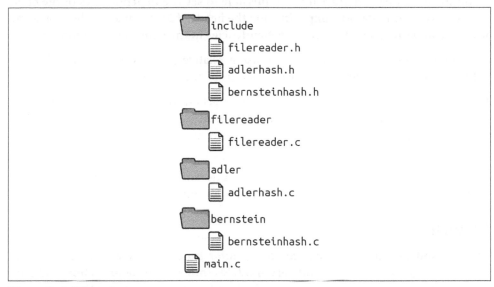

Figure 8-6. File overview

Now, even if you rename one of the directories, you do not have to touch the implementation files. So you decoupled the implementations a bit more.

Next, you want to extend the code. You want to use the hash functions not only to hash the content of the files but also in another application context, calculating a pseudorandom number based on the hash function. You want to make it possible to develop the two applications, which both use the hash functions, independently from each other, maybe even by independent development teams.

Having to share one global include directory with another development team is not an option, as you don't want to mix the code files between the different teams. You want to separate the two applications as far as possible from each other. To do that, organize them as Self-Contained Components.

Self-Contained Component

Context

You have Software-Module Directories and maybe a Global Include Directory. The number of software-modules keeps growing, and your code becomes larger.

Problem

From the directory structure it is not possible to see the dependencies in the code. Any software-module can simply include the header files from any other software-module, so it's impossible to check dependencies in the code via the compiler.

Including header files can be done by using relative paths, which means that any software-module can include the header files from any other software-module.

Keeping an overview of the software-modules gets difficult as their number grows. Just like before you used Software-Module Directories, where you had too many files in a single directory, now you have too many Software-Module Directories.

As with the dependencies, it is also not possible to see the code responsibility from the code structure. If multiple development teams work on the code, you might want to define who is responsible for which software-module.

Solution

Identify software-modules that contain similar functionality and that should be deployed together. Put these software-modules into a common directory and have a designated subdirectory for their header files that are relevant for the caller.

Furthermore, such a group of software-modules including all their header files will be called a *component*. Compared to software-modules, a component is usually bigger and could be deployed independently from the rest of the codebase.

When grouping the software-modules, check which part of your code could be independently deployed from the rest of the codebase. Check which part of the code is developed by separate teams and thus might be developed in a way to only have loose coupling to the rest of the codebase. Such software-module groups are candidates for components.

If you have one Global Include Directory, move all header files from your component from that directory and put them inside the designated directory in your component (for example, *myComponent/include*). Developers who use the component can add this path to their global include paths in their toolchain or can modify the Makefile and compiler command accordingly.

You can use the toolchain to check if the code in one of the components only uses functionality that it is allowed to use. For example, if you have a component that abstracts the operating system, you might want all other code to use that abstraction and to not use operating system–specific functions. You can configure your toolchain to set the include paths to the operating system–specific functions only for your component that abstracts the operating system. For all other code, only the directory with the interface of your operating-system abstraction is configured as the include path. Then an unexperienced developer who does not know that there is an operating system abstraction and tries to use the operating system–specific functions directly would have to use the relative include path to these function declarations to get the code compiling (and this will hopefully discourage the developer from doing that).

Figure 8-7 and the following code show the file structure and the include filepaths.

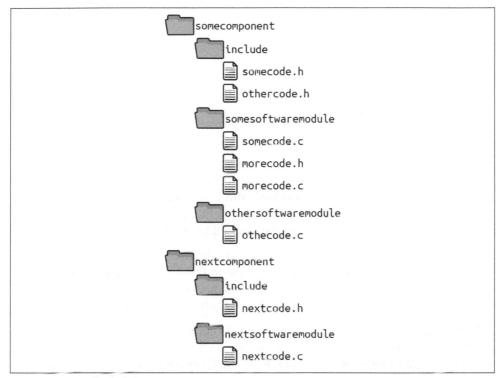

Figure 8-7. File overview

Configured global include paths:

- */somecomponent/include*
- */nextcomponent/include*

somecode.c

```
#include <somecode.h>
#include <othercode.h>
#include "morecode.h"
...
```

morecode.c

```
#include "morecode.h"
...
```

othercode.c

```
#include <othercode.h>
...
```

nextcode.c

```
#include <nextcode.h>
#include <othercode.h> // use API of other component
...
```

Consequences

The software-modules are well organized, and it is easier to find software-modules that belong together. If the components are well split, then it should also be clear to which component which kind of new code should be added.

Having everything that belongs together in a single directory makes it easier to configure specific things for that component in the toolchain. For example, you can have stricter compiler warnings for new components that you create in your codebase, and you can automatically check code dependencies between components.

When developing the code in multiple teams, component directories make it easier to set the responsibilities between the teams because these components usually have very low coupling between each other. Even the functionality for the overall product might not depend on these components. It is easier to split responsibilities on a component level than on a software-module level.

Known Uses

The following examples show applications of this pattern:

- The GCC code has separate components with their own directories gathering its header files. For example, */libffi/include* or *libcpp/include*.

- The operating system RIOT organizes its drivers into well-separated directories. For example, the directories */drivers/xbee* and */drivers/soft_spi* each contain an *include* subdirectory that contains all interfaces for that software-module.

- The Radare reverse engineering framework has well-separated components, each with its own *include* directory that contains all its interfaces.

Applied to Running Example

You added the implementation of pseudorandom numbers that uses one of the hash functions. Apart from that, you isolated three different parts of your code:

- The hash functions
- The hash calculation of a file content
- The pseudorandom number calculation

All three parts of the code are now well separated and could easily be developed by different teams or could even be deployed independently from one another:

main.c

```c
#include <stdio.h>
#include <stdlib.h>
#include <adlerhash.h>
#include <bernsteinhash.h>
#include <filereader.h>
#include <pseudorandom.h>

int main(int argc, char* argv[])
{
  char* buffer = malloc(100);
  getFileContent(buffer, 100);

  unsigned int hash = adler32hash(buffer, 100);
  printf("Adler32 hash value: %u", hash);

  hash = bernsteinHash(buffer, 100);
  printf("Bernstein hash value: %u", hash);

  unsigned int random = getRandomNumber(50);
  printf("Random value: %u", random);

  return 0;
}
```

randrandomapplication/include/pseudorandom.h

```c
#ifndef PSEUDORANDOM_H
#define PSEUDORANDOM_H
/* Returns a pseudo random number lower than the
   provided maximum number (parameter `max')*/
unsigned int getRandomNumber(int max);
#endif
```

randomapplication/pseudorandom/pseudorandom.c

```c
#include <pseudorandom.h>
#include <adlerhash.h>

unsigned int getRandomNumber(int max)
{
  char* seed = "seed-text";
  unsigned int random = adler32hash(seed, 10);
  return random % max;
}
```

Your code now has the following directory structure. Note how each part of the code files is well separated from the other parts. For example, all code related to hashes is in one directory. For a developer using these functions, it is easy to spot where to find the API to these functions, which are in the *include* directory as shown in Figure 8-8.

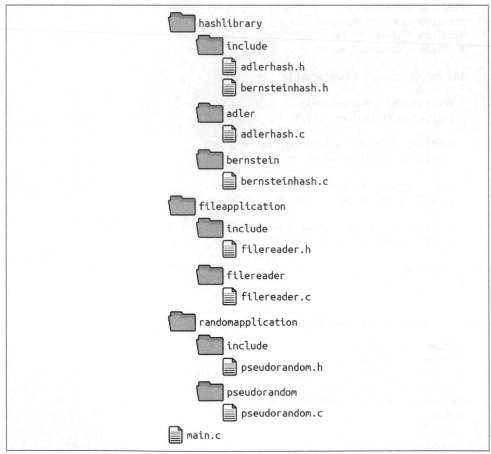

Figure 8-8. File overview

For this code, the following global include directories are configured in the toolchain:

- */hashlibrary/include*
- */fileapplication/include*
- */randomapplication/include*

Now the code is well separated into different directories, but there are still dependencies that you could remove. Have a look at the include paths. You have one codebase and all include paths are used for all that code. However, for the code of the hash functions, there is no need to have the file handling include path.

Also, you compile all code and simply link all the objects into one executable file. However, you might want to split that code and independently deploy it. You might want to have one application that prints the hash output and one application that prints the pseudorandom number. Those two applications should be independently developed, but both should use, for example, the same hash function code, which you do not want to duplicate.

To decouple the applications and have a defined way to access the functionality from other parts without having to share private information, like include paths to those parts, you should have an API Copy.

API Copy

Context

You have a large codebase with different teams developing it. In the codebase, the functionality is abstracted via header files that are organized in Software-Module Directories. Best case is that you have well-organized Self-Contained Components, and the interfaces have existed for some time, so you are quite sure they are stable.

Problem

You want to develop, version, and deploy the parts of your codebase independently from one another. However, to do that, you need clearly defined interfaces between the code parts and the ability to separate that code into different repositories.

If you have Self-Contained Components then you are nearly there. The components have well-defined interfaces, and all code for those components is already in separate directories, so they could easily be checked in to separate repositories.

But there is still a directory structure dependency between the components: the configured include path. That path still includes the full path to the code of the other component and, for example, if the name of that component changes, you have to change the configured include path. That is a dependency you do not want to have.

Solution

To use the functionality of another component, copy its API. Build that other component separately and copy the build artifacts and its public header files. Put these files into a directory inside your component and configure that directory as a global include path.

Copying code may seem like a bad idea. In general it is, but here you only copy the interface of another component. You copy the function declarations of the header files, so there are no multiple implementations. Think about what you do when you install a third-party library: you also have a copy of its interfaces to access its functionality.

In addition to the copied header files, you have to use other build artifacts during the build of your component. You could version and deploy the other component as a separate library that you'd have to link to your component. Figure 8-9 and the following code show the overview of the involved files.

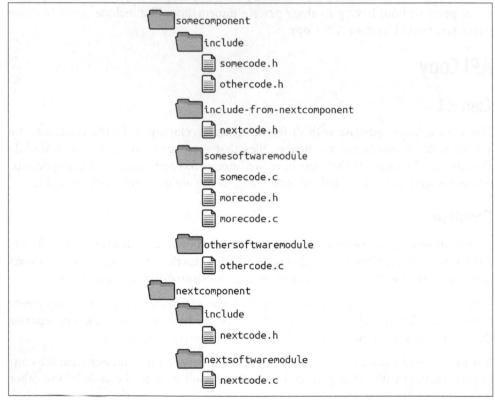

Figure 8-9. File overview

Configured global include paths for `somecomponent`:

- */include*
- */include-from-nextcomponent*

somecode.c

```
#include <somecode.h>
#include <othercode.h>
#include "morecode.h"
...
```

morecode.c

```
#include "morecode.h"
...
```

othercode.c

```
#include <othercode.h>
...
```

Configured global include path for `nextcomponent`:

- */include*

nextcode.c

```
#include <nextcode.h>
...
```

Note that the preceding code is now split into two different code blocks. It is now possible to split the code and put it into separate repositories, or in other words: to have separate codebases. There are no more dependencies involving the directory structure between the components. However, now you are in the situation that different versions of the components have to ensure that their interfaces stay compatible even if their implementations change. Depending on your deployment strategy, you have to define which kind of interface compatibility (API compatible or ABI compatible) you want to provide. To keep your interfaces flexible while being compatible, you can use Handles, Dynamic Interfaces, or Function Controls.

Interface Compatibility

The *application programming interface* (API) stays compatible if there is no need to change anything in the caller's code. You break API compatibility if you, for example, add another parameter to an existing function, or if you change the type of the return value or the parameters.

The *application binary interface* (ABI) stays compatible if there is no need to recompile the caller's code. You break the ABI compatibility if you, for example, change the platform for which you compile your code, or if you update your compiler to a newer version that has a different function, calling convention compared to previous compiler versions.

Consequences

Now there are no more dependencies involving the directory structure between the components. It is possible to rename one of the components without having to change the include directives of the code from other components (or as you can call them now, other codebases).

Now the code can be checked into different repositories, and there is absolutely no need to know the path to other components in order to include their header files. To get to the header files of another component, you copy it. So initially you have to know from where to get the header files and build artifacts. Maybe the other component provides some kind of setup installer, or maybe it just provides a versioned list of all required files.

You need an agreement that the interfaces of the components will stay compatible in order to use the main benefit of the split codebases: independent development and versioning. The requirement for compatible interfaces restricts the development of components providing such interfaces, because once a function can be used by others, it cannot be freely changed anymore. Even compatible changes, like adding a new function to an existing header file, could become more difficult. This is because then you'd provide a different set of functionality with different versions of that header file, which makes it more difficult for your callers to know which version of the header file they should use. It also makes it difficult to write code that works with any version of your header file.

You buy the flexibility of separate codebases with the additional complexity of having to cope with API compatibility requirements and with more complexity in the build procedure (copying header files, keeping them in sync, linking the other component, versioning the interfaces).

Version Numbers

The way you version your interfaces should specify if a new version brings incompatible changes. Commonly, *semantic versioning* (*https://semver.org*) is used to indicate in the version number whether there are major changes. With semantic versioning you have a three-digit version number for your interface (for example, 1.0.7), and only a change in the first number means an incompatible change.

Known Uses

The following examples show applications of this pattern:

- Wireshark copies the APIs of the independently deployed Kazlib to use its exception emulation functionality.

- The B&R Visual Components software accesses functionality from the underlying Automation Runtime operating system. The Visual Components software is independently deployed and versioned from Automation Runtime. To access the Automation Runtime functionality, its public header files are copied into the Visual Components codebase.

- The Education First company develops digital learning products. In their C code, they copy include files into a global include directory when building the software in order to decouple the components in their codebase.

Applied to Running Example

Now the different parts of the code are well separated. The hash implementation has a well-defined interface to the code for printing file hashes and to the code for generating pseudorandom numbers. Additionally, these parts of the code are well separated into directories. Even the APIs of other components are copied, so that all code that has to be accessed by one of the components is in its own directory. The code for each of the components could even be stored in its own repository and deployed and versioned independently from the other components.

The implementations did not change at all. Only the APIs of other components were copied and the include paths for the codebases changed. The hashing code is now isolated from even the main application. The hashing code is treated as an independently deployed component and is only linked to the rest of the application. Example 8-1 shows the code of your main application, which is now separated from the hash library.

Example 8-1. Code of the main application

main.c

```c
#include <stdio.h>
#include <stdlib.h>
#include <adlerhash.h>
#include <bernsteinhash.h>
#include <filereader.h>
#include <pseudorandom.h>

int main(int argc, char* argv[])
{
  char* buffer = malloc(100);
  getFileContent(buffer, 100);

  unsigned int hash = adler32hash(buffer, 100);
  printf("Adler32 hash value: %u\n", hash);

  hash = bernsteinHash(buffer, 100);
  printf("Bernstein hash value: %u\n", hash);

  unsigned int random = getRandomNumber(50);
  printf("Random value: %u\n", random);

  return 0;
}
```

randomapplication/include/pseudorandom.h

```c
#ifndef PSEUDORANDOM_H
#define PSEUDORANDOM_H
/* Returns a pseudorandom number lower than the provided maximum number
   (parameter `max')*/
unsigned int getRandomNumber(int max);
#endif
```

randomapplication/pseudorandom/pseudorandom.c

```c
#include <pseudorandom.h>
#include <adlerhash.h>

unsigned int getRandomNumber(int max)
{
  char* seed = "seed-text";
  unsigned int random = adler32hash(seed, 10);
  return random % max;
}
```

fileapplication/include/filereader.h

```
#ifndef FILEREADER_H
#define FILEREADER_H
/* Reads the content of a file and stores it in the provided "buffer"
   if is is long enough according to its provided "length" */
void getFileContent(char* buffer, int length);
#endif
```

*_fileapplication/filereader/filereader.c_*

```
#include <stdio.h>
#include "filereader.h"

void getFileContent(char* buffer, int length)
{
  FILE* file = fopen("SomeFile", "rb");
  fread(buffer, length, 1, file);
  fclose(file);
}
```

This code has the directory structure and include path shown in Figure 8-10 and the following code example. Note that no source code regarding the hash implementation is part of this codebase anymore. The hash functionality is accessed by including the copied header files, and then the *.a* file has to be linked to the code in the build process.

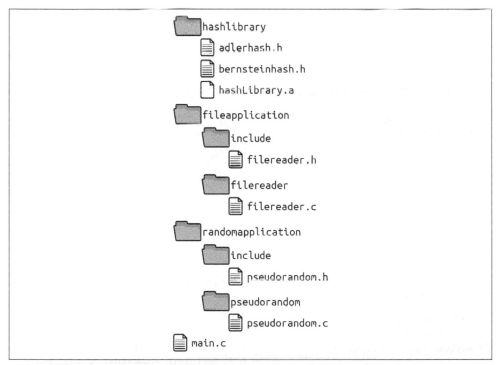

Figure 8-10. File overview

Configured include paths:

- */hashlibrary*
- */fileapplication/include*
- */randomapplication/include*

Example 8-2 for the hash implementation is now managed in its own repository. Every time the code changes, a new version of the hash library can be shipped. That means that the object file compiled for that library has to be copied into the other code, and as long as the API of the hash library does not change, there is nothing more to do.

Example 8-2. Code of the hash library

inc/adlerhash.h

```
#ifndef ADLERHASH_H
#define ADLERHASH_H
/* Returns the hash value of the provided "buffer" of size "length".
   The hash is calculated according to the Adler32 algorithm. */
unsigned int adler32hash(const char* buffer, int length);
#endif
```

adler/adlerhash.c

```
#include "adlerhash.h"

unsigned int adler32hash(const char* buffer, int length)
{
  unsigned int s1=1;
  unsigned int s2=0;
  int i=0;

  for(i=0; i<length; i++)
  {
    s1=(s1+buffer[i]) % 65521;
    s2=(s1+s2) % 65521;
  }
  return (s2<<16) | s1;
}
```

inc/bernsteinhash.h

```
#ifndef BERSTEINHASH_H
#define BERNSTEINHASH_H
/* Returns the hash value of the provided "buffer" of size "length".
   The hash is calculated according to the D.J. Bernstein algorithm. */
```

```
unsigned int bernsteinHash(const char* buffer, int length);
#endif
```

bernstein/bernsteinhash.c

```c
#include "bernsteinhash.h"

unsigned int bernsteinHash(const char* buffer, int length)
{
  unsigned int hash = 5381;
  int i;
  for(i=0; i<length; i++)
  {
    hash = 33 * hash ^ buffer[i];
  }
  return hash;
}
```

This code has the directory structure and include path shown in Figure 8-11. Note that source code regarding the file handling or the pseudorandom number calculation is not part of this codebase anymore. The codebase here is generic and could be used in other contexts as well.

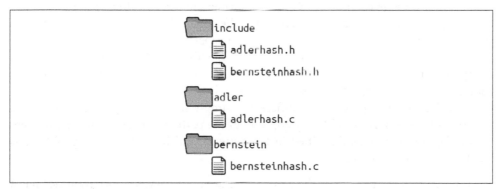

Figure 8-11. File overview

Configured include paths:

- */include*

Starting from a simple hash application, we ended up with this code, which lets you develop and deploy the hash code separately from its application. Going one step further, the two applications could even be split into separate parts, which can be separately deployed.

Organizing the directory structure as proposed in this example is not at all the most important issue in making the code modular. There are many more important issues that are not explicitly addressed in this chapter and in this running example, like code dependencies, which can be addressed by applying the SOLID principles. However, once the dependencies are set in a way that makes the code modular, the directory structure as shown in this example makes it easier to split the ownership of the code and to version and deploy the code independently from other parts of the codebase.

Summary

This chapter presented patterns on how to structure source and header files in order to build large modular C programs.

The Include Guard pattern makes sure header files are not included multiple times. Software-Module Directories suggests putting all files for a software-module into one directory. Global Include Directory suggests having all header files that are used by multiple software-modules in one global directory. For larger programs, Self-Contained Component suggests instead having one global header file directory per component. In order to decouple these components, API Copy suggests copying the header files and build artifacts that are used from other components.

The presented patterns to some extent build on one another. The later patterns in this chapter can be applied more easily if the former ones were already applied. After applying all of the patterns to your codebase, the codebase reaches a high level of flexibility for developing and deploying parts of it separately. However, that flexibility is not always needed and it does not come for free: with each of these patterns, you add complexity to your codebase. For very small codebases in particular, it will not be required to deploy parts of the codebase separately, so it will likely not be necessary to apply API Copy. It might even be sufficient to simply stop after applying Header Files and Include Guard. Do not blindly apply all of the patterns. Instead, only apply them if you face the problems described in the patterns and if solving these problems is worth the additional complexity.

With these patterns as part of the programming vocabulary, a C programmer has a toolbox and step-by-step guidance on how to build modular C programs and organize their files.

Outlook

The next chapter covers an aspect of many large-scale programs: handling multiplatform code. The chapter presents patterns on how to implement code in a way that makes it easier to have a single codebase for multiple processor architectures or multiple operating systems.

CHAPTER 9

Escaping #ifdef Hell

C is widespread, in particular with systems where high-performance or hardware-near programming is required. With hardware-near programming comes the necessity of dealing with hardware variants. Aside from hardware variants, some systems support multiple operating systems or cope with multiple product variants in the code. A commonly used approach to addressing these issues is to use #ifdef statements of the C preprocessor to distinguish variants in the code. The C preprocessor comes with this power, but with this power also comes the responsibility to use it in a well-structured way.

However, that is where the weakness of the C preprocessor with its #ifdef statements shows up. The C preprocessor does not support any methods to enforce rules regarding its usage. That is a pity, because it can very easily be abused. It is very easy to add another hardware variant or another optional feature in the code by adding yet another #ifdef. Also, #ifdef statements can easily be abused to add quick bug fixes that only affect a single variant. That makes the code for different variants more diverse and leads to code that increasingly has to be fixed for each of the variants separately.

Using #ifdef statements in such an unstructured and ad-hoc way is the certain path to hell. The code becomes unreadable and unmaintainable, which all developers should avoid. This chapter presents approaches to escape from such a situation or avoid it altogether.

This chapter gives detailed guidance on how to implement variants, like operating system variants or hardware variants, in C code. It discusses five patterns on how to cope with code variants as well as how to organize or even get rid of #ifdef statements. The patterns can be viewed as an introduction to organizing such code or as a guide on how to refactor unstructured #ifdef code.

Figure 9-1 shows the way out of the #ifdef nightmare, and Table 9-1 provides a short summary of the patterns discussed in this chapter.

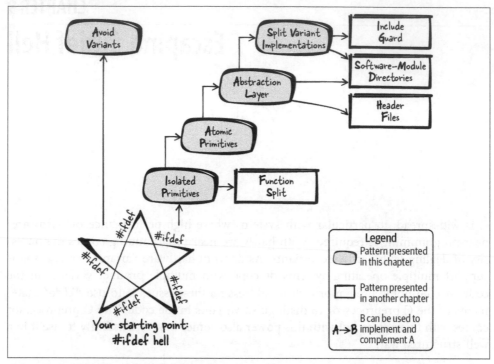

Figure 9-1. The way out of #ifdef hell

Table 9-1. Patterns on how to escape #ifdef hell

Pattern name	Summary
Avoid Variants	Using different functions for each platform makes the code harder to read and write. The programmer is required to initially understand, correctly use, and test these multiple functions in order to achieve a single functionality across multiple platforms. Therefore, use standardized functions that are available on all platforms. If there are no standardized functions, consider not implementing the functionality.
Isolated Primitives	Having code variants organized with #ifdef statements makes the code unreadable. It is very difficult to follow the program flow, because it is implemented multiple times for multiple platforms. Therefore, isolate your code variants. In your implementation file, put the code handling the variants into separate functions and call these functions from your main program logic, which then contains only platform-independent code.
Atomic Primitives	The function that contains the variants and is called by the main program is still hard to comprehend because all the complex #ifdef code was only put into this function in order to get rid of it in the main program. Therefore, make your primitives atomic. Only handle exactly one kind of variant per function. If you handle multiple kinds of variants—for example, operating system variants and hardware variants—then have separate functions for each.

Pattern name	Summary
Abstraction Layer	You want to use the functionality that handles platform variants at several places in your codebase, but you do not want to duplicate the code of that functionality. Therefore, provide an API for each functionality that requires platform-specific code. Define only platform-independent functions in the header file and put all platform-specific #ifdef code into the implementation file. The caller of your functions includes only your header file and does not have to include any platform-specific files.
Split Variant Implementations	The platform-specific implementations still contain #ifdef statements to distinguish between code variants. That makes it difficult to see and select which part of the code should be built for which platform. Therefore, put each variant implementation into a separate implementation file and select per file what you want to compile for which platform.

Running Example

Let's say you want to implement the functionality to write some text into a file to be stored in a newly created directory that, depending on a configuration flag, is either created in the current or in the home-directory. To make things more complicated, your code should run on Windows systems as well as on Linux systems.

Your first attempt is to have one implementation file that contains all the code for all configurations and operating systems. To do that, the file contains many #ifdef statements to distinguish between the code variants:

```c
#include <string.h>
#include <stdio.h>
#include <stdlib.h>
#ifdef __unix__
  #include <sys/stat.h>
  #include <fcntl.h>
  #include <unistd.h>
#elif defined _WIN32
  #include <windows.h>
#endif

int main()
{
  char dirname[50];
  char filename[60];
  char* my_data = "Write this data to the file";
  #ifdef __unix__
    #ifdef STORE_IN_HOME_DIR
      sprintf(dirname, "%s%s", getenv("HOME"), "/newdir/");
      sprintf(filename, "%s%s", dirname, "newfile");
    #elif defined STORE_IN_CWD
      strcpy(dirname, "newdir");
      strcpy(filename, "newdir/newfile");
    #endif
    mkdir(dirname,S_IRWXU);
    int fd = open (filename, O_RDWR | O_CREAT, 0666);
    write(fd, my_data, strlen(my_data));
    close(fd);
```

```
    #elif defined _WIN32
       #ifdef STORE_IN_HOME_DIR
          sprintf(dirname, "%s%s%s", getenv("HOMEDRIVE"), getenv("HOMEPATH"),
                 "\\newdir\\");
          sprintf(filename, "%s%s", dirname, "newfile");
       #elif defined STORE_IN_CWD
          strcpy(dirname, "newdir");
          strcpy(filename, "newdir\\newfile");
       #endif
       CreateDirectory (dirname, NULL);
       HANDLE hFile = CreateFile(filename, GENERIC_WRITE, 0, NULL,
                                 CREATE_NEW, FILE_ATTRIBUTE_NORMAL, NULL);
       WriteFile(hFile, my_data, strlen(my_data), NULL, NULL);
       CloseHandle(hFile);
    #endif
    return 0;
}
```

This code is chaos. The program logic is completely duplicated. This is not operating system-independent code; instead, it is only two different operating system–specific implementations put into one file. In particular, the orthogonal code variants of different operating systems and different places for creating the directory make the code ugly because they lead to nested #ifdef statements, which are very hard to understand. When reading the code, you have to constantly jump between the lines. You have to skip the code from other #ifdef branches in order to follow the program logic. Such duplicated program logic invites programmers to fix errors or to add new features only in the code variant that they currently work on. That causes the code pieces and the behavior for the variants to drift apart, which makes the code hard to maintain.

Where to start? How to clean this mess up? As a first step, if possible, you can use standardized functions in order to Avoid Variants.

Avoid Variants

Context

You write portable code that should be used on multiple operating system platforms or on multiple hardware platforms. Some of the functions you call in your code are available on one platform, but are not available in exactly the same syntax and semantics on another platform. Because of this, you implement code variants—one for each platform. Now you have different pieces of code for your different platforms, and you distinguish between the variants with #ifdef statements in your code.

Problem

Using different functions for each platform makes the code harder to read and write. The programmer is required to initially understand, correctly use, and test these multiple functions in order to achieve a single functionality across multiple platforms.

Quite often it is the aim to implement functionality that should behave exactly the same on all platforms, but when using platform-dependent functions, that aim is more difficult to achieve and might require writing additional code. This is because not only the syntax but also the semantics of the functions might differ slightly between the platforms.

Using multiple functions for multiple platforms makes the code more difficult to write, read, and understand. Distinguishing between the different functions with #ifdef statements makes the code longer and requires the reader to jump across lines to find out what the code does for a single #ifdef branch.

With any piece of code that you have to write, you can ask yourself if it is worth the effort. If the required functionality is not an important one, and if platform-specific functions make it very difficult to implement and support that functionality, then it is an option to not provide that functionality at all.

Solution

Use standardized functions that are available on all platforms. If there are no standardized functions, consider not implementing the functionality.

Good examples of standardized functions that you can use are the C standard library functions and the POSIX functions. Consider which platforms you want to support and check that these standardized functions are available on all your platforms. If possible, such standardized functions should be used instead of more specific platform-dependent functions as shown in the following code:

Caller's code

```
#include <standardizedApi.h>

int main()
{
  /* just a single function is called instead of multiple via
     ifdef distinguished functions */
  somePosixFunction();
  return 0;
}
```

Standardized API

```
    /* this function is available on all operating systems
       that adhere to the POSIX standard */
    somePosixFunction();
```

Again, if no standardized functions exist for what you want, you probably shouldn't implement the requested functionality. If there are only platform-dependent functions available for the functionality you want to implement, then it might not be worth the implementation, testing, and maintenance effort.

However, in some cases you do have to provide functionality in your product even if there are no standardized functions available. That means you have to use different functions across different platforms or maybe even implement features on one platform that are already available on another. To do that in a structured way, have Isolated Primitives for your code variants and hide them behind an Abstraction Layer.

To avoid variants you can, for example, use C standard library file access functions like `fopen` instead of using operating system–specific functions like Linux's `open` or Windows' `CreateFile` functions. As another example, you can use the C standard library time functions. Avoid using operating system–specific time functions like Windows' `GetLocalTime` and Linux's `localtime_r`; use the standardized `localtime` function from *time.h* instead.

Consequences

The code is simple to write and read because a single piece of code can be used for multiple platforms. The programmer does not have to understand different functions for different platforms when writing the code, and they don't have to jump between `#ifdef` branches when reading the code.

Since the same piece of code is being used across all platforms, functionality doesn't differ. But the standardized function might not be the most efficient or high-performance way to achieve the required functionality on each of the platforms. Some platforms might provide other platform-specific functions that, for example, use specialized hardware on that platform to achieve higher performance. These advantages may not be used by the standardized functions.

Known Uses

The following examples show applications of this pattern:

- The code of the VIM text editor uses the operating system–independent functions `fopen`, `fwrite`, `fread`, and `fclose` to access files.

- The OpenSSL code writes the current local time to its log messages. To do that, it converts the current UTC time to local time using the operating system–independent function localtime.

- The OpenSSL function BIO_lookup_ex looks up the node and service to connect to. This function is compiled on Windows and Linux and uses the operating system–independent function htons to convert a value to network byte order.

Applied to Running Example

For your functionality to access files, you are in a lucky position because there are operating system–independent functions available. You now have the following code:

```
#include <string.h>
#include <stdio.h>
#include <stdlib.h>
#ifdef __unix__
  #include <sys/stat.h>
#elif defined _WIN32
  #include <windows.h>
#endif

int main()
{
  char dirname[50];
  char filename[60];
  char* my_data = "Write this data to the file";
  #ifdef __unix__
    #ifdef STORE_IN_HOME_DIR
      sprintf(dirname, "%s%s", getenv("HOME"), "/newdir/");
      sprintf(filename, "%s%s", dirname, "newfile");
    #elif defined STORE_IN_CWD
      strcpy(dirname, "newdir");
      strcpy(filename, "newdir/newfile");
    #endif
    mkdir(dirname,S_IRWXU);
  #elif defined _WIN32
    #ifdef STORE_IN_HOME_DIR
      sprintf(dirname, "%s%s%s", getenv("HOMEDRIVE"), getenv("HOMEPATH"),
            "\\newdir\\");
      sprintf(filename, "%s%s", dirname, "newfile");
    #elif defined STORE_IN_CWD
      strcpy(dirname, "newdir");
      strcpy(filename, "newdir\\newfile");
    #endif
    CreateDirectory(dirname, NULL);
  #endif
  FILE* f = fopen(filename, "w+"); ❶
  fwrite(my_data, 1, strlen(my_data), f);
  fclose(f);
```

```
    return 0;
}
```

❶   The functions fopen, fwrite, and fclose are part of the C standard library and
    are available on Windows as well as on Linux.

The standardized file-related function calls in that code made things a lot simpler
already. Instead of having the separate file access calls for Windows and for Linux,
you now have one common code. The common code ensures that the calls perform
the same functionality for both operating systems, and there is no danger that two
different implementations run apart after bug fixes or added features.

However, because your code is still dominated by #ifdefs, it is very difficult to read.
Therefore, make sure that your main program logic does not get obfuscated by code
variants. Have Isolated Primitives separating the code variants from the main program logic.

Isolated Primitives

Context

Your code calls platform-specific functions. You have different pieces of code for different platforms, and you distinguish between the code variants with #ifdef statements. You cannot simply Avoid Variants because there are no standardized
functions available that provide the feature you need in a uniform way on all your
platforms.

Problem

**Having code variants organized with #ifdef statements makes the code unread-
able. It is very difficult to follow the program flow, because it is implemented multiple times for multiple platforms.**

When trying to understand the code, you usually focus on only one platform, but the
#ifdefs force you to jump between the lines in the code to find the code variant you
are interested in.

The #ifdef statements also make the code difficult to maintain. Such statements
invite programmers to only fix the code for the one platform they are interested in
and to not touch any other code because of the danger of breaking it. But only fixing
a bug or introducing a new feature for one platform means that the behavior of the
code on the other platforms drifts apart. The alternative—to fix such a bug on all platforms in different ways—requires testing the code on all platforms.

Testing code with many code variants is difficult. Each new kind of #ifdef statement doubles the testing effort because all possible combinations have to be tested. Even worse, each such statement doubles the number of binaries that can be built and have to be tested. That brings in a logistic problem because build times increase and the number of binaries provided to the test department and to the customer increases.

Solution

Isolate your code variants. In your implementation file, put the code handling the variants into separate functions and call these functions from your main program logic, which then only contains platform-independent code.

Each of your functions should either only contain program logic or only cope with handling variants. None of your functions should do both. So either there is no #ifdef statement at all in a function, or there are #ifdef statements with a single variant-dependent function call per #ifdef branch. Such a variant could be a software feature that is turned on or off by a build configuration, or it could be a platform variant as shown in the following code:

```
void handlePlatformVariants()
{
  #ifdef PLATFORM_A
    /* call function of platform A */
  #elif defined PLATFORM_B ❶
    /* call function of platform B */
  #endif
}

int main()
{
  /* program logic goes here */
  handlePlatformVariants();
  /* program logic continues */
}
```

❶ Similar to else if statements, mutually exclusive variants can be expressed nicely using #elif.

Utilizing a single function call per #ifdef branch should make it possible to find a good abstraction granularity for the functions handling the variants. Usually the granularity is exactly at the level of the available platform-specific or feature-specific functions to be wrapped.

If the functions that handle the variants are still complicated and contain #ifdef cascades (nested #ifdef statements), it helps to make sure you only have Atomic Variants.

Consequences

The main program logic is now easy to follow, because the code variants are separated from it. When reading the main code, it is no longer necessary to jump between the lines to find out what the code does on one specific platform.

To determine what the code does on one specific platform, you have to look at the called function that implements this variant. Having that code in a separately called function has the advantage that it can be called from other places in the file, and thus code duplications can be avoided. If the functionality is also required in other implementation files, then an Abstraction Layer has to be implemented.

No program logic should be introduced in the functions handling the variants, so it is easier to pinpoint bugs that do not occur on all platforms, because it is easy to identify the places in the code where the behavior of the platforms differs.

Code duplication becomes less of an issue since the main program logic is well separated from the variant implementations. There is no temptation to duplicate the program logic anymore, so there is no threat of then accidentally only making bug fixes in one of these duplications.

Known Uses

The following examples show applications of this pattern:

- The code of the VIM text editor isolates the function `htonl2` that converts data to network byte order. The program logic of VIM defines `htonl2` as a macro in the implementation file. The macro is compiled differently depending on the platform endianness.

- The OpenSSL function `BIO_ADDR_make` copies socket information into an internal `struct`. The function uses `#ifdef` statements to handle operating system–specific and feature-specific variants distinguishing between Linux/Windows and IPv4/IPv6. The function isolates these variants from the main program logic.

- The function `load_rcfile` of GNUplot reads data from an initialization file and isolates operating system–specific file access operations from the rest of the code.

Applied to Running Example

Now that you have Isolated Primitives, your main program logic is a lot easier to read and doesn't require the reader to jump between the lines to keep the variants apart:

```
void getDirectoryName(char* dirname)
{
  #ifdef __unix__
    #ifdef STORE_IN_HOME_DIR
      sprintf(dirname, "%s%s", getenv("HOME"), "/newdir/");
```

```
    #elif defined STORE_IN_CWD
      strcpy(dirname, "newdir/");
    #endif
  #elif defined _WIN32
    #ifdef STORE_IN_HOME_DIR
      sprintf(dirname, "%s%s%s", getenv("HOMEDRIVE"), getenv("HOMEPATH"),
              "\\newdir\\");
    #elif defined STORE_IN_CWD
      strcpy(dirname, "newdir\\");
    #endif
  #endif
}

void createNewDirectory(char* dirname)
{
  #ifdef __unix__
    mkdir(dirname,S_IRWXU);
  #elif defined _WIN32
    CreateDirectory (dirname, NULL);
  #endif
}

int main()
{
  char dirname[50];
  char filename[60];
  char* my_data = "Write this data to the file";
  getDirectoryName(dirname);
  createNewDirectory(dirname);
  sprintf(filename, "%s%s", dirname, "newfile");
  FILE* f = fopen(filename, "w+");
  fwrite(my_data, 1, strlen(my_data), f);
  fclose(f);
  return 0;
}
```

The code variants are now well isolated. The program logic of the main function is very easy to read and understand without the variants. However, the new function getDirectoryName is still dominated by #ifdefs and is not easy to comprehend. It may help to only have Atomic Primitives.

Atomic Primitives

Context

You implemented variants in your code with #ifdef statements, and you put these variants into separate functions in order to have Isolated Primitives that handle these variants. The primitives separate the variants from the main program flow, which makes the main program well structured and easy to comprehend.

Problem

The function that contains the variants and is called by the main program is still hard to comprehend because all the complex #ifdef code was only put into this function in order to get rid of it in the main program.

Handling all kinds of variants in one function becomes difficult as soon as there are many different variants to handle. If, for example, a single function uses #ifdef statements to distinguish between different hardware types and operating systems, then adding an additional operating system variant becomes difficult because it has to be added for all hardware variants. Each variant cannot be handled in one place anymore; instead, the effort multiplies with the number of different variants. That is a problem. It should be easy to add new variants at one place in the code.

Solution

Make your primitives atomic. Only handle exactly one kind of variant per function. If you handle multiple kinds of variants—for example, operating system variants and hardware variants—then have separate functions for each.

Let one of these functions call another that already abstracts one kind of variant. If you abstract a platform-dependence and a feature-dependence, then let the feature-dependent function be the one calling the platform-dependent function, because you usually provide features across all platforms. Therefore, platform-dependent functions should be the most atomic functions, as shown in the following code:

```
void handleHardwareOfFeatureX()
{
  #ifdef HARDWARE_A
   /* call function for feature X on hardware A */
  #elif defined HARDWARE_B || defined HARDWARE_C
   /* call function for feature X on hardware B and C */
  #endif
}

void handleHardwareOfFeatureY()
{
  #ifdef HARDWARE_A
   /* call function for feature Y on hardware A */
  #elif defined HARDWARE_B
   /* call function for feature Y on hardware B */
  #elif defined HARDWARE_C
   /* call function for feature Y on hardware C */
  #endif
}

void callFeature()
{
  #ifdef FEATURE_X
```

```
      handleHardwareOfFeatureX();
   #elif defined FEATURE_Y
      handleHardwareOfFeatureY();
   #endif
}
```

If there is a function that clearly has to provide a functionality across multiple kinds of variants as well as handle all these kinds of variants, then the function scope might be wrong. Perhaps the function is too general or does more than one thing. Split the function as suggested by the Function Split pattern.

Call Atomic Primitives in your main code containing the program logic. If you want to use the Atomic Primitives in other implementation files with a well-defined interface, then use an Abstraction Layer.

Consequences

Each function now only handles one kind of variant. That makes each of the functions easy to understand because there are no more cascades of #ifdef statements. Each of the functions now only abstracts one kind of variant and does no more than exactly that one thing. So the functions follow the single-responsibility principle.

Having no #ifdef cascades makes it less tempting for programmers to simply handle one additional kind of variant in one function, because starting an #ifdef cascade is less likely than extending an existing cascade.

With separate functions, each kind of variant can easily be extended for an additional variant. To achieve this, only one #ifdef branch has to be added in one function, and the functions which handle other kinds of variants do not have to be touched.

Known Uses

The following examples show applications of this pattern:

- The OpenSSL implementation file *threads_pthread.c* contains functions for thread handling. There are separate functions to abstract operating systems and separate functions to abstract whether pthreads are available at all.

- The code of SQLite contains functions to abstract operating system–specific file access (for example, the fileStat function). The code abstracts file access–related compile-time features with other separate functions.

- The Linux function boot_jump_linux calls another function that performs different boot actions depending on the CPU architecture that is handled via #ifdef statements in that function. Then the function boot_jump_linux calls another function that uses #ifdef statements to select which configured resources (USB, network, etc.) have to be cleaned up.

Applied to Running Example

With Atomic Primitives you now have the following code for your functions to determine the directory path:

```
void getHomeDirectory(char* dirname)
{
  #ifdef __unix__
    sprintf(dirname, "%s%s", getenv("HOME"), "/newdir/");
  #elif defined _WIN32
    sprintf(dirname, "%s%s%s", getenv("HOMEDRIVE"), getenv("HOMEPATH"),
            "\\newdir\\");
  #endif
}

void getWorkingDirectory(char* dirname)
{
  #ifdef __unix__
    strcpy(dirname, "newdir/");
  #elif defined _WIN32
    strcpy(dirname, "newdir\\");
  #endif
}

void getDirectoryName(char* dirname)
{
  #ifdef STORE_IN_HOME_DIR
    getHomeDirectory(dirname);
  #elif defined STORE_IN_CWD
    getWorkingDirectory(dirname);
  #endif
}
```

The code variants are now very well isolated. To obtain the directory name, instead of having one complicated function with many #ifdefs, you now have several functions that only have one #ifdef each. That makes it a lot easier to understand the code because now each of these functions only performs one thing instead of distinguishing between several kinds of variants with #ifdef cascades.

The functions are now very simple and easy to read, but your implementation file is still very long. In addition, one implementation file contains the main program logic as well as code to distinguish between variants. This makes parallel development or separate testing of the variant code next to impossible.

To improve things, split the implementation file up into variant-dependent and variant-independent files. To do that, create an Abstraction Layer.

Abstraction Layer

Context

You have platform variants that are distinguished with #ifdef statements in your code. You may have Isolated Primitives to separate the variants from the program logic and made sure that you have Atomic Primitives.

Problem

You want to use the functionality which handles platform variants at several places in your codebase, but you do not want to duplicate the code of that functionality.

Your callers might be used to work directly with platform-specific functions, but you don't want that anymore because each of the callers has to implement platform variants on their own. Generally, callers should not have to cope with platform variants. In the callers' code, it should not be necessary to know anything about implementation details for the different platforms, and the callers should not have to use any #ifdef statements or include any platform-specific header files.

You are even considering working with different programmers (not the ones responsible for the platform-independent code) to separately develop and test the platform-dependent code.

You want to be able to change the platform-specific code later on without requiring the caller of this code to care about this change. If programmers of the platform-dependent code perform a bug fix for one platform or if they add an additional platform, then this must not require changes to the caller's code.

Solution

Provide an API for each functionality that requires platform-specific code. Define only platform-independent functions in the header file and put all platform-specific #ifdef code into the implementation file. The caller of your functions only includes your header file and does not have to include any platform-specific files.

Try to design a stable API for the abstraction layer, because changing the API later on requires changes in your caller's code and sometimes that is not possible. However, it is very difficult to design a stable API. For platform abstractions, try looking around at different platforms, even ones you don't yet support. After you have a sense of how they work and what the differences are, you can create an API to abstract features for these platforms. That way, you won't need to change the API later, even when you're adding support for different platforms.

Make sure to document the API thoroughly. Add comments to each function describing what the function does. Also, describe on which platforms the functions are supported if that is not clearly defined elsewhere for your whole codebase.

The following code shows a simple Abstraction Layer:

caller.c

```
#include "someFeature.h"

int main()
{
  someFeature();
  return 0;
}
```

someFeature.h

```
/* Provides generic access to someFeature.
   Supported on platform A and platform B. */
void someFeature();
```

someFeature.c

```
void someFeature()
{
  #ifdef PLATFORM_A
    performFeaturePlatformA();
  #elif defined PLATFORM_B
    performFeaturePlatformB();
  #endif
}
```

Consequences

The abstracted features can be used from anywhere in the code and not only from one single implementation file. In other words, now you have distinct roles of caller and callee. The callee has to cope with platform variants, and the caller can be platform independent.

The benefit to this setup is the caller does not have to cope with platform-specific code. The caller simply includes the provided header file and does not have to include any platform-specific header files. The downside is the caller cannot directly use all platform-specific functions anymore. If the caller is accustomed to these functions, then the caller might not be satisfied with using the abstracted functionality and may find it difficult to use or suboptimal in functionality.

The platform-specific code can now be developed and even tested separately from the other code. Now the testing effort is manageable, even with many platforms, because you can mock the hardware-specific code in order to write simple tests for the platform-independent code.

When building up such APIs for all platform-specific functions, the sum of these functions and APIs is the platform abstraction layer for the codebase. With a platform abstraction layer, it is very clear which code is platform dependent and which is platform independent. A platform abstraction layer also makes it clear which parts of the code have to be touched in order to support an additional platform.

Known Uses

The following examples show applications of this pattern:

- Most larger-scale code that runs on multiple platforms has a hardware Abstraction Layer. For example, Nokia's Maemo platform has such an Abstraction Layer to abstract which actual device drivers are loaded.

- The function `sock_addr_inet_pton` of the lighttpd web server converts an IP address from text to binary form. The implementation uses `#ifdef` statements to distinguish between code variants for IPv4 and IPv6. Callers of the API do not see this distinction.

- The function `getprogname` of the gzip data compression program returns the name of the invoking program. The way to obtain this name depends on the operating system and is distinguished via `#ifdef` statements in the implementation. The caller does not have to care on which operating system the function is called.

- A hardware abstraction is used for the Time-Triggered Ethernet protocol described in the bachelor's thesis "Hardware-Abstraction of an Open Source Real-Time Ethernet Stack—Design, Realisation and Evaluation" (*https://oreil.ly/hs0Jh*) by Flemming Bunzel. The hardware abstraction layer contains functions for accessing interrupts and timers. The functions are marked as `inline` to not lose performance.

Applied to Running Example

Now you have a much more streamlined piece of code. Each of the functions only performs one action, and you hide implementation details about the variants behind APIs:

directoryNames.h

```
/* Copies the path to a new directory with name "newdir"
   located in the user's home directory into "dirname".
   Works on Linux and Windows. */
void getHomeDirectory(char* dirname);
```

```
/* Copies the path to a new directory with name "newdir"
   located in the current working directory into "dirname".
   Works on Linux and Windows. */
void getWorkingDirectory(char* dirname);
```

directoryNames.c

```
#include "directoryNames.h"
#include <stdio.h>
#include <stdlib.h>
#include <string.h>

void getHomeDirectory(char* dirname)
{
  #ifdef __unix__
    sprintf(dirname, "%s%s", getenv("HOME"), "/newdir/");
  #elif defined _WIN32
    sprintf(dirname, "%s%s%s", getenv("HOMEDRIVE"), getenv("HOMEPATH"),
            "\\newdir\\");
  #endif
}

void getWorkingDirectory(char* dirname)
{
  #ifdef __unix__
    strcpy(dirname, "newdir/");
  #elif defined _WIN32
    strcpy(dirname, "newdir\\");
  #endif
}
```

directorySelection.h

```
/* Copies the path to a new directory with name "newdir" into "dirname".
   The directory is located in the user's home directory, if STORE_IN_HOME_DIR
   is set or it is located in the current working directory, if STORE_IN_CWD
   is set. */
void getDirectoryName(char* dirname);
```

directorySelection.c

```
#include "directorySelection.h"
#include "directoryNames.h"

void getDirectoryName(char* dirname)
{
  #ifdef STORE_IN_HOME_DIR
    getHomeDirectory(dirname);
  #elif defined STORE_IN_CWD
```

```
      getWorkingDirectory(dirname);
    #endif
}
```

directoryHandling.h

```
/* Creates a new directory of the provided name ("dirname").
   Works on Linux and Windows. */
void createNewDirectory(char* dirname);
```

directoryHandling.c

```
#include "directoryHandling.h"
#ifdef __unix__
  #include <sys/stat.h>
#elif defined _WIN32
  #include <windows.h>
#endif

void createNewDirectory(char* dirname)
{
  #ifdef __unix__
    mkdir(dirname,S_IRWXU);
  #elif defined _WIN32
    CreateDirectory (dirname, NULL);
  #endif
}
```

main.c

```
#include <stdio.h>
#include <string.h>
#include "directorySelection.h"
#include "directoryHandling.h"

int main()
{
  char dirname[50];
  char filename[60];
  char* my_data = "Write this data to the file";
  getDirectoryName(dirname);
  createNewDirectory(dirname);
  sprintf(filename, "%s%s", dirname, "newfile");
  FILE* f = fopen(filename, "w+");
  fwrite(my_data, 1, strlen(my_data), f);
  fclose(f);
  return 0;
}
```

Your file with the main program logic is finally completely independent from the operating system; operating system–specific header files are not even included here. Separating the implementation files with an Abstraction Layer makes the files easier to comprehend and makes it possible to reuse the functions in other parts of the code. Also, development, maintenance, and testing can be split for the platform-dependent and platform-independent code.

If you have Isolated Primitives behind an Abstraction Layer and you've organized them according to the kind of variant that they abstract, then you'll end up with a hardware abstraction layer or operating system abstraction layer. Now that you have a lot more code files than before—particularly those handling different variants—you may want to consider structuring them into Software-Module Directories.

The code that uses the API of the Abstraction Layer is very clean now, but the implementations below that API still contain `#ifdef` code for different variants. This has the disadvantage that these implementations have to be touched and will grow if, for example, additional operating systems have to be supported. To avoid touching existing implementation files when adding another variant, you could Split Variant Implementations.

Split Variant Implementations

Context

You have platform variants hidden behind an Abstraction Layer. In the platform-specific implementation, you distinguish between the code variants with `#ifdef` statements.

Problem

The platform-specific implementations still contain #ifdef statements to distinguish between code variants. That makes it difficult to see and select which part of the code should be built for which platform.

Because code for different platforms is put into a single file, it is not possible to select the platform-specific code on a file-basis. However, that is the approach taken by tools such as Make, which are usually responsible for selecting via Makefiles which files should be compiled in order to come up with variants for different platforms.

When looking at the code from a high-level view, it is not possible to see which parts are platform-specific and which are not, but that would be very desirable when porting the code to another platform, in order to quickly see which code has to be touched.

The open-closed principle says that to bring in new features (or to port to a new platform), it should not be necessary to touch existing code. The code should be open for such modifications. However, having platform variants separated with `#ifdef` statements requires that existing implementations have to be touched when introducing a new platform, because another `#ifdef` branch has to be placed into an existing function.

Solution

Put each variant implementation into a separate implementation file and select per file what you want to compile for which platform.

Related functions of the same platform can still be put into the same file. For example, there could be a file gathering all socket handling functions on Windows and one such file doing the same for Linux.

With separate files for each platform, it is OK to use `#ifdef` statements to determine which code is compiled on a specific platform. For example, a *someFeatureWindows.c* file could have an `#ifdef _WIN32` statement across the whole file similar to Include Guards:

someFeature.h

```
/* Provides generic access to someFeature.
   Supported on platform A and platform B. */
someFeature();
```

someFeatureWindows.c

```
#ifdef _WIN32
  someFeature()
  {
    performWindowsFeature();
  }
#endif
```

someFeatureLinux.c

```
#ifdef __unix__
  someFeature()
  {
    performLinuxFeature();
  }
#endif
```

Alternatively to using `#ifdef` statements across the whole file, other platform-independent mechanisms such as Make can be used to decide on a file-basis which code to compile on a specific platform. If your IDE helps with generating Makefiles, that alternative might be more comfortable for you, but be aware that when changing the IDE, you might have to reconfigure which files to compile on which platform in the new IDE.

With separate files for the platforms comes the question of where to put these files and how to name them:

- One option is to put platform-specific files per software-module next to each other and name them in a way that makes it clear which platform they cover (for example *fileHandlingWindows.c*). Such Software-Module Directories provide the advantage that the implementations of the software-modules are in the same place.

- Another option is to put all platform-specific files from the codebase into one directory and to have one subdirectory for each platform. The advantage of this is that all files for one platform are in the same place and it becomes easier to configure in your IDE which files to compile on which platform.

Consequences

Now it is possible to not have any `#ifdef` statements at all in the code but to instead distinguish between the variants on a file-basis with tools such as Make.

In each implementation file there is now just one code variant, so there is no need to jump between the lines when reading the code in order to only read the `#ifdef` branch you are looking for. It is much easier to read and understand the code.

When fixing a bug on one platform, no files for other platforms have to be touched. When porting to a new platform, only new files have to be added, and no existing file or existing code has to be modified.

It is easy to spot which part of the code is platform-dependent and which code has to be added in order to port to a new platform. Either all platform-specific files are in one directory, or the files are named in a way that makes it clear they are platform-dependent.

However, putting each variant into a separate file creates many new files. The more files you have, the more complex your build procedure gets and the longer the compile time for your code gets. You will need to think about structuring the files, for example, with Software-Module Directories.

Known Uses

The following examples show applications of this pattern:

- The Simple Audio Library presented in the book *Write Portable Code: An Introduction to Developing Software for Multiple Platforms* by Brian Hook (No Starch

Press, 2005) uses separate implementation files to provide access to threads and Mutexes for Linux and OS X. The implementation files use #ifdef statements to ensure that only the correct code for the platform is compiled.

- The Multi-Processing-Module of the Apache web server, which is responsible for handling accesses to the web server, is implemented in separate implementation files for Windows and Linux. The implementation files use #ifdef statements to ensure that only the correct code for the platform is compiled.

- The code of the U-Boot bootloader puts the source code for each hardware platform it supports into a separate directory. Each of these directories contains, among others, the file *cpu.c*, which contains a function to reset the CPU. A Makefile decides which directory (and which *cpu.c* file) has to be compiled—there are no #ifdef statements in these files. The main program logic of U-Boot calls the function to reset the CPU and does not have to care about hardware platform details at that point.

Applied to Running Example

After Splitting Variant Implementations, you'll end up with the following final code for your functionality to create a directory and write data to a file:

directoryNames.h

```
/* Copies the path to a new directory with name "newdir"
   located in the user's home directory into "dirname".
   Works on Linux and Windows. */
void getHomeDirectory(char* dirname);

/* Copies the path to a new directory with name "newdir"
   located in the current working directory into "dirname".
   Works on Linux and Windows. */
void getWorkingDirectory(char* dirname);
```

directoryNamesLinux.c

```
#ifdef __unix__
  #include "directoryNames.h"
  #include <string.h>
  #include <stdio.h>
  #include <stdlib.h>

  void getHomeDirectory(char* dirname)
  {
    sprintf(dirname, "%s%s", getenv("HOME"), "/newdir/");
  }

  void getWorkingDirectory(char* dirname)
  {
```

```
        strcpy(dirname, "newdir/");
    }
#endif
```

directoryNamesWindows.c

```c
#ifdef _WIN32
  #include "directoryNames.h"
  #include <string.h>
  #include <stdio.h>
  #include <windows.h>

  void getHomeDirectory(char* dirname)
  {
    sprintf(dirname, "%s%s%s", getenv("HOMEDRIVE"), getenv("HOMEPATH"),
        "\\newdir\\");
  }

  void getWorkingDirectory(char* dirname)
  {
    strcpy(dirname, "newdir\\");
  }
#endif
```

directorySelection.h

```c
/* Copies the path to a new directory with name "newdir" into "dirname".
   The directory is located in the user's home directory, if STORE_IN_HOME_DIR
   is set or it is located in the current working directory, if STORE_IN_CWD
   is set. */
void getDirectoryName(char* dirname);
```

directorySelectionHomeDir.c

```c
#ifdef STORE_IN_HOME_DIR
  #include "directorySelection.h"
  #include "directoryNames.h"

  void getDirectoryName(char* dirname)
  {
    getHomeDirectory(dirname);
  }
#endif
```

directorySelectionWorkingDir.c

```c
#ifdef STORE_IN_CWD
  #include "directorySelection.h"
  #include "directoryNames.h"

  void getDirectoryName(char* dirname)
  {
```

```
      return getWorkingDirectory(dirname);
    }
  #endif
```

directoryHandling.h

```
/* Creates a new directory of the provided name ("dirname").
   Works on Linux and Windows. */
void createNewDirectory(char* dirname);
```

directoryHandlingLinux.c

```
#ifdef __unix__
  #include <sys/stat.h>

  void createNewDirectory(char* dirname)
  {
    mkdir(dirname,S_IRWXU);
  }
#endif
```

directoryHandlingWindows.c

```
#ifdef _WIN32
  #include <windows.h>

  void createNewDirectory(char* dirname)
  {
    CreateDirectory(dirname, NULL);
  }
#endif
```

main.c

```
#include "directorySelection.h"
#include "directoryHandling.h"
#include <string.h>
#include <stdio.h>

int main()
{
  char dirname[50];
  char filename[60];
  char* my_data = "Write this data to the file";
  getDirectoryName(dirname);
  createNewDirectory(dirname);
  sprintf(filename, "%s%s", dirname, "newfile");
  FILE* f = fopen(filename, "w+");
  fwrite(my_data, 1, strlen(my_data), f);
  fclose(f);
```

```
    return 0;
}
```

There are still #ifdef statements present in this code. Each of the implementation files has one huge #ifdef in order to make sure that the correct code is compiled for each platform and variant. Alternatively, the decision regarding which files should be compiled could be put into a Makefile. That would get rid of the #ifdefs, but you'd simply use another mechanism to chose between variants. Deciding which mechanism to use is not so important. It is much more important, as described throughout this chapter, to isolate and abstract the variants.

While the code files would look cleaner when using other mechanisms to handle the variants, the complexity would still be there. Putting the complexity into Makefiles can be a good idea because the purpose of Makefiles is to decide which files to build. In other situations, it's better to use #ifdef statements. For example, if you're building operating system–specific code, maybe a proprietary IDE for Windows and another IDE for Linux is used to decide which files to build. In that circumstance, using the solution with #ifdef statements in the code is much cleaner; configuring which files should be built for which operating system is only done once by the #ifdef statements, and there is no need to touch that when changing to another IDE.

The final code of the running example showed very clearly how code with operating system–specific variants or other variants can be improved step by step. Compared to the first code example, this final piece of code is readable and can easily be extended with additional features or ported to additional operating systems without touching any of the existing code.

Summary

This chapter presented patterns on how to handle variants, like hardware or operating system variants, in C code and how to organize and get rid of #ifdef statements.

The Avoid Variants pattern suggests using standardized functions instead of self-implemented variants. This pattern should be applied anytime it is applicable, because it resolves issues with code variants in one blow. However, there is not always a standardized function available, and in such cases, programmers have to implement their own function to abstract the variant. As a start, Isolated Primitives suggests putting variants into separate functions, and Atomic Primitives suggests only handling one kind of variant in such functions. Abstraction Layer takes the additional step to hide the implementations of the primitives behind an API. Split Variant Implementations suggests putting each variant into a separate implementation file.

With these patterns as part of the programming vocabulary, a C programmer has a toolbox and step-by-step guidance on how to tackle C code variants in order to structure code and escape from #ifdef hell.

For experienced programmers, some of the patterns might look like obvious solutions and that is a good thing. One of the tasks of patterns is to educate people on how to do the right thing; once they know how to do the right thing, the patterns are not necessary anymore because people then intuitively do as suggested by the patterns.

Further Reading

If you're ready for more, here are some resources that can help you further your knowledge of platform and variant abstractions.

- The book *Write Portable Code: An Introduction to Developing Software for Multiple Platforms* by Brian Hook (No Starch Press, 2005) describes how to write portable code in C. The book covers operating system variants and hardware variants by giving advice for specific situations, like coping with byte ordering, data type sizes, or line-separator tokens.

- The article "#ifdef Considered Harmful" (*https://oreil.ly/eZ2CW*) by Henry Spencer and Geoff Collyer is one of the first that skeptically discusses the use of #ifdef statements. The article elaborates on problems that arise when using them in an unstructured way and provides alternatives.

- The article "Writing Portable Code" (*https://oreil.ly/XkTbj*) by Didier Malenfant describes how to structure portable code and which functionality should be put below an abstraction layer.

Outlook

You are now equipped with more patterns. Next, you'll learn how to apply these patterns as well as the patterns from the previous chapters. The next chapters cover larger code examples that show the application of all these patterns.

Pattern Stories

Telling stories is an inherent and natural way to convey information. In the world of patterns, it is sometimes difficult to see how the described patterns can be applied in a real-world context. To show an example of such pattern application, this second part of the book tells you stories of applying the C programming patterns from the first part of the book to implement larger programs. You'll learn how to build such programs bit by bit, and you'll see how the patterns make your life easier by providing you with guidance on good design decisions.

CHAPTER 10

Implementing Logging Functionality

Choosing the right patterns in the right situations helps a lot when designing software. But sometimes it is difficult to find the right pattern and to decide when to apply it. You can find guidance for that in the context and problem sections of the patterns from Part I of this book. But usually it is much easier to understand how to do something by looking at a concrete example.

This chapter tells the story of applying the patterns from Part I of this book to a running example that was abstracted from an industrial-strength implementation of a logging system. To keep the example code easy to grasp, not all aspects of the original industrial-strength code are covered. For example, the code design does not focus on performance or testability aspects. Still, the example nicely shows how to build a logging system piece by piece by applying patterns.

The Pattern Story

Imagine you have a C program out in the field that you have to maintain. If an error occurs, you get into your car, drive to the customer, and debug the program. This works fine until your customer moves to another city. The car ride now takes several hours, which is not at all satisfactory.

You'd prefer to solve the problem from your desk to save both time and nerves. In some instances, you can utilize remote debugging. In other instances, you need detailed data about the exact software states in which the error occurred, which is very hard to get via a remote connection—especially in instances of sporadic errors.

Perhaps you've already guessed what the solution is to avoiding your long car rides. Your solution is to implement a logging functionality and to ask your customer in case of error to send you the log files containing the debug information. In other words, you want to implement the Log Errors pattern to be able to analyze bugs after they occur, which allows you to more easily fix those bugs without having to reproduce them. While this sounds simple, there are many crucial design decisions you'll need to make to implement logging functionality.

File Organization

To get started, organize the header and implementation files that you expect to need. You already have a large codebase, so you want to clearly separate these files from the rest of your code. How should you organize the files? Should you put all your logging-related files into the same directory? Should you put all the header files of your code into a single directory?

To answer these questions, you search for patterns on organizing files and find them in Chapters 6 and 8. You read through the problem statements of these patterns, and you trust in the knowledge provided in the described solutions. You end up with the following three patterns that nicely address your problems:

Pattern name	Summary
Software-Module Directories	Put header files and implementation files that belong to a tightly coupled functionality into one directory. Name that directory after the functionality that is provided via the header files.
Header Files	Provide function declarations in your API for any functionality you want to provide to your user. Hide any internal functions, internal data, and your function definitions (the implementations) in your implementation file and don't provide this implementation file to the user.
Global Include Directory	Have one global directory in your codebase that contains all software-module APIs. Add this directory to the global include paths in your toolchain.

Create a Software-Module Directory for your implementation files and put the Header File of your logging software-module into the already existing Global Include Directory of your codebase. Having this header file in the Global Include Directory has the advantage that the callers of your code will definitely know which header file they are supposed to use.

Your file structure should appear as shown in Figure 10-1.

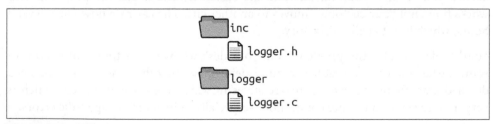

Figure 10-1. File structure

With this file structure, you can put any implementation files that only concern your logging software-module into the *logger* directory. You can put the interface, which can be used from other parts of your program, into the *inc* directory.

Central Logging Function

As a start, implement a central function for error logging that takes custom error texts, adds the current timestamp to the texts, and prints it to the standard output. The timestamp information will make it easier for you to analyze the error texts later on.

Put the function declaration into the *logger.h* file. To protect your header file against multiple inclusion, add an Include Guard. There is no need to store any information in that code or to initialize it; simply implement a Stateless Software-Module. Having a stateless logger brings many benefits: you keep your logging code simple, and things get easier when calling the code in a multithreaded environment.

Pattern name	Summary
Include Guard	Protect the content of your header files against multiple inclusion so that the developer using the header files does not have to care whether it is included multiple times. Use an interlocked `#ifdef` statement or a `#pragma` once statement to achieve this.
Stateless Software-Module	Keep your functions simple and don't build up state information in your implementation. Put all related functions into one header file and provide the caller this interface to your software-module.

logger.h

```
#ifndef LOGGER_H
#define LOGGER_H
void logging(const char* text);
#endif
```

Caller's code

```
logging("Some text to log");
```

To implement the function in your *logger.h* file, call a `printf` to write the timestamp and the text to `stdout`. But what if the caller of your function provides invalid logging input like a `NULL` pointer? Should you check for such invalid input and provide error information to the caller? Adhere to the Samurai Principle, according to which you should not return error information about programming errors.

Pattern name	Summary
Samurai Principle	Return from a function victorious or not at all. If there is a situation for that you know that an error cannot be handled, then abort the program.

Forward the provided text to the `printf` function, and in case of invalid input your program simply crashes, which makes it easy for the caller to find out programming errors regarding invalid input:

logger.c

```
void logging(const char* text)
{
  time_t mytime = time(NULL);
  printf("%s %s\n", ctime(&mytime), text);
}
```

And what if you call the function in the context of a multithreaded program? Can the string provided to the function be changed by other threads, or is it necessary for the string to remain unchanged until the logging function is finished? In the preceding code example, the caller has to provide `text` as input for the `logging` function and is responsible for ensuring that the string is valid until the function returns. So we have a Caller-Owned Buffer here. That behavior has to be documented in the function's interface.

Pattern name	Summary
Caller-Owned Buffer	Require the caller to provide a buffer and its size to the function that returns the large, complex data. In the function implementation, copy the required data into the buffer if the buffer size is large enough.

logger.h

```
/* Prints the current timestamp followed by the provided string to stdout.
   The string must be valid until this function returns. */
void logging(const char* text);
```

Logging Source Filter

Now imagine that every software-module calls the logging function in order to log some information. The output can become quite messy, especially if you have a multithreaded program.

To make it easier to get the information you are looking for, you want to make it possible to configure the code so that it only prints the logging information for configured software-modules. To achieve this, add an additional parameter to your function which identifies the current software-module. Add a function to enable printing output for a software-module. If that function is called, all future logging output for that software-module will be printed:

logger.h

```
/* Prints the current timestamp followed by the provided string to stdout.
   The string must be valid until this function returns. The provided module
   identifies the software-module that calles this function. */
void logging(const char* module, const char* text);
```

```
/* Enables printing output for the provided module. */
bool enableModule(const char* module);
```

Caller's code

```
logging("MY-SOFTWARE-MODULE", "Some text to log");
```

How will you keep track of which software-modules' logging information should be printed? Should you store that state information in a global variable, or is each global variable a code smell? Or in order to avoid global variables, should you pass an additional parameter to all your functions that stores this state information? Should the required memory be allocated throughout the whole lifetime of your program? The answer to these questions involves implementing a Software-Module with Global State using Eternal Memory.

Pattern name	Summary
Software-Module with Global State	Have one global instance to let your related functions share common resources. Put all functions that operate on this instance into one header file and provide the caller this interface to your software-module.
Eternal Memory	Put your data into memory that is available throughout the whole lifetime of your program.

logger.c

```
#define MODULE_SIZE 20
#define LIST_SIZE 10
typedef struct
{
  char module[MODULE_SIZE];
}LIST;
static LIST list[LIST_SIZE];
```

The list in the preceding code example is populated by enabling software-modules with the following function:

logger.c

```
bool enableModule(const char* module)
{
  for(int i=0; i<LIST_SIZE; i++)
  {
    if(strcmp(list[i].module, "") == 0)
    {
      strcpy(list[i].module, module);
      return true;
    }
    if(strcmp(list[i].module, module) == 0)
    {
      return false;
    }
```

```
    }
    return false;
}
```

The preceding code adds the software-module name to the list if a slot in the list is empty and if that name is not already in the list. The caller sees through the Return Value whether an error occurred but does not see which of these errors occurred. You don't Return Status Codes; you only Return Relevant Errors, because there is no relevant scenario in which the caller could react differently to the described error situations. You should also document this behavior in your function definition.

Pattern name	Summary
Return Value	Simply use the one C mechanism intended to retrieve information about the result of a function call: the Return Value. The mechanism to return data in C copies the function result and provides the caller access to this copy.
Return Relevant Errors	Only return error information to the caller if that information is relevant to the caller. Error information is only relevant to the caller if the caller can react to that information.

logger.h

```
/* Enables printing output for the provided module. Returns true on success
   and false on error (no more modules can be enabled or module was already
   enabled). */
bool enableModule(const char* module);
```

Conditional Logging

Now, with the activated software-modules in your list, you can conditionally log information depending on the activated modules, as shown in the following code:

logger.c

```
void logging(const char* module, const char* text)
{
    time_t mytime = time(NULL);
    if(isInList(module))
    {
        printf("%s %s\n", ctime(&mytime), text);
    }
}
```

But how do you implement the `isInList` function? There are several ways to iterate through a list. You could have a Cursor Iterator that provides a `getNext` method to abstract the underlying data structure. But is that necessary here? After all, you only go through an array in your own software-module. Because the iterated data is not carried across API boundaries that might have to be kept compatible, you can apply a much simpler solution here. Index Access directly uses an index to access the elements you want to iterate:

Pattern name	Summary
Index Access	Provide a function that takes an index to address the element in your underlying data structure and return the content of this element. The user calls this function in a loop to iterate over all elements.

logger.c

```c
bool isInList(const char* module)
{
  for(int i=0; i<LIST_SIZE; i++)
  {
    if(strcmp(list[i].module, module) == 0)
    {
      return true;
    }
  }
  return false;
}
```

Now all your code for software-module-specific logging is written. The code simply iterates the data structure by incrementing an index. The same kind of iteration was already used in your `enableModule` function.

Multiple Logging Destinations

Next, you want to provide different destinations for your log entries. Until now, all output is logged to the `stdout`, but you want your caller to be able to configure your code to directly log into a file. Such a configuration is usually done before the action to be logged is started. Start with a function that allows you to configure the logging destination for all future loggings:

logger.h

```c
/* All future log messages will be logged to stdout */
void logToStdout();

/* All future log messages will be logged to a file */
void logToFile();
```

To implement this log destination selection, you could simply have an `if` or `switch` statement to call the right function depending on the configured logging destination. However, each time you add another logging destination, you'd have to touch that piece of code. That is not a good solution according to the open-closed principle. A much better solution is to implement a Dynamic Interface.

Pattern name	Summary
Dynamic Interface	Define a common interface for the deviating functionalities in your API and require the caller to provide a callback function for that functionality which you then call in your function implementation.

logger.c

```c
typedef void (*logDestination)(const char*);
static logDestination fp = stdoutLogging;

void stdoutLogging(const char* buffer)
{
  printf("%s", buffer);
}

void fileLogging(const char* buffer)
{
  /* not yet implemented */
}

void logToStdout()
{
  fp = stdoutLogging;
}

void logToFile()
{
  fp = fileLogging;
}

#define BUFFER_SIZE 100
void logging(const char* module, const char* text)
{
  char buffer[BUFFER_SIZE];
  time_t mytime = time(NULL);
  if(isInList(module))
  {
    sprintf(buffer, "%s %s\n", ctime(&mytime), text);
    fp(buffer);
  }
}
```

A lot changed in the existing code, but now additional log destinations can be added without any changes to the logging function. In the preceding code, the stdoutLogging function is already implemented, but the fileLogging function is still missing.

File Logging

To log to a file, you could simply open and close the file each time you log a message. But that is not very efficient, and if you want to log a lot of information, that approach takes a lot of time. So what alternative do you have? You could simply open the file once and then leave it open. But how do you know when to open the file? And when would you close it?

After reviewing the patterns in this book, you cannot find one that solves your problem. However, a quick Google search will lead you to the pattern that solves your problem: Lazy Acquisition. In the first call to your `fileLogging` function, open the file once and then leave it open. You can store the file descriptor in Eternal Memory.

Pattern name	Summary
Lazy Acquisition	Implicitly initialize the object or data the first time it is used (see *Pattern-Oriented Software Architecture: Volume 3: Patterns for Resource Management* by Michael Kirchner and Prashant Jain [Wiley, 2004])
Eternal Memory	Put your data into memory that is available throughout the whole lifetime of your program.

logger.c

```
void fileLogging(const char* buffer)
{
  static int fd = 0; ❶
  if(fd == 0)
  {
    fd = open("log.txt", O_RDWR | O_CREAT, 0666);
  }
  write(fd, buffer, strlen(buffer));
}
```

❶ Such `static` variables are only initialized once and not each time the function is called.

To keep the code example simple, it does not target thread safety. In order to be thread-safe, the code would have to protect the Lazy Acquisition with a Mutex to make sure that the acquisition only happens once.

What about closing the file? For some applications, like the one in this chapter, not closing the file is a valid option. Imagine that you want to log as long as your application is running, and when you shut the application down, you rely on the operating system to clean up the file that you left open. If you are afraid that the information is not stored in case of a system crash, you could even flush the file content from time to time.

Cross-Platform Files

The code so far implements logging to a file on Linux systems, but you also want to use your code on Windows platforms, for which the current code won't yet work.

To support multiple platforms, you first consider to Avoid Variants so that you only have common code for all platforms. That would be possible for writing files by simply using the `fopen`, `fwrite`, and `fclose` functions, which are available on Linux as well as on Windows systems.

Pattern name	Summary
Avoid Variants	Use standardized functions that are available on all platforms. If there are no standardized functions, consider not implementing the functionality.

However, you want to make your file logging code as efficient as possible and using the platform-specific functions for accessing files is more efficient. But how do you implement platform-specific code? Duplicating your codebase to have one full code version for Windows and one full code version for Linux is not an option because future changes and maintenance of duplicated code can become a nightmare.

You decide to use `#ifdef` statements in your code to differentiate between the platforms. But isn't that a code duplication as well? After all, when you have huge `#ifdef` blocks in your code, all the program logic in these statements is duplicated. How can you avoid code duplication while still supporting multiple platforms?

Again the patterns show you the way. First, define platform-independent interfaces for the functionality that requires the platform-dependent functions. In other words, define an Abstraction Layer.

Pattern name	Summary
Abstraction Layer	Provide an API for each functionality that requires platform-specific code. Define only platform-independent functions in the header file and put all platform-specific `#ifdef` code into the implementation file. The caller of your functions includes only your header file and does not have to include any platform-specific files.

logger.c

```
void fileLogging(const char* buffer)
{
  void* fileDescriptor = initiallyOpenLogFile();
  writeLogFile(fileDescriptor, buffer);
}

/* Opens the logfile at the first call.
   Works on Linux and on Windows systems */
void* initiallyOpenLogFile()
{
  ...
}

/* Writes the provided buffer to the logfile.
   Works on Linux and on Windows systems */
void writeLogFile(void* fileDescriptor, const char* buffer)
{
  ...
}
```

Behind this Abstraction Layer you have Isolated Primitives of your code variants. That means you don't use #ifdef statements across several functions, but you stick to one #ifdef for one function. Should you have an #ifdef statement across the whole function implementation or just across the platform-specific part?

The solution is to have both. You should have Atomic Primitives. The functions should be on a granularity so that they only contain platform-specific code. If they don't, then you can split these functions up further. That is the best way to keep platform-dependent code manageable.

Pattern name	Summary
Isolated Primitives	Isolate your code variants. In your implementation file, put the code handling the variants into separate functions and call these functions from your main program logic, which then contains only platform-independent code.
Atomic Primitives	Make your primitives atomic. Only handle exactly one kind of variant per function. If you handle multiple kinds of variants, for example, operating system variants and hardware variants, then have separate functions for that.

The following code shows the implementations of your Atomic Primitives:

logger.c

```
void* initiallyOpenLogFile()
{
#ifdef __unix__
  static int fd = 0;
  if(fd == 0)
  {
    fd = open("log.txt", O_RDWR | O_CREAT, 0666);
  }
  return fd;
#elif defined _WIN32
  static HANDLE hFile = NULL;
  if(hFile == NULL)
  {
    hFile = CreateFile("log.txt", GENERIC_WRITE, 0, NULL,
                       CREATE_NEW, FILE_ATTRIBUTE_NORMAL, NULL);
  }
  return hFile;
#endif
}

void writeLogFile(void* fileDescriptor, const char* buffer)
{
#ifdef __unix__
  write((int)fileDescriptor, buffer, strlen(buffer));
#elif defined _WIN32
  WriteFile((HANDLE)fileDescriptor, buffer, strlen(buffer), NULL, NULL);
#endif
}
```

The preceding code doesn't look great. But then again, any platform-dependent code rarely looks nice. Is there anything else you can do to make that code easier to read and maintain? A possible approach to improve things is to Split Variant Implementations into separate files.

Pattern name	Summary
Split Variant Implementations	Put each variant implementation into a separate implementation file and select per file what you want to compile for which platform.

fileLinux.c

```
#ifdef __unix__
void* initiallyOpenLogFile()
{
  static int fd = 0;
  if(fd == 0)
  {
    fd = open("log.txt", O_RDWR | O_CREAT, 0666);
  }
  return fd;
}

void writeLogFile(void* fileDescriptor, const char* buffer)
{
  write((int)fileDescriptor, buffer, strlen(buffer));
}
#endif
```

fileWindows.c

```
#ifdef _WIN32
void* initiallyOpenLogFile()
{
  static HANDLE hFile = NULL;
  if(hFile == NULL)
  {
    hFile = CreateFile("log.txt", GENERIC_WRITE, 0, NULL,
                       CREATE_NEW, FILE_ATTRIBUTE_NORMAL, NULL);
  }
  return hFile;
}

void writeLogFile(void* fileDescriptor, const char* buffer)
{
  WriteFile((HANDLE)fileDescriptor, buffer, strlen(buffer), NULL, NULL);
}
#endif
```

Both of the shown code files are a lot easier to read compared to the code where Linux and Windows code is mixed within a single function. Also, instead of conditionally compiling the code on a platform via #ifdef statements, it is now possible to eliminate all #ifdef statements and to use Makefiles to select which files to compile.

Using the Logger

With these final changes to your logging functionality, your code can now log messages for configured software-modules to stdout or to cross-platform files. The following code shows how to use the logging functionality:

```
enableModule("MYMODULE");
logging("MYMODULE", "Log to stdout");
logToFile();
logging("MYMODULE", "Log to file");
logging("MYMODULE", "Log to file some more");
```

After you finish making all these coding decisions and then implementing them, you are very relieved. You take your hands off the keyboard and look at the code in admiration. You are astonished at how some of your initial questions that seemed difficult to you were easily resolved by the patterns. The benefit to utilizing the patterns is that they remove the burden of making hundreds of decisions by yourself.

The long car rides to fix bugs on site are in the past. Now you simply get the debug information that you need via the log files. That makes your customer happy, because they get quicker bug fixes. More importantly, it makes your own life better. You can provide more professional software, and you now have the time to get home from work early.

Summary

You constructed the code for this logging functionality step by step by applying the patterns presented in Part I in order to solve one problem after another. At the start you had many questions on how to organize the files or how to cope with error handling. The patterns showed you the way. They gave you guidance and made it easier to construct this piece of code. They also provide understanding as to why the code looks and behaves the way it does. Figure 10-2 shows an overview of the decisions that the patterns helped you make.

There are, of course, still a lot of potential feature improvements for your code. The code, for example, doesn't handle maximum file sizes or rotation of logfiles, and doesn't support configuration of a log level to skip very detailed logging. To keep things simple and easier to grasp, these features are not covered but could be added to the code examples.

The next chapter will tell another story on how to apply the patterns to build another larger industrial-strength piece of code.

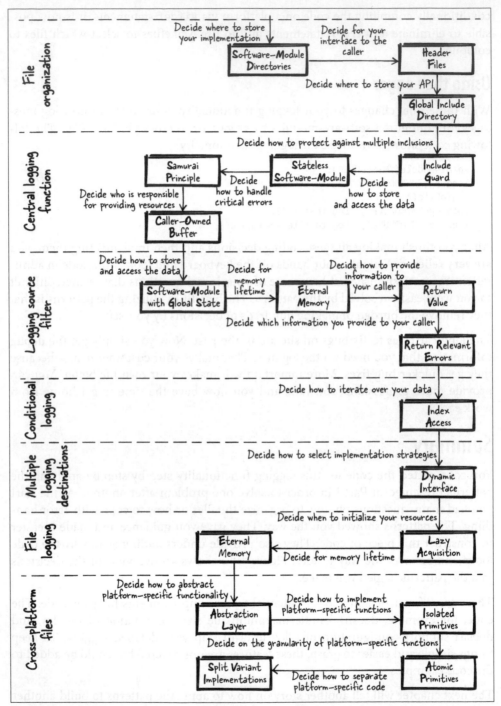

Figure 10-2. The patterns applied throughout this story

CHAPTER 11

Building a User Management System

This chapter tells the story of applying the patterns from Part I of this book to a running example. With that example, it illustrates how design choices made with the aid of patterns provide benefits and support for programmers. This chapter's running example is abstracted from an industrial-strength implementation of a user management system.

The Pattern Story

Imagine you are fresh from university and start working for a software development company. Your boss hands you a product specification for a piece of software that stores usernames and passwords and tells you to implement it. The software should provide functionality to check whether a provided password for a user is correct and functionality to create, delete, and view existing users.

You are eager to show your boss that you are a good programmer, but before you even start, your mind fills with questions. Should you write all code into a single file? You know from your studies that this is bad practice, but what's a good number of files? Which parts of the code will you put into the same files? Should you check the input parameters for each function? Should your functions return detailed error information? At university you learned how to build a software program that works, but you did not learn how to write good code that is maintainable. So what should you do? How do you start?

Data Organization

To answer your questions, start by reviewing the patterns in this book to get guidance on how to build good C programs. Begin with the part of your system that stores the usernames and passwords. Your questions should now focus on how to store the data in your program. Should you store it in global variables? Should you hold the data in local variables inside a function? Should you allocate dynamic memory?

First, consider the exact problem that you want to solve in your application: you are not sure how to store the username data. Currently, there is no need to make this data persistent; you simply want to be able to build up and access this data at runtime. Also, you don't want the caller of your functions to have to cope with explicit allocation and initialization of the data.

Next, look for patterns that address your specific problem. Review the C patterns on data lifetime and ownership from Chapter 5, which addresses the issue of who is responsible of holding which data. Read through all the problem sections of these patterns and find one pattern that matches your problem very well and describes consequences which are acceptable to you. That pattern is the Software-Module with Global State pattern, which suggests having Eternal Memory in the form of global variables with scope limited to the file in order for that data to be accessed from within that file.

Pattern name	Summary
Software-Module with Global State	Have one global instance to let your related functions share common resources. Put all functions that operate on this instance into one header file and provide the caller this interface to your software-module.
Eternal Memory	Put your data into memory that is available throughout the whole lifetime of your program.

```
#define MAX_SIZE 50
#define MAX_USERS 50

typedef struct
{
  char name[MAX_SIZE];
  char pwd[MAX_SIZE];
}USER;

static USER userList[MAX_USERS]; ❶
```

❶ The userList contains the data for your users. It is accessible within the implementation file. Because it is kept in the static memory, there is no need to manually allocate it (which would make the code more flexible, but also more complicated).

Storing Passwords

In this simplified example, we keep the password in plain text. Never, ever do this in real-life applications. When storing passwords, you should instead store a salted hash value (*https://oreil.ly/5y7yO*) of the plain text password.

File Organization

Next, define an interface for your caller. Make sure that it is easy for you to change your implementation later on without requiring the caller to change any code. Now you have to decide which part of your program should be defined in the interface and which part should be defined in your implementation file.

Solve this problem by using Header Files. Put as few things as possible (only those things that are relevant to the caller) into the interface (*.h* file). All the rest goes into your implementation files (*.c* files). To protect against multiple inclusion of header files, implement an Include Guard.

Pattern name	Summary
Header Files	Provide function declarations in your API for any functionality you want to provide to your user. Hide any internal functions, internal data, and your function definitions (the implementations) in your implementation file and don't provide this implementation file to the user.
Include Guard	Protect the content of your header files against multiple inclusion so that the developer using the header files does not have to care whether it is included multiple times. Use an interlocked #ifdef statement or a #pragma once statement to achieve this.

user.h

```
#ifndef USER_H
#define USER_H

#define MAX_SIZE 50

#endif
```

user.c

```
#include "user.h"

#define MAX_USERS 50

typedef struct
{
  char name[MAX_SIZE];
  char pwd[MAX_SIZE];
}USER;

static USER userList[MAX_USERS];
```

Now the caller can use the defined MAX_SIZE to know how long the strings provided to the software-module can be. By convention, the caller knows that everything in the *.h* file can be used but that nothing in the *.c* file should be used.

Next, make sure that your code files are well separated from your caller's code to avoid name clashes. Should you put all your files into one directory, or should you, for example, have all .h files in the whole codebase in one directory to make it easier to include them?

Create a Software-Module Directory and put all your files for your software-module, the interfaces and the implementations, into one directory.

Pattern name	Summary
Software-Module Directories	Put header files and implementation files that belong to a tightly coupled functionality into one directory. Name that directory after the functionality that is provided via the header files.

With the directory structure shown in Figure 11-1, it is now possible to easily spot all files that are related to your code. Now you don't have to worry that the names of your implementation files will clash with other filenames.

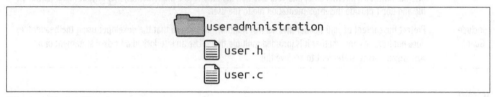

useradministration
user.h
user.c

Figure 11-1. File structure

Authentication: Error Handling

Now it is time to implement the first functionality to access the data. Start by implementing a function that checks whether a provided password matches the previously saved password for a provided user. Define the behavior of the function by declaring the function in the header file and documenting that behavior with code comments next to the function declaration.

The function should let the caller know whether the provided password is correct for a provided user. Tell the caller by using the Return Value of the function. But which information should you return? Should you provide the caller with any error information that occurs?

Only Return Relevant Errors because for any security-related functionality, it is common to provide only the information that you must provide and no more. Don't let the caller know whether the provided user does not exist or whether the provided password is wrong. Instead, simply tell the caller whether authentication worked or not.

Pattern name	Summary
Return Value	Simply use the one C mechanism intended to retrieve information about the result of a function call: the Return Value. The mechanism to return data in C copies the function result and provides the caller access to this copy.

Pattern name	Summary
Return Relevant Errors	Only return error information to the caller if that information is relevant to the caller. Error information is only relevant to the caller if the caller can react to that information.

user.h

```
/* Returns true if the provided username exists and
   if the provided password is correct for that user. */
bool authenticateUser(char* username, char* pwd);
```

This code defines which value is returned by the function very well, but it does not specify the behavior in case of invalid input. How should you cope with invalid input like NULL pointers? Should you check against NULL pointers, or should you simply ignore invalid input?

Require your user to provide valid input, because invalid input would be a programming error of that user, and such errors should not go unnoticed. According to the Samurai Principle, you abort the program in case of invalid input and document that behavior in the header file.

Pattern name	Summary
Samurai Principle	Return from a function victorious or not at all. If there is a situation for which you know that an error cannot be handled, then abort the program.

user.h

```
/* Returns true if the provided username exists and
   if the provided password is correct for that user,
   returns false otherwise. Asserts in case of invalid
   input (NULL string) */
bool authenticateUser(char* username, char* pwd);
```

user.c

```
bool authenticateUser(char* username, char* pwd)
{
  assert(username);
  assert(pwd);

  for(int i=0; i<MAX_USERS; i++)
  {
    if(strcmp(username, userList[i].name) == 0 &&
       strcmp(pwd, userList[i].pwd) == 0)
    {
      return true;
    }
  }
  return false;
}
```

With the Samurai Principle, you take the burden from your caller of checking for specific return values indicating invalid input. Instead, for invalid input the program crashes. You chose to use explicit `assert` statements instead of letting the program crash in an uncontrolled way (e.g., by passing invalid input to the `strcmp` function), In the context of security-critical applications, you want your program to have a defined behavior even in error situations.

At first glance, letting the program crash looks like a brutal solution, but with that behavior, calls with invalid parameters do not go unnoticed. Over the long term, this strategy makes the code more reliable. It does not let subtle bugs, like invalid parameters, manifest and show up somewhere else in the caller's code.

Authentication: Error Logging

Next, keep track of callers who provide you with the wrong password. Log Errors if your `authenticateUser` function fails so this information is available for security audits later on. For logging, either take the code from Chapter 10 or implement a simpler version for logging as shown in the following.

Pattern name	Summary
Log Errors	Use different channels to provide error information that is relevant for the calling code and error information that is relevant for the developer. For example, write debug error information into a log file and don't return the detailed debug error information to the caller.

It is difficult to provide this logging mechanism on different platforms—for example on Linux as well as on Windows—because the different operating systems provide different functions for accessing files. Also, multiplatform code is hard to implement and maintain. So how can you implement your logging functionality as simply as possible? Make sure to Avoid Variants and to use standardized functions, which are available on all platforms.

Pattern name	Summary
Avoid Variants	Use standardized functions that are available on all platforms. If there are no standardized functions, consider not implementing the functionality.

Luckily, the C standard defines functions for accessing files, and these can be used on Windows and Linux systems. While there are operating system–specific functions for accessing files which might be more performant or might provide you with operating system–specific features, these are not necessary here. Simply use the file access functions defined by the C standard.

To implement your logging functionality, call the following function if the wrong password was provided:

user.c

```
static void logError(char* username)
{
  char logString[200];
  sprintf(logString, "Failed login. User:%s\n", username);
  FILE* f = fopen("logfile", "a+"); ❶
  fwrite(logString, 1, strlen(logString), f);
  fclose(f);
}
```

❶ Use the platform-independent functions fopen, fwrite, and fclose. This code works on Windows and Linux platforms, and there are no nasty #ifdef statements to handle the platform variants.

For storing the log information, the code uses Stack First, because the log message is small enough to fit on the stack. This is also easiest for you because you don't have to deal with memory cleanup.

Pattern name	Summary
Stack First	Simply put your variables on the stack by default to profit from automatic cleanup of stack variables.

Adding Users: Error Handling

Looking at the whole code, you now have a function to check whether a password is correct for a username stored in your list, but your list of users is still empty. To fill your list of users, implement a function that allows the caller to add new users.

Make sure that the usernames are unique, and let the caller know whether adding the new user worked or not, either because the username already exists or because there is no more space in your user list.

Now you have to decide how you want to inform the caller about these error situations. Should you use the Return Value to return this information, or should you set the errno variable? Additionally, what kind of information will you provide the caller, and what data type will you use to return that information?

In this instance, Return Status Codes because you have different error situations and you want to inform your caller about these different situations. In addition, in case of invalid parameters, abort the program (Samurai Principle). Define the error codes in your interface to allow you and your caller to have a mutual understanding of how the error codes map to different error situations so the caller can react accordingly.

Pattern name	Summary
Return Status Codes	Use the Return Value of a function to return status information. Return a value that represents a specific status. Both of you as the callee and the caller must have a mutual understanding of what the value means.

user.h

```
typedef enum{
  USER_SUCCESSFULLY_ADDED,
  USER_ALREADY_EXISTS,
  USER_ADMINISTRATION_FULL
}USER_ERROR_CODE;

/* Adds a new user with the provided `username' and the provided password
   `pwd' (asserts on NULL). Returns USER_SUCCESSFULLY_ADDED on success,
   USER_ALREADY_EXISTS if a user with the provided username already exists
   and USER_ADMINISTRATION_FULL if no more users can be added. */
USER_ERROR_CODE addUser(char* username, char* pwd);
```

Next, implement the addUser function. Check whether such a user already exists and then add the user. To separate these tasks, perform a Function Split to split the different tasks and responsibilities into different functions. First, implement a function to check whether the user already exists.

Pattern name	Summary
Function Split	Split up the function. Take a part of a function that seems useful on its own, create a new function with that, and call that function.

user.c

```
static bool userExists(char* username)
{
  for(int i=0; i<MAX_USERS; i++)
  {
    if(strcmp(username, userList[i].name) == 0)
    {
      return true;
    }
  }
  return false;
}
```

This function can now be called inside the function that adds new users in order to add new users only if they don't yet exist. Should you check for existing users at the beginning of the function or right before you add the user to the list? Which of these alternatives would make your function easier to read and maintain?

Implement a Guard Clause at the beginning of the function that will return immediately if the action cannot be performed because the user already exists. A check right at the beginning of the function makes it easier to follow the program flow.

Pattern name	Summary
Guard Clause	Check whether you have pre-conditions and immediately return from the function if these pre-conditions are not met.

user.c

```
USER_ERROR_CODE addUser(char* username, char* pwd)
{
  assert(username);
  assert(pwd);

  if(userExists(username))
  {
    return USER_ALREADY_EXISTS;
  }

  for(int i=0; i<MAX_USERS; i++)
  {
    if(strcmp(userList[i].name, "") == 0)
    {
      strcpy(userList[i].name, username);
      strcpy(userList[i].pwd, pwd);
      return USER_SUCCESSFULLY_ADDED;
    }
  }

  return USER_ADMINISTRATION_FULL;
}
```

With the implemented code fragments so far, you can fill your user administration with users and to check whether a provided password is correct for these users.

Iterating

Next, provide some functionality to read out all usernames by implementing an iterator. While you may want to simply provide an interface that lets the caller access the userList array by index, you'd be in trouble if the underlying data structure changes (for example, to a linked list), or if the caller wants to access the array while another caller modifies the array.

To provide an iterator interface to the caller that solves the mentioned issues, implement a Cursor Iterator, which uses a Handle to hide the underlying data structure from the caller.

Pattern name	Summary
Cursor Iterator	Create an iterator instance that points to an element in the underlying data structure. An iteration function takes this iterator instance as argument, retrieves the element the iterator currently points to, and modifies the iteration instance to point to the next element. The user then iteratively calls this function to retrieve one element at a time.
Handle	Have a function to create the context on which the caller operates and return an abstract pointer to internal data for that context. Require the caller to pass that pointer to all your functions, which can then use the internal data to store state information and resources.

```
typedef struct ITERATOR* ITERATOR;

/* Create an iterator instance. Returns NULL on error. */
ITERATOR createIterator();

/* Retrieves the next element from an iterator instance. */
char* getNextElement(ITERATOR iterator);

/* Destroys an iterator instance. */
void destroyIterator(ITERATOR iterator);
```

The caller has full control of when to create and destroy the iterator. Thus, you have Dedicated Ownership with a Caller-Owned Instance. The caller can simply create the iterator Handle and use it to access the list of usernames. If creation fails, then the Special Return Value NULL indicates this. Having this Special Return Value instead of explicit error codes makes using the function easier because no additional function parameters are needed to return error information. When the caller is done with iterating, the caller can destroy the Handle.

Pattern name	Summary
Dedicated Ownership	Right at the time when you implement memory allocation, clearly define where it's going to be cleaned up and who is going to do that.
Caller-Owned Instance	Require the caller to pass an instance, which is used to store resource and state information, along to your functions. Provide explicit functions to create and destroy these instances, so that the caller can determine their lifetime.
Special Return Values	Use the Return Value of your function to return the data computed by the function. Reserve one or more special values to be returned if an error occurs.

Because the interface provides the caller with explicit functions to create and destroy the iterator, this naturally leads to separate functions for initializing and cleaning up the resources for your iterator in the implementation. This Object-based Error Handling brings the advantage of nicely separated responsibilities in your functions, which makes them easier to extend if necessary later on. You can see this separation in the following code where all initialization code is in one function, and all cleanup code is in another function.

Pattern name	Summary
Object-Based Error Handling	Put initialization and cleanup into separate functions, similar to the concept of constructors and destructors in object-oriented programming.

user.c

```
struct ITERATOR
{
  int currentPosition;
  char currentElement[MAX_SIZE];
};

ITERATOR createIterator()
{
  ITERATOR iterator = (ITERATOR) calloc(sizeof(struct ITERATOR),1);
  return iterator;
}

char* getNextElement(ITERATOR iterator)
{
  if(iterator->currentPosition < MAX_USERS)
  {
    strcpy(iterator->currentElement,userList[iterator->currentPosition].name);
    iterator->currentPosition++;
  }
  else
  {
    strcpy(iterator->currentElement, "");
  }
  return iterator->currentElement;
}

void destroyIterator(ITERATOR iterator)
{
  free(iterator);
}
```

When implementing the preceding code, how should you provide the username data to the caller? Should you simply provide the caller with a pointer to that data? If you copy that data into a buffer, who should allocate it?

In this situation, the Callee Allocates the string buffer. This makes it possible for the caller to have full access to that string without having the possibility of changing the data in the userList. Additionally, the caller avoids accessing data that might be changed by other callers at the same time.

Pattern name	Summary
Callee Allocates	Allocate a buffer with the required size inside the function that provides the large, complex data. Copy the required data into the buffer and return a pointer to that buffer.

Using the User Management System

You have now completed your user management code. The following code shows how to use that user management system:

```
char* element;
addUser("A", "pass");
addUser("B", "pass");
addUser("C", "pass");

ITERATOR it = createIterator();

while(true)
{
  element = getNextElement(it);
  if(strcmp(element, "") == 0)
  {
    break;
  }

  printf("User: %s ", element);
  printf("Authentication success? %d\n", authenticateUser(element, "pass"));
}

destroyIterator(it);
```

Throughout this chapter, the patterns helped you to design this final piece of code. Now you can tell your boss you completed the task of implementing the requested system for storing usernames and passwords. By utilizing pattern-based design for that system, you rely on documented solutions that are proven in use.

Summary

You constructed the code in this chapter step by step by applying the patterns presented in Part I in order to solve one problem after another. At the start you had many questions on how to organize the files and how to cope with error handling. The patterns showed you the way. They gave you guidance and made it easier to construct this piece of code. They also provide understanding as to why the code looks and behaves the way it does. Throughout this chapter, you applied the patterns shown in Figure 11-2. In the figure, you can see how many decisions you had to make and how many decisions were guided by the patterns.

The constructed user administration system contains basic functionalities to add, find, and authenticate users. Again, there are many other functionalities that could be added to that system, like the functionality to change passwords, to not store them in plain text, or to check that the passwords meet some security criteria. The advanced functionality is not addressed in this chapter to make the pattern application easier to grasp.

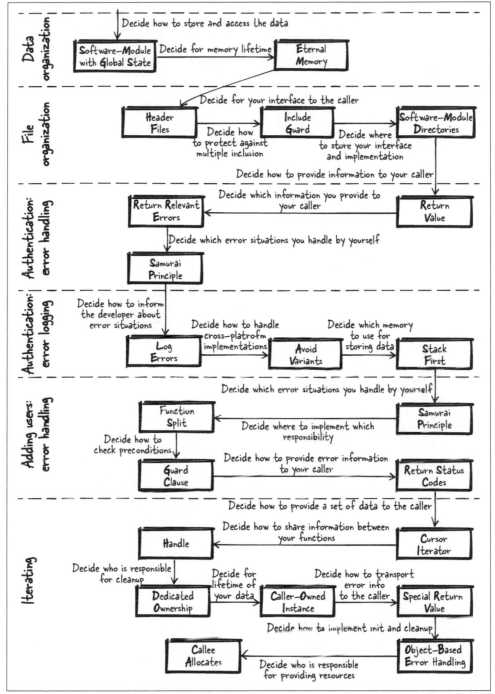

Figure 11-2. *The patterns applied throughout this story*

CHAPTER 12

Conclusion

What You've Learned

After reading this book, you are now familiar with several advanced C programming concepts. When looking at larger code examples, you now know why the code looks the way it does. You now know the reasoning behind the design decisions made in that code. For example, in the Ethernet driver sample code presented in the Preface of this book, you now understand why there is an explicit `driverCreate` method and why there is a `DRIVER_HANDLE` that holds state information. The patterns from Part I guided the decisions made in this example and many others discussed throughout the book.

The pattern stories from Part II showed you the benefits of applying the patterns from this book and how to grow code bit by bit through the application of patterns. When facing your next C programming problem, review the problem sections of the patterns and see whether one of them matches your problem. In that case, you are very lucky because then you can benefit from the guidance provided by the patterns.

Further Reading

This book helps C programming novices to become advanced C programmers. Here are some other books that particularly helped me improve my C programming skills:

- *Clean Code: A Handbook of Agile Software Craftsmanship* by Robert C. Martin (Prentice Hall, 2008) discusses the basic principles of how to implement high-quality code that lasts over time. It is a good read for any programmer and covers topics like testing, documentation, code style, and others.

- *Test-Driven Development for Embedded C* by James W. Grenning (Pragmatic Bookshelf, 2011) uses a running example to explain how to implement unit-tests with C in the context of hardware-near programs.

- *Expert C Programming* by Peter van der Linden (Prentice Hall, 1994) is an early book on advanced C programming guidance. It describes how the C syntax works in detail and how to avoid common pitfalls. It also discusses concepts like C memory management and tells you how the linker works.

- Closely related to my book is the book *Patterns in C* by Adam Tornhill (Leanpub, 2014). It also presents patterns and focuses on how to implement the Gang of Four design patterns with C.

Closing Remarks

Compared to a C programmer fresh out of their studies, you now have advanced knowledge on which techniques to use to compose larger-scale and industrial-strength C code. You can now:

- perform error handling, even though you don't have a mechanism like exceptions

- manage your memory, even though you don't have a garbage collector and you don't have destructors to clean up the memory

- implement flexible interfaces, even though you don't have native abstraction mechanisms

- structure files and code, even though you don't have classes or packages

You are now able to work with C, despite it lacking some of the conveniences of modern programming languages.

Index

About the Author

Christopher Preschern organizes design pattern conferences and initiatives to improve pattern writing. As a C programmer at the company ABB, he gathered and documented hands-on knowledge on how to write industrial-strength code. He has lectured on coding and quality at Graz University of Technology and holds a PhD in computer science.

Colophon

The animal on the cover of *Fluent C* is a Major Mitchell's cockatoo (*Lophochroa leadbeateri*), also known as Leadbeater's cockatoo or the pink cockatoo. This medium-sized cockatoo is named after Major Thomas Mitchell, a surveyor and explorer of southeastern Australia. It is native to the arid and semi-arid parts of Australia, preferring wooded areas where it can forage for seeds. Its plumage is primarily white and a pale salmon pink, with deeper pink under its wings and a bright red, yellow, and white crest. Males and females look almost identical, though males are usually a little larger and have brown eyes, while females have reddish-pink eyes and broader yellow stripes in their crests.

Major Mitchell's cockatoos are popular as pets, though they are very social birds that require a great deal of attention from their owners. In the wild, they nest in pairs and require large territories, making their habitats vulnerable to fragmentation. Although they are considered a species of least concern, their numbers have declined as woodlands have been cleared. They are also threatened by illegal trapping for the pet trade. Many of the animals on O'Reilly covers are endangered; all of them are important to the world.

The cover illustration is by Karen Montgomery, based on an antique line engraving from *Cassell's Natural History*. The cover fonts are Gilroy Semibold and Guardian Sans. The text font is Adobe Minion Pro; the heading font is Adobe Myriad Condensed; and the code font is Dalton Maag's Ubuntu Mono.

O'REILLY®

Learn from experts.
Become one yourself.

Books | Live online courses
Instant Answers | Virtual events
Videos | Interactive learning

Get started at oreilly.com.

Milton Keynes UK
Ingram Content Group UK Ltd.
UKHW011501030924
447785UK00002B/2

9 781492 097334